D1050744

ECONOMICS
OF
SOCIAL ISSUES

ECONOMICS
OF
SOCIAL ISSUES

RICHARD H. LEFTWICH
ANSEL M. SHARP

Both of
the Department of Economics
Oklahoma State University

 1974

BUSINESS PUBLICATIONS, INC.
Dallas, Texas   75224
Irwin-Dorsey International   London, England   WC2H 9NJ
Irwin-Dorsey Limited   Georgetown, Ontario   L7G 4B3

First Printing, April 1974
Second Printing, August 1974

ISBN 0–256–01606–2
Library of Congress Catalog Card No. 74–76458

Printed in the United States of America

PREFACE

THE TRADITIONAL Principles of Economics course with its emphasis on abstract formal theory has succeeded over the years in turning off untold thousands of students. To a large extent, students take the course because it is required. It inspires only a few to dig further into the discipline. "Difficult," "dry," "dull," and "irrelevant" are some of the responses it evokes.

This is unfortunate because economics has much of importance to say about almost all of the social issues of our day. Many mistakes in social and economic policy making are directly traceable to widespread economic illiteracy. That more students major in economics is not important. What is important is that a much larger proportion of students take enough economics to know what the economic consequences of various kinds of social and economic policies will be. This means that for most students their first exposure to economics should be "of moderate difficulty," "interesting," and "relevant."

This book is an outgrowth of three years of experimentation with the lower division economics courses at Oklahoma State University. In the fall of 1971 the traditional six-hour course in principles at the sophomore level was abandoned in favor of a three-hour course entitled "Economics of Social Issues," plus a concentrated three-hour principles course. The major objective of the Economics of Social Issues course and of this book is to create student interest in economics and to arouse a desire for further study in the field.

A major question raised by the introduction of the issues-oriented course in lieu of three hours of traditional principles is how much, if any, economics learning is sacrificed. To answer the question and to evaluate other aspects of the experiment, a research project was developed under the co-sponsorship of the Joint Council on Economic Education and the Oklahoma State University College of Business Administration. The broad conclusions reached are that the issues-oriented approach results in (1) an insignificant learning loss; (2) a significantly higher level of interest on the part of students enrolled in the course; and (3) a substantial increase in enrollments in the courses.

We attempt in this book to discuss a set of issues that is interesting and stimulating, and that lends itself to learning economics. We do not presume to have selected *the* best set of issues. But we find that our mix of issues holds the interest of students and permits a systematic presentation of economic principles.

In presenting each issue certain elementary economic principles and concepts basic to the analysis of that issue are introduced, explained, and applied. The issues themselves are ordered so as to facilitate a logical, systematic development of principles and concepts. The Introduction, Chapter 1, on population growth, discusses the insatiability of wants, the relative scarcity of resources, and the nature of economic activity as the fundamental concepts needed to understand and to appraise the problem. Part I, consisting of chapters on agriculture, higher education, crime, pollution, and health issues, brings out and utilizes principles related to pricing, resource allocation, and economic efficiency. Part II, dealing with issues of poverty and discrimination, is concerned with principles of income distribution and their applications in the achievement of the social goal of some degree of equity. Part III, on issues of unemployment and inflation, enables us to develop basic principles of national income determination, the causes of economic instability, and the fiscal-monetary principles that are useful in the control of instability.

Each chapter begins with a checklist of economic concepts and principles and an outline of the chapter. The checklist will alert students to the concepts and principles that should be looked for in the chapter. The outline shows the organization and coverage of the chapter.

The book is intended as the text for a one-term issues-oriented course; as the text for the first term in a two-term principles sequence, stressing issues in the first term and theory in the second term; or as a supplemental readings book for a traditional two-term principles course. For a one-term course, we have learned that eleven issues are about all that can be fruitfully examined. For those instructors who desire to delete an issue or two in order to probe more thoroughly into certain other issues, the supplementary readings list at the end of each chapter should prove helpful.

In the classroom, we find it useful to proceed more slowly with unemployment and inflation in Chapters 9 and 10 than with the other issues in the book. These are very important social issues to a generation of students who have experienced and puzzled over both during almost all of their adult lives. But they are not just social issues—in and of themselves they form the content of a very large part of fundamental economic theory. We have tried to provide a simple but useful macroeconomic framework for their analysis. The presentation is packed full but our experience shows us that if it is handled carefully it works well. Student response has been excellent.

We now come to the point in a preface where claims of originality are often made. The issues approach is not new. In traditional texts authors have for many years tried to put life into principles by the application of principles to problems. A casual observation of recently published principles texts and revisions of the old standbys shows an increasing proportion of space devoted to issues. Although it may not long remain true, we make a modest claim of originality in having attempted to introduce principles systematically by means of an issues-oriented book.

We have benefited greatly from the encouragement, advice, and plain hard work of other people on the manuscript as it developed. Arthur G. Welsh of the Joint Council on Economic Education has made valuable suggestions regarding the evaluation of results of our approach and our teaching methods. Professor Charles M. Hargrove, Department of Economics, University of Texas at Arlington, and Professor Harry S. Walker, Department of Economics, Texas Technological University, Lubbock, provided helpful criticisms of manuscript drafts. Judy Leftwich drafted the Chapter 2 Appendix and provided valuable critiques of the first five chapters. We are heavily indebted to our colleague, Donald L. Bumpass, and to our graduate assistants, Shiu-Fang Yu and Douglas McNiel, for the many hours they spent helping with research and myriad other tasks connected with the writing and preparation of the manuscript. Various members of the economics faculty who have taught the Economics of Social Issues course have contributed their expertise and we are grateful to them. Peggy Wooden, our secretary, rendered invaluable service in typing the manuscript and in keeping its various drafts orderly. As usual, as much as we would like to do so, we cannot escape the direct responsibility for any shortcomings that may remain.

March 1974   RICHARD H. LEFTWICH
                                                ANSEL M. SHARP

CONTENTS

Part IV. EPILOGUE

INTRODUCTION

Chapter 1

POPULATION GROWTH

CHECKLIST OF ECONOMIC CONCEPTS

Economic Activity
Insatiability of Wants
Scarce Resources
Labor
Capital
Technology
Gross National Product
Production Possibilities Curve
Per Capita GNP
Economic Growth

1

POPULATION GROWTH
Can the Earth Hold Us All?

PEDRO was happy to see the wild afternoon come to a close so he could escape from the people who swarmed the supermarket where he worked as a stockboy. They seemed to hold him personally responsible when the market ran out of the popular sizes of several different items. So he breathed a sigh of relief as he walked toward the bus stop where he would catch the No. 6 bus for his home.

Pedro was not the only one waiting for the No. 6 bus. He squeezed on when it stopped, but he was lucky. The seats and aisles were full, and when the doors closed a sizable group was left to wait for the next bus. Pedro stood in the aisle, hanging onto the back of a seat for the hour-long ride home.

Pedro's home neighborhood was crowded and dirty. Kids playing baseball in the street ran into him as he walked from the bus stop to his home. There was not much yard space around the apartment houses in which the hordes of youngsters could work off their excess energy, so the only place where Pedro, his two brothers, his three sisters, and the neighbors' kids had elbow room was in the streets. The family's cramped apartment provided little more than a place to eat and sleep.

It often occurred to Pedro (as it has to many of us) that there may be too many people running around in this world.

WHAT ARE WE AFRAID OF?

General concern over population problems is of fairly recent origin. There have been some persistent worriers for a long time, dating at least back to the late 1700s, but they were in the minority until World War II. In fact, many people—especially those in state governments—looked with great favor on population growth prior to that time. The post World War II emphasis on economic development seems to have brought about some changes in thinking. Newspapers, telecasts, magazines, books, and everyday conversation refer to the "population problem" time and again. In all these media, at least three main fears about population growth surface: (1) it strains the capacity of the world to provide adequate food supplies, (2) it causes ever-increasing levels of pollution, and (3) it causes excessive crowding.

Pressures on Food Supplies

Population pressure on the food supply has evoked the most concern over time. We are told persistently that the world's capacities to produce food cannot keep pace with its growing population, that the day of reckoning is at hand, and that massive famines are in the offing unless we mend our reproductive ways.[1] These dire predictions are not new. In the late 1700s a British clergyman-sociologist-economist, Thomas Robert Malthus, was voicing the same set of ideas.[2] He presented the issues logically and systematically, and his analysis is well known today as the Malthusian theory.

Malthus believed that the world's population tends to increase faster than its food supply, keeping the bulk of the population at the verge of starvation or subsistence. He argued that an unrestrained population tends to increase in *geometric* progression; that is, in the series 2–4–8–16–32 . . . The food supply increases in *arithmetic* progression 2–4–6–8–10 . . . This being the case, living standards can never rise far above subsistence levels because of constant population pressure on the food supply.

Malthus pointed to two sets of checks or restraints that operate on

---

[1] Paul R. Ehrlich, *The Population Bomb*, rev. ed. (New York: Ballantine Books, 1971).

[2] Thomas Robert Malthus, *On Population*, ed. Gertrude Himmelfarb (New York: Modern Library, 1960). Originally published, 1798.

the total population. The first consists of *natural* checks—starvation, disease or pestilence, and war. All of these are the natural outgrowth of population pressure on the food supply and serve to limit the size of the total population. The second is made up of *positive* restraints that man can use to limit population growth. Chief among them are celibacy, late marriage, and birth control. Do these ideas seem to have a familiar, modern ring?

Pollution Levels

Concentrations of population are expected by many to affect the environment adversely—at least in the immediate vicinity of the concentration and sometimes well beyond it. As people produce and consume goods and services, they create wastes. These must be disposed of, and the environment—land, atmosphere, and water—serves as the wastebasket or the sewer. Biochemical processes work on the wastes, transforming some of them back into usable forms. But if a growing population increases the rate at which wastes are dumped into and on the environment above the rate at which it can process them, pollution problems are created. The air becomes smoggy; the rivers and lakes lose their capacities to support aquatic life; and the land may be stripped of valuable resources, to say nothing of the destruction of its beauty.

Crowding

There can be no doubt that crowding and congestion are commonplace throughout the world. Try going home at 5:00 P.M. in Los Angeles, New York City, or Stillwater, Oklahoma. Drive through the ghetto of any major U.S. city, walk through the bazaar areas in Old Delhi or Hong Kong, or ride a train through the Japanese countryside. Any of these experiences would provide ample evidence of crowding and congestion. They are cited as examples of the adverse effects of population growth.

POPULATION AND ECONOMICS

The common theme of the three foregoing fears about population growth is that it affects living standards adversely. Clearly, population pressure on the food supply, if it occurs as predicted, will result in lower living standards than we now enjoy in the

United States. Increases in pollution levels result in a deterioration in the quality of life—some even go so far as to say pollution will eventually destroy life. Similarly, increasing levels of crowding and congestion are expected to decrease the quality of life. These are economic themes—they sum up what the study of economics is all about.

An explicit understanding of the foundations of economic activity is essential to an analysis and assessment of population problems—whether or not there really are population problems and, if they exist, where they are and how serious they are. Consequently, in this section we shall sketch out the fundamental aspects of economic activity and of economics as an intellectual discipline.

Our Insatiable Wants

Economic activity springs from human wants and desires. Humans want the things necessary to keep them alive—food and protection from the elements of nature. They want a great many other things, too, and the fulfillment of these wants and desires is the end toward which economic activity is directed.

As nearly as we can tell, human wants in the aggregate are unlimited or insatiable. Why? Because once our basic needs are met, we desire variety in the way they are met—variety in foods, in housing, in clothing, and in entertainment. Additionally, as we look around, we see other people enjoying things that we do not have (ten-speed bicycles, for example) and we think that our level of well-being would be elevated if we had those things, too. But most important of all, want-satisfying activity itself generates new wants. A new house generates wants for new furnishings—the old ones look shabby in the new setting. A college or university education opens the doors to wants that would never have existed if we had stayed on the farm or in the machine shop. To be sure, any one of us can saturate ourselves—temporarily, at least—with any one kind of good or service, but almost all would like to have more than they now have and better qualities than they can obtain.

Our Limited Means

The fundamental economic problem is that the means available for satisfying wants are scarce or limited relative to the extent of those wants. The amounts of goods and services per year that the economic system can produce are limited because (1) the resources available to produce them cannot be increased by any great amount in any given year and (2) the technology available for production is also subject to a limited degree of annual improvement.

An economy's *resources* are the ingredients that go into the making of goods (like automobiles) and services (like physical examinations). Production is a bit like cooking. Resources (ingredients) are brought together; technology is used to process these resources in certain ways (stir and cook them); and then out comes a good or service (a cake, perhaps). Some outputs of production processes are used directly to satisfy wants. Others become inputs for additional production processes. The resources available in an economy are usually divided into two broad classifications: (1) labor and (2) capital.

Labor resources consist of all the efforts of mind and muscle that can be used in production processes. The ditch digger's output as well as that of the heart surgeon and the university professor are included. There are many kinds and grades of labor resources; their main common characteristic is that they are human.

Capital resources consist of all the nonhuman ingredients that go into the production of goods and services. They include land which provides space for production facilities, elements that enable it to grow crops, and many useful mineral deposits. They also include buildings and equipment that have been built up over time, along with the economy's stock of tools. In addition, all of the raw and semifinished materials that exist in the economy at any given time and that are available for use in production are capital resources. Sheets of steel and grocery store inventories are examples of semifinished materials.

Resources are always scarce relative to the total amounts of human wants. Consider the U.S. economy. We have a population of over 200 million persons wanting more of all sorts of things than they now have. Can the economy increase next year's production enough to fulfill all of these wants? Obviously not. The labor force available from the present population cannot be increased substantially. Its quantity can be increased slowly over time by increasing the population, but this increases total wants, too. The stocks of buildings, machines, tools, raw and semifinished materials, and usable land are not susceptible to rapid increase, either, but are accumulated slowly over time.

Technology refers to the known means and methods available for combining resources to produce goods and services. Given the quantities of an economy's labor and capital resources, the better its technology, the greater the annual volume of goods and services it can turn out. Usually improvements in technology in an economic system result from increasing the scope and depth of its educational processes and from an ample supply of capital that provides, among other things, a laboratory for experimentation and practice.

The Capacity of the Economy to Produce

Gross National Product. The value of an economy's annual output of goods and services is called its *gross national product,* or GNP. For any given year the upper limits of GNP are determined by the quantities of resources available to the economy and by the level of technology that can be utilized. A picture of the economy's performance over time—whether it is expanding, contracting, or remaining stationary—is provided by GNP data for the appropriate series of years.

Production Possibilities. Given an economy's available stocks of resources and its level of technology, there are any number of combinations of goods and services that can comprise its GNP. Suppose, for example, that it produces only two items—bread and milk. All of its resources are devoted to the production of these two things. The line *AE* in Figure 1–1 represents all possible combinations of bread and milk that can be produced. It is appropriately called the economy's *production possibilities curve.* Thus, GNP may consist of 100,000 loaves of bread per year as shown by point *A,* or 100,000 quarts of milk per year as shown by point *E.* Or it may consist of any combination on the curve, such as *B,* containing 90,000 loaves of bread and 40,000 quarts of milk, or *C,* containing 50,000 loaves of bread and 80,000 quarts of milk, or some combination under the curve such as *F.*

If an economy's GNP is a combination of goods and services such as *F,* which lies below its production possibilities curve, the economic system is not operating efficiently. Some of its resources may be unemployed, used in the wrong places, or wasted. It also may not be using the best available techniques of production.

FIGURE 1–1
Production Possibilities Curve for an Economy

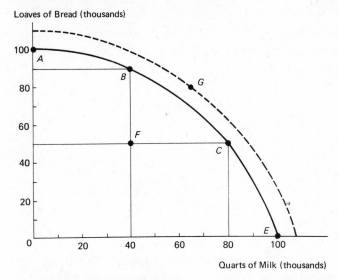

Line *AE* shows all combinations of bread and milk that the economy's available resources and techniques of production can produce annually. Combinations such as *F* imply unemployment of resources or inefficiency in production. Those such as *G* are not attainable.

Combinations of goods and services such as *G,* lying above the production possibilities curve, are not currently attainable. The economy does not have sufficient quantities and qualities of resources and/or good enough techniques of production to push its GNP out to that level. Over time, perhaps, it can accumulate enough resources and/or improve its technique and press its production possibilities curve outward to the dotted line. Then combination *G* would become a feasible level of GNP.

For the combinations of bread and milk making up line *AE,* all of the resources of the economy are employed and the best possible techniques are used. If all resources were used to produce bread and no milk were produced, the result would be the 100,000 loaves per year shown at point *A.* If some milk is desired, some resources must be withdrawn from the production of bread and used to produce milk. Suppose, for example, a decision is made to produce 40,000 quarts of milk. Bread production must be reduced by 10,000 loaves in order to release enough resources to produce the milk. The new combination of milk and bread is represented by point B on the diagram. By giving up 40,000 more loaves of bread, an additional 40,000 quarts of milk can be produced, leaving the economy with the 50,000 loaves of bread and the 80,000 quarts of milk shown by point C. At point E all of the economy's resources are being used to produce milk.

Living Standards

Gross national product data alone indicate little about how well an economy can provide for its inhabitants. If the economy's GNP is divided by its population for any given year, the result is *per capita GNP*. This concept is a rough measure of individual well-being. For any one country, per capita GNP for a series of years is indicative of whether or not the performance of the economy in terms of the well-being of its inhabitants is improving. Among countries, the comparative per capita GNPs are indicative of the comparative economic performances of the countries.

Per capita GNP is a measure of an economy's standard of living, but it is in no sense a perfect measure. It fails to take into account such things as the distribution of the economy's output among the population. If a few people get the bulk of the output while the masses are at subsistence level, per capita or average figures provide a distorted picture of individual well-being. But by and large, they are the best measure currently available.

It should be obvious now that concern over population growth is to a very large extent economic in nature. Given a country's GNP, the larger its population the lower its average standard of living, as measured by per capita GNP, will be. If a country's living standards are to increase over time, its GNP must increase at a faster rate than its population.

HOW POPULATION GROWTH IS MEASURED

Demographers, who study population characteristics, have developed a standard set of concepts for measuring and analyzing population growth. The most important ones for our purposes are (1) the rate of natural increase, (2) the net migration rate, (3) the rate of population increase, and (4) the fertility rate.

The Rate of Natural Increase

Measurements of population growth usually start with the concept of the *crude birth rate,* or CBR. The CBR is defined as the number of babies born per year per 1,000 people in the country's population. In Table 1–1, column 2 shows the crude birth rate for the United States from 1935 through 1972.

TABLE 1–1
Measures of Population Growth in the United States, 1935–72 (annual rates per 1,000 of midyear population)

(1)	(2)	(3)	(4)	(5)	(6)	(7)
				Net	Rate of	
	Crude	Crude	Rate of	Mi-	Popu-	General
	Birth	Death	Natural	gration	lation	Fertility
Period	Rate	Rate	Increase	Rate	Increase	Rate
1935–39	18.8	11.0	7.8	.4	8.2	77.6
1940–44	21.2	10.8	10.4	.8	11.4	87.5
1945–49	24.1	10.1	14.0	1.6	15.7	103.1
1950–54	24.8	9.5	15.2	1.8	17.1	113.1
1955–59	24.8	9.4	14.4	1.8	17.2	120.7
1960–64	22.6	9.4	13.2	1.9	14.9	113.2
1965–69	18.3	9.5	8.8	2.1	10.7	89.9
1970	18.2	9.4	8.8	2.1	10.9	88.0
1971	17.2	9.3	7.9	1.8	9.7	82.6
1972	15.7	9.4	6.3	N.A.	N.A.	

Sources: U.S. Department of Commerce, Bureau of the Census, *Estimates and Projections,* Current Population Reports, Series P–25, No. 481 (April 1972), and *Statistical Abstract of the United States, 1972,* p. 10; U.S. Department of Health, Education, and Welfare, National Center for Health Statistics, *Vital Statistics Report,* Vol. 21, No. 11 (January 30, 1973).

The CBR of a country is determined by a complex of forces. The percentage of the population that is composed of women in the childbearing age bracket, generally defined as ages 15 through 44 years, is very important. Add in the social beliefs or values of the population—attitudes toward early or late marriages, sexual permissiveness, children born out of wedlock, abortion and birth control, working wives, and a variety of other attitudes. Religious beliefs are also important; witness the birth rate in the predominantly Catholic Latin American countries. Then, certainly, the level of technical knowledge of birth control and the facilities available for dispensing birth control information, medicines, and devices are critical. All of these factors work together in determining the CBR.

Next we consider the country's *crude death rate,* or CDR, which is the number of deaths per year per 1,000 of the country's population. U.S. CDR data for the years 1935 through 1972 are shown in Table 1–1, column 3.

The crude death rate of a country also is influenced by a complex of forces. Perhaps the most important one is the society's level of medical and sanitary knowledge, together with the facilities available for putting that knowledge into practice. Where these are at low levels, infant mortality rates are high and life spans are short. Another important factor will be the productivity of the country's economy: Can it produce enough goods and services to provide an adequate diet? The country need not be agriculturally oriented, but it must be productive enough to grow or trade for an adequate supply of food. Social beliefs and values also affect the CDR. They help shape the diet that the population eats and the exercise regimen it follows—and these contribute importantly to the general state of health. They also influence the kinds of medical and sanitary practices that are acceptable. For example, it is widely accepted in one part of the world that fresh cow manure is good medicine for an open sore.

A country's CDR is substracted from its CBR to obtain its annual *rate of natural increase,* or RNI. The RNI for the United States from 1935 through 1972 is shown in column 4 of Table 1–1. The measurements are obtained by subtracting column 3 from column 2 for each group of years. For example, in 1970 the CBR was 18.2 and the CDR was 9.4 per 1,000 persons. Consequently, the RNI was 8.8. Some can see more readily what this means if it is put in percentage terms—the RNI is divided by ten to make this conversion. In 1970 the *percentage* rate of natural increase was 0.88. Certainly it looks less startling this way.

The Net Migration Rate

If we want to know how fast a country's population is growing, we must take its *net migration rate* as well as its RNI into account. First its *crude in-migration rate,* the number of persons coming into the country per year per 1,000 of its population, is considered. Then its *crude out-migration rate,* the number per 1,000 population leaving annually, is determined. The difference between the two is its net migration rate, or NMR, which may be either positive or negative. For the United States, as column 5 of Table 1–1 shows, it was positive for the years indicated.

The Rate of Population Increase

A country's RNI and its NMR are added together to obtain its annual *rate of population increase,* or RPI. The RPI of the United States from 1935 through 1972 is presented in Table 1–1, column 6. It also can be converted to percentage terms by dividing it by ten. Thus in 1970 the population increase was 1.09 percent. The rate of population increase as a measurement concept is most useful for describing what has been and is now occurring with respect to a country's population. In other words, it is a better device for recording events than for predicting them.

The Fertility Rate

The measurement concept most useful in predicting the future course of population growth is the *fertility rate.* This concept is defined as the number of births annually per 1,000 females in the childbearing age—that is, 15 through 44 years of age. The annual fertility rates for the United States for the years 1935 through 1972 are shown in Table 1–1, column 7.

Fertility rate trends of a country provide valuable information for forecasting total population trends over time. Suppose, for example, that the annual fertility rate of a country has been stable over a series of years, and then it falls. This does not affect the number of women of childbearing age immediately; in fact, it will be 15 years before it does so. Consequently, the immediate effect is on the number of children being fed into the population from those potential mothers. Eventually the lower fertility rate also causes the number of mothers to be lower than it would otherwise be, thus augmenting its effects.

The annual fertility rate figure can be converted easily into the average number of children born per woman during her childbearing years. Consider the 1971 fertility rate of 82.6 children per year per 1,000 women. Dividing by 1,000 indicates that each woman has 0.0826 children per year. When this is multiplied by 30—the years comprising ages 15 through 44—it can be determined that the average number of children borne by each woman during her life span is 2.478.

Population experts estimate that an average of 2.11 children per woman will result eventually in a *zero population growth,* or ZPG, abstracting from net migration. Two children would replace the parents, and the 0.11 of a child makes allowance for those who die before reaching adulthood.[3]

POPULATION GROWTH FROM THE ECONOMIC VIEWPOINT

In examining the prospects for future population growth and the economic implications of those prospects, we shall consider first the impact of population growth on living standards. Then we shall turn to the crowding and pollution aspects of population growth. Finally, we shall consider the possible impact of zero population growth on economic activity.

World Population Growth

Is population growth a serious threat to living standards? Has it kept them from rising, or does it seem to be a significant factor in holding down their rate of increase? Is there any evidence that it has caused them to deteriorate? Per capita GNP data over the years should provide important clues to the answers to these questions.

To analyze the effects of population growth around the globe, a sampling of countries can be grouped according to level of per capita GNP.[4] Those with per capita GNP below $200 per year can be classified as *underdeveloped,* those with per capita GNP between $200 and $1,000 as *moderately developed,* and those with per capita GNP above $1,000 as *developed* countries. A random sample of countries in each classification is shown in Table 1–2.

---

3 "Population Heads for a Zero Growth Rate," *Business Week,* October 24, 1970, pp. 102–4.

4 Actually the correct term is per capita gross domestic product, a concept used by the United Nations in gathering data on the output of different countries. The differences from per capita GNP are not significant for our purposes, however, and we will use the latter term.

TABLE 1-2
Population Trends and Per Capita GNP for Selected Countries

	Population Estimate (1971)	(1963–71) Annual Rate of Population Increase (percent)	Population Density (per square kilometer)	Per Capita GNP* (1970)	Annual Growth Rate of Real Per Capita GNP (percent)
Underdeveloped countries					
India	550,374,000	2.2%	168	$ 94†	0.5% (1960–70)
Indonesia	124,894,000	2.8	84	115	0.6 (1960–70)
Kenya	11,694,000	3.1	20	140	4.1 (1964–70)
Pakistan	116,598,000	2.1	123	149†	3.2 (1960–69)
Tanzania, United Republic of	13,634,000	2.6	14	97	2.6 (1964–70)
Moderately developed countries					
Argentina	23,552,000	1.5	8	974†	2.4 (1960–69)
Brazil	95,408,000	2.8	11	362	1.2 (1960–68)
Chile	8,992,000	1.4	12	681	1.8 (1960–70)
Colombia	21,772,000	3.2	19	401	1.7 (1960–69)
Philippines	37,959,000	3.0	127	377	1.4 (1960–70)
South Africa	22,092,000	3.1	18	864	3.7 (1960–70)
Taiwan	13,161,023§	2.6†	390§	389	7.1 (1960–70)
Venezuela	8,144,000||	3.6†	11§	979	2.3 (1960–70)
Developed countries					
Australia	12,728,000	1.9	2	2,708†	3.4 (1960–69)
Canada	21,786,000	1.8	2	3,676	3.7 (1961–70)
France	51,260,000	0.9	94	2,901	4.6 (1960–70)
Italy	54,078,000	0.8	180	1,727	4.4 (1960–69)
Japan	104,661,000	1.1	283	1,911	9.4 (1960–69)
Sweden	8,105,000	0.8	18	4,055	3.5 (1960–70)
United Kingdom ...	55,566,000	0.4	228	2,128	2.2 (1960–69)
United States	207,006,000	1.1	22	4,734	3.2 (1960–70)
West Germany	59,175,000	0.8	239	3,034	3.6 (1960–70)

* At market prices (U.S. dollars).   † 1963–70.   ‡ 1969.   § 1970. || 1963.
Sources: United Nations, *Demographic Yearbook, 1971*, pp. 112–24, and *Statistical Yearbook, 1971*, pp. 568–91, 600–602.

Underdeveloped Countries. The sample of underdeveloped countries indicates that their average annual rates of population growth for most of the decade of the sixties ranged from 2.2 to 3.1 percent per year. Their population densities varied from 14 persons per square kilometer in Tanzania to 168 in India. The lowest average annual rate of growth in per capita GNP for the decade was 0.5 percent for India, and the highest was reported as 4.1 percent for Kenya. But Kenya's per capita GNP in 1970 was still at an extremely low figure, $140.

While nothing conclusive comes from the foregoing data, a few supplementary observations may be in order. In the underdeveloped countries, population growth is occurring. Death rates are high because nutrition, sanitation, and medical knowledge and facilities are at low levels. But birth rates are even higher. Population densities appear to be relatively high in Pakistan and India, yet Pakistan reported a 3.2 percent annual increase in per capita GNP. Tanzania, with a much lower population density than Pakistan, also reported a lower annual rate of increase in per capita GNP.

Moderately Developed Countries. The sample of moderately developed countries indicates that with the exception of Argentina and Chile, the range of population growth rates is higher than that for the underdeveloped countries. The higher levels of per capita GNP are conducive to better nutrition, better sanitation, and improvements in the quantity and quality of medical services available. Infant and child mortality has decreased and life expectancy has increased. Thus, the death rate is lower. Birth rates, however, remain high, causing population growth rates to be generally higher for this group of countries.

The higher population growth rates of some of the moderately developed countries may impede their economic development or play a significant part in holding down the rate of increase in per capita GNP. Increases in per capita GNP are for the most part low; Taiwan and South Africa provide significant exceptions. Further, Taiwan, with a population density more than twice that of India and with a higher rate of population growth, has a very high 7.1 percent annual growth rate in per capita GNP.

Developed Countries. The developed countries are characterized by slow population growth. Their death rates are low, and they have come to accept measures that hold the birth rate down. The general range of growth rates in per capita income is higher than for the underdeveloped and moderately developed countries. The population density characteristics differ widely among the countries of the sample.

Summary. The data on population growth, population density, levels of per capita GNP, and growth in per capita GNP do not indicate that population growth plays a dominant part in holding living standards down in countries around the world. If problems of population pressure on living standards do occur, they are most likely in moderately developed countries that have not yet brought their birth rates down to correspond to the lower death rates that their moderate affluence permits. Thus their further growth may be impeded. The developed countries appear to have little or no population pressure on their living standards. Almost all of them, except sparsely populated Canada and Australia, have relatively low rates of population growth, indicating that slow population growth is indeed characteristic of developed countries.

U.S. Population Growth

We will look more closely at population growth and living standards in the United States. Data on population growth are shown in Table 1–3 and on per capita income (as measured by GNP) in Table 1–4.

The population growth trends in the United States are far from frightening; they contain little or no hint of any sort of population explosion. Three estimates of population growth patterns to the year 2020, based on different assumptions as to what the fertility rate will be from now until that year, are shown in Table 1–3.

The medium Series D projection appears to pick up the trend evidenced through 1972, carrying it through the year 2020. This projection is based on the assumption that each woman by the end of her childbearing period will have had 2.1 children. The actual fertility rate for the 12-month period ending with February 1973 was 72.3, which converts to 2.17 children per woman. For the month of February 1973 alone it was 70.9, which means 2.13 children per woman and closely approaches the assumed fertility rate for the

TABLE 1–3
U.S. Population Trends

Year	Population (millions)	Average Annual Increase
1800	5.3	—%
1850	23.2	—
1900	76.0	—
1950	152.3	2.5
1960	180.7	2.9
1970	204.9	2.2
1971	207.0	2.1
1972	208.8	1.8

Year	Projected Population (millions)* High (Series C) Millions	Average Annual Increase	Medium (Series D) Millions	Average Annual Increase	Low (Series E) Millions	Average Annual Increase
1975	215.9	2.7%	213.9	1.9%	213.4	1.6%
1980	231.0	3.4	224.1	2.3	221.8	1.8
1985	248.7	3.6	235.7	2.3	230.9	1.7
1990	266.2	3.3	246.6	2.0	239.1	1.4
1995	282.8	3.3	256.0	1.7	245.6	1.1
2000	300.4	3.5	264.4	1.7	250.7	1.0
2005	321.0	4.1	273.1	1.7	255.2	0.9
2010	344.1	4.6	282.0	1.8	259.3	0.8
2015	368.0	4.8	290.4	1.7	262.6	0.7
2020	392.0	4.8	297.7	1.5	264.6	0.4

* High, medium, and low projections are based on assumptions of 2.8, 2.1, and 1.8 children, respectively, for each woman in the population at the end of her childbearing age.

Sources: U.S. Department of Commerce, Bureau of the Census, *Statistical Abstract of the United States, 1972*, p. 10, *Estimates of the Population of the United States and Components of Change: 1940 to 1972*, Current Population Reports, Series P–25, No. 481 (April 1972), and *Projections of the Population of the United States by Age and Sex: 1972 to 2020*, Current Population Reports, Series P–25, No. 493 (December 1972).

Series D projection.[5] If the medium projection is more or less correct, the United States will eventually reach a zero population growth rate. This would occur during the last half of the 2000s at a population level between 300 and 400 million.

Fertility rates can be volatile over time, but much evidence points toward permanence of the assumed rate or to a rate even lower. We noted previously that the rates of population growth tend to be much lower in the developed countries of the world than in those that are less developed. In the United States a number of factors point in the direction of lower fertility rates: later marriages, higher divorce rates, an increasing number of women in the labor force, improvements in contraceptive devices, and liberalization of abortion laws.

Effects on Living Standards. There is no evidence that population growth, either experienced or projected, has had or is likely to have adverse effects on living standards as evidenced by per capita GNP. Trends in per capita GNP are shown in Table 1–4. The effects of inflation or rising prices have been removed from the data by quoting the value of per capita output of goods and services for each of the years in terms of 1958 prices. During the 1950s per

TABLE 1–4
Per Capita GNP in the United States, 1950–72

Year	Per Capita GNP (at 1958 prices)	Rate of Annual Increase (percent)
1950	$2,342	
1955	2,650	1.4%
1960	2,699	
1965	3,181	
1967	3,399	
1968	3,522	3.2
1969	3,577	
1970	3,516	
1971	3,583	1.9
1972	3,782	5.6
1973*	3,991	5.5

* Estimate for the first quarter only.
Sources: U.S. Department of Commerce, Bureau of the Census, *Statistical Abstracts of the United States, 1972*, p. 315; U.S. Department of Commerce, Bureau of Economic Analysis, *Survey of Current Business*, Vol. 53, No. 4 (April 1973), p. 5–1.

---

5 U.S. Department of Health, Education, and Welfare, Public Health Service, *Monthly Vital Statistics Report*, Vol. 22, No. 2 (April 1973).

capita income growth was relatively low, but this was not due to
population growth but to recessions or periods of slack economic
activity following the Korean War and again in the late 1950s.
Through the 1960s the growth rate of per capita GNP was substantially higher, although the population growth rate did not slow
appreciably until the end of the decade.

Forecasting very far into the future is an uncertain business, but
in general the outlook is certainly not dismal. The population projections referred to above indicate an eventual leveling off of the
total population at around 350 million persons—not even double
the present population. At this point the population density would
still be less than 40 persons per square kilometer, which is relatively
low as compared to many countries with similar or higher per capita
GNP growth rates.

Crowding. How serious are the crowding problems engendered
by population growth? Population density is the usual measure of
the extent to which crowding occurs, but the density levels at which
crowding can be said to occur differ, depending upon who is defining the term. Daniel Boone felt crowded when he could see the
smoke from a neighbor's fire, but many people who live in New
York City are not happy in more sparsely populated environments.

Many countries have a population density that far exceeds that of
the United States. The population density of Taiwan, for example,
was 390 persons per square kilometer in 1970. In Japan it was 280
persons per square kilometer. In both countries people are accustomed to living in close quarters. Is it likely that they *feel* more
crowded than do people in the United States where population
density is only 22 persons per square kilometer?

Crowding and congestion occur in some places—particularly in
urban areas—but not in others. A flight over New Mexico, Arizona,
Colorado, or Utah will reveal thousands of square miles of empty
land. In Texas, Oklahoma, Kansas, Missouri, and almost any other
state there are vast areas with ample elbow room. Similarly, around
the world there are vast areas that are sparsely populated. Why do
people put up with crowding? All things considered, they apparently believe their living standards are higher than they would be
in the more sparsely populated areas.

Pollution. Population concentrations have always had adverse
effects on the environment in which the concentration occurs.

Anthropologists have speculated that the abandonment of old Indian cities like Chichén Itzá in Yucatán and Machu Picchu in Peru may have resulted partly from waste accumulations. Terrible pollution problems existed in the cities of Asia, Europe, and Africa in ancient and medieval times, resulting in plagues and epidemics that wiped out thousands of persons.

Pollution can also be observed in the crowded areas of the United States, and we sometimes confuse the pollution problem with population problems. Certainly the more people that occupy a given area, the more wastes there will be to dispose of. But the amount of pollution that occurs also depends upon the means available to dispose of wastes. We shall treat the pollution problem in detail in a later chapter. At this point, we can say with some degree of confidence that intolerable levels of pollution of the environment are not the inevitable consequences of the population growth projected for the United States in the foreseeable future.

Some Economic Implications of ZPG

Although a zero population growth situation is not expected to occur in the United States before 2050, its economic implications are interesting. These implications follow primarily from the changes in the age distribution of the population as we move toward zero population growth.

Age Distribution of the Population. It is possible to project what will happen to the number of people in different age brackets as the population grows to its zero growth rate level. First, there will be little growth in the number of people under 25 years of age. Second, there will be a marked increase in the number between 25 and 65, as well as in the number over 65. The median age of the population will rise from about 28 to 37 years.

Growth of GNP. Gross national product will continue to increase, both while the population is growing and after it reaches its stationary level. Since the proportion of the population between the ages of 25 and 65 will be increasing, the labor force will tend to increase faster than the population as a whole. In addition, the economy can be expected to continue accumulating capital resources both while the population is increasing and after it becomes stationary. After the population becomes stationary, GNP will continue to grow as capital is accumulated and as the quality of the labor force is improved—if it is improved.

Changes in the Pattern of Demand. The demand pattern of the population will change as its age composition changes. For example, a ZPG fertility rate means that the diaper and pacifier industries will cease to grow. The lower growth rate of the school-age population means that the demand for school facilities will grow relatively more slowly than demand in general, soon tapering off to a zero rate of increase unless educational efforts become more intensive. Presumably, as the proportion of the population over 65 increases, demand for medical facilities, drugs, nursing homes, travel, and leisure-time activities will increase more rapidly than demand in general.

These changes in demand patterns are no cause for alarm. Demand patterns are always changing over time as new inventions and innovations come to the market. The changing age distribution of the population will be gradual enough so that it will not bring about sudden changes in demand. In fact, the demand changes stemming from the changing age distribution are likely to be swamped or hidden by those that occur in the normal course of events over time.

THE ROLE OF GOVERNMENT

What, if anything, should governments do to influence population growth? Public opinion in the United States and in other countries is not unanimous in answering this question. Most people agree that governments can take steps that will reduce fertility rates and, eventually population growth; but questions of what is ethical, what is moral, and what is socially acceptable cause divided opinions with regard to what should be done. We shall consider two alternative courses of possible government action. The first consists of positive programs to influence or coerce people to limit family size. The second consists of programs for birth control education and action in which final judgments are left to the individuals concerned.

Programs to Influence Family Size Decisions

A government may use its taxing powers to induce people to limit their family size. It could, for example, levy a heavy tax on each minor child over and above some specified number, say two children. The costs of additional children could be made heavy enough to induce many to seek out and use birth control information, devices, and methods.

Such a tax would place poor people at a disadvantage in relation to rich people. The incentives *not* to have children would tend to be greater for the poor than for the rich if the tax on all children in excess of two were the same for everyone, because the tax on a child would constitute a larger proportion of the income of a poor person than that of a rich person. Further, the use of birth control devices and techniques can be overlooked, as some are not 100 percent effective. Consequently, some unintended pregnancies and births over and above the limit are likely to occur, and taxation of these would place a greater burden on the poor than on the rich.

Subsidy payments provide another means of governmental influence on fertility rates. The government of India, for example, has been paying a subsidy to each male who undergoes a vasectomy, provided he has fathered two children. An interesting facet of this program is that a like subsidy is paid to any individual who induces another to have a vasectomy, so a supply of procurers of patients is developed. Subsidies can also be used to encourage females to be sterilized. Again, the primary incidence of efforts to reduce the fertility rate will be among the poor.

Programs for Birth Control Education and Action[6]

Population experts estimate that some 20 percent of total births in the United States are unwanted, an unwanted birth being defined as one in which either contraception failed or, in the absence of contraception, there was no intent that the woman become pregnant. Most of these result either from an absence of knowledge on the part of those engaging in sexual intercourse or from the unavailability at the time of intercourse of reliable contraceptive devices. Obviously, if every birth were the result of deliberate informed choice the fertility rate would be below its present level, and progress toward zero population growth would be more rapid than it is now.

---

[6] This section is based on Ansley J. Coale, "Man and His Environment," *Science* 170 (October 2, 1970): 132–36.

The ultimate objective of birth control education and action programs is precisely that of making every birth the result of deliberate, informed choice. At a minimum, birth control education would be aimed at providing information on the causes and consequences of childbearing and on the availability and reliability of contraceptive devices and techniques, but it by no means needs to be limited to these areas. It would be universal and introduced before young people reach the childbearing age.

Education would be supplemented by birth control clinics, which would make reliable contraceptive devices available to all who want them. They would be staffed by trained medical personnel capable of rendering sound medical advice on the pros and cons of different means of contraception. They would also be available for all of the routine medical examinations necessary for effective contraceptive practices.

For every birth to be indeed a matter of deliberate choice, it would be necessary to use abortions as a last resort to terminate unwanted pregnancies, some of which would occur despite widespread dissemination of birth control information and use of contraceptive practices. The moral issues raised by abortion are without doubt more pronounced than those raised by any other means of preventing unwanted births. Until very recently most states have had antiabortion laws, but antiabortion sentiment is changing. Some state antiabortion laws have been declared unconstitutional, and others have been made less stringent. Some states—New York, for example—make abortion a private matter between the doctor and the patient.

The Appropriate Course

Unfortunately, the appropriate course of action for all governments to take in influencing population growth is not clearly evident. The impact of population growth is not the same for all countries. Within any given country the web of moral, ethical, and social values will determine what is feasible at any given time. There will seldom be unanimity among the population of a country; it considers the alternatives and makes its choices. Then we engage in discussion with our fellow citizens to try to come to a meeting of the minds on what courses of action to take or, perhaps, on whether no action at all should be pursued by the government.

SUMMARY

Many people are concerned about population growth because they fear it will reduce living standards, raise pollution levels to unbearable levels, and cause excessive crowding. These fears are to a large extent economic in nature, and a knowledge of the nature of economic activity is essential to their analysis.

Economic activity is generated by the wants of mankind, which seem to be insatiable in the aggregate. The means available in any economy for satisfying the wants of its population are scarce. They consist of the economy's resources—its labor and its capital—along with its available technology. The supplies of resources, together with the level of technology available, determine the maximum GNP that the country can turn out to satisfy wants. Dividing a country's GNP by its population yields its per capita GNP, which is a rough measure of its standard of living. Thus an assessment of the impact of population growth over time on living standards is largely an assessment of whether or not it has any appreciable impact on the growth of per capita GNP over time. The population growth rate of a country, or its rate of population increase, is made up of two components, the rates of natural increase and net migration. Predictions of the future population growth rate hinge on the country's anticipated fertility rate.

There is not much evidence that population growth by itself has impinged significantly on the living standards of countries around the world. Moderately developed countries may provide an exception. Developed countries have already achieved very low population growth rates.

Neither does population growth appear to be a serious problem in the United States. Fertility rates are now and should continue to be low enough to result in zero population growth at less than twice the present population level. Meanwhile per capita GNP continues to grow at a very satisfactory rate. Crowding is a problem only for those who choose to make it so. Pollution is not an inevitable outcome of foreseeable population growth in the United States.

As zero population growth is approached in the United States, the distribution of population among age brackets will shift upward. Gross national product and per capita GNP should continue to grow, but demand patterns will change. These will likely be swamped by "normal" changes in demand patterns.

Governmental policies and actions may be used to influence fertility rates and population growth rates. They may be aimed at influencing directly family size decisions or disseminating birth control information and techniques. Whatever course of action the government pursues will most certainly be surrounded by controversy, for this is a morally sensitive area.

SUPPLEMENTARY READINGS

Bogue, Donald J. *Principles of Demography*. New York: John Wiley & Sons, 1969.

A comprehensive book covering the entire field of population studies, written to be comprehensible to all levels of college and university students. Each chapter is more or less self-contained and thus can be read and understood independently.

Coale, Ansley J. "Man and His Environment." *Science* 170 (October 2, 1970): 132–36.

A thoughtful treatise on population growth and environmental problems. Coale is a population expert who understands economic principles. His treatment of appropriate governmental policies relative to human fertility is especially good.

Ehrlich, Paul R. *The Population Bomb*. Rev. ed. New York: Ballantine Books, 1971.

A scare book written by a biologist with little understanding of economics. It is an important book, however, worthy of the attention of anyone seriously concerned with population problems.

Enke, Stephen. "*ZPG*: Good or Bad for Business?" *Wall Street Journal*, Tuesday, May 18, 1971, p. 20.

A report on some of the findings at Tempo, General Electric's center for advanced studies at Santa Barbara, Cal. The impact of a zero population growth fertility rate on GNP and the structure of demand is examined.

"Population Heads for a Zero Growth Rate." *Business Week*, October 24, 1970, pp. 102–4.

The possibility of zero population growth is discussed, and its consequences for the economy are projected. The article then considers possible governmental policies to reduce the fertility rate.

Part I

RESOURCE ALLOCATION

Chapter 2

AGRICULTURAL ISSUES

CHECKLIST OF ECONOMIC CONCEPTS

Demand
Supply
Equilibrium Price
Shortage
Surplus
Per Capita Income
Economic Instability
Price Elasticity of Demand
Changes in Demand
Changes in Supply
Price Support
Subsidy
Economies of Size
Income Distribution
Change in Quantity Demanded
Change in Quantity Supplied
Economic Efficiency

2

AGRICULTURAL ISSUES
Should We Subsidize the Rich?

IT LOOKED to old Joe Henderson as if the long winter ahead would be a hard one. Smut and borers had hit the corn crop, but at least he had the fodder left to help hold the cattle through the winter. It might do the job if the winter wheat would give him a break and provide a little more pasture than usual. The wheat crop hadn't been too bad, and the government loan check had been very welcome. But for a small farmer like Joe the check had been small—he just didn't have enough total bushels to get a very large government loan for it. He had wanted to get the tractor overhauled this winter, but that seemed to be out of the question now. If they should get enough rain next spring to make another good wheat crop he could get it done next winter. The tractor would make it through the year, even though the gas and oil costs would be a little higher.

They wouldn't starve to death. Sally's garden had been a good one, and she had canned large quantities of vegetables. They could butcher a couple of hogs and a beef or so. These food supplies, together with what the milk and egg money would buy in town, would take care of their personal needs quite well. If only they could just get a little money ahead to expand and modernize their buildings and machinery as well as take care of maintenance and repairs on what they have!

IS THERE AN AGRICULTURAL PROBLEM?

Over the years the Joes and Sallys of the United States have evoked a great deal of public and congressional concern. Spurred by the Great Depression of the 1930s, the U.S. Department of Agriculture has been built into a large bureaucratic organization pumping out large sums of money to alleviate the "farm problem." But what is the problem—what is it that the government presumably alleviates? Spokesmen for agriculture usually point to two phenomena: (1) low farm incomes, or poverty on the farm, and (2) instability of farm incomes over time.

Farm Poverty

Poverty is usually singled out as the primary problem in agriculture. Farm incomes are thought to be too low relative to incomes in the rest of the economy, and farmers are therefore thought to be entitled to governmental assistance. Are farm incomes really all that low? We will look at some of the evidence.

Per Capita Income. Per capita disposable income of farm and nonfarm residents for selected years since 1935 is shown in Table 2–1. The per capita disposable income concept refers to what is available per person to spend per year. It consists roughly of a person's money income from all sources, less the taxes he must pay.

TABLE 2–1
Per Capita Disposable Personal Income, Farm and Nonfarm,
Selected Years, 1935–72

Year	Farm, from All Sources (dollars)	Nonfarm, from All Sources (dollars)	Farm, as a Percentage of Nonfarm
1935	$ 237	$ 535	44.3%
1940	245	573	36.5
1945	655	1,162	56.4
1950	841	1,458	57.7
1955	854	1,772	48.2
1960	1,100	2,017	54.5
1965	1,772	2,481	71.4
1969	2,406	3,169	75.9
1970	2,600	3,404	76.4
1971	2,832	3,623	78.0
1972	3,179	3,837	82.9

Source: U.S. Department of Agriculture, Economic Research Service, *Farm Income Situation,* July 1972, p. 50, and February 1973, p. 7.

The data confirm that per capita farm income has indeed been lower than per capita nonfarm income over the entire series of years considered. It increased from less than 50 percent of per capita nonfarm income in the 1930s and 1940s to about 83 percent in 1972. But per capita farm disposable income is simply the average disposable income of those living on farms. It provides no information on how many, if any, are poor—or rich.

Income Distribution. We can build a better picture of the farm income situation from information on its distribution among farms. In Table 2–2 farms are classified by the total value of the products

TABLE 2–2
Distribution of Farms by Value of Sales, 1971

Classification by Value of Sales	Number of Farms (000 omitted)	Percent of Farms	Cash Receipts from Farming (000,000 omitted)	Percent of Receipts	Realized Net Income per Farm (dollars)
Under $10,000					
$2,500 or less	1,184	40.5%	$ 1,344	2.6%	$ 1,059
2,500–4,999	260	8.9	1,113	2.1	2,049
5,000–9,999	370	12.7	3,060	5.8	3,492
Subtotal	1,814	62.1%	$ 5,517	10.5%	
$10,000 or more					
$10,000–19,999	513	17.5%	$ 8,259	15.6%	6,208
20,000–39,999	374	12.8	11,346	21.4	9,208
40,000 and over	223	7.6	27,826	52.5	25,664
Subtotal	1,110	37.9%	$47,431	89.5%	
Total	2,924	100.0%	$52,948	100.0%	

Source: U.S. Department of Agriculture, Economic Research Service, *Farm Income Situation*, July 1972, pp. 68–71.

they sell annually. The table shows the number of farms in each classification and the percent of all farms this number represents, the total cash receipts of the farms in each classification, and the percentage of all total receipts each classification generates. The last column shows the average realized net income (after deduction of all expenses) per farm in each classification.

Most families living on farms generating less than $10,000 cash receipts per year are living in poverty as it is defined by federal government agencies. Realized net income per farm is less than $3,500. Note that over 60 percent of the total number of farms in

existence are poverty farms and that these generate only slightly
more than 10 percent of total farm cash receipts. Poverty farms are
typically small, infertile, poorly equipped, and managed by persons
with low levels of educational attainment.

Nonpoverty farms generating annual cash receipts of $10,000 or
more make up less than 40 percent of the total number of farms. But
notice the large share of total farm cash receipts they generate—
almost 90 percent. These farms are for the most part well-managed,
efficient business enterprises. They take advantage of advanced agricultural technology in the areas of soil care, fertilization, plant and
animal genetics, and equipment.

Most nonpoverty farms are large, so that they can use cost-saving
technology. As Table 2–3 shows, the size of the average farm in

TABLE 2–3
Average Farm Size, 1935–71

Year	Size (acres)	Year	Size (acres)
1935	155	1960	297
1940	167	1965	342
1945	191	1970	383
1950	213	1971	389
1955	258		

Source: U.S. Department of Commerce, Bureau of the Census, *Statistical Ab-stract of the United States, 1972*, p. 573.

the United States increased from 297 acres in 1960 to 389 acres in
1971, evidencing the advantages of size as technology has been
improved.

Instability of Farm Incomes

Farm incomes are generally thought to be less stable than nonfarm incomes; that is, they are thought to vary more from year to
year. To test the validity of this idea, we compiled the lengthy data
series presented in Table 2–4. This table's bark is worse than its
bite—the relevant columns for our purposes are 3 and 5, which
show the percentage changes from year to year in per capita net
income from farming for the farm population and in disposable
income for the nonfarm population. Per capita net income from
farming *does not* constitute the total per capita net income of the

TABLE 2–4

Per Capita Net Income from Farming for Farm Population and Per Capita Disposable Income for Nonfarm Population, 1934–71

(1)	(2)	(3)	(4)	(5)
	Per Capita Net Income From Farming*, Farm Population	*Annual Rate of Change*	*Per Capita Disposable Income Nonfarm Population*	*Annual Rate of Change*
Year	*(dollars)*	*(percent)*	*(dollars)*	*(percent)*
1934	$ 78		$ 500	
1935	149	90.0%	535	7.0%
1936	128	—14.0	614	14.8
1937	183	42.9	638	3.9
1938	129	—29.7	590	—7.5
1939	122	— 5.4	630	6.8
1940	126	3.7	671	6.5
1941	200	58.3	801	19.4
1942	321	60.8	973	21.5
1943	427	32.8	1,063	9.2
1944	444	4.1	1,151	8.3
1945	477	7.5	1,162	1.0
1946	566	18.7	1,217	4.7
1947	584	3.1	1,267	4.1
1948	715	22.5	1,365	7.7
1949	522	—27.1	1,362	—0.2
1950	582	11.7	1,458	7.0
1951	719	23.4	1,548	6.2
1952	681	— 5.3	1,609	3.9
1953	649	— 4.7	1,677	4.2
1954	646	— 0.6	1,678	0.1
1955	590	— 8.6	1,772	5.6
1956	586	— 0.8	1,850	4.4
1957	591	0.9	1,902	2.8
1958	731	23.6	1,915	0.7
1959	653	—10.6	1,998	4.3
1960	732	12.1	2,017	1.0
1961	787	7.5	2,050	1.6
1962	814	3.5	2,128	3.8
1963	873.7	7.4	2,193	3.1
1964	796	— 8.9	2,343	20.5
1965	1,033	29.9	2,481	5.9
1966	1,147	11.0	2,643	6.5
1967	1,113	— 3.0	2,791	5.6
1968	1,120	0.6	2,985	7.0
1969	1,304	16.4	3,169	6.2
1970	1,388	6.4	3,404	7.4
1971	1,546	11.4	3,632	6.7

* Excludes government payments and income of farm population from nonfarm sources.
Source: U.S. Department of Agriculture, Economic Research Service, *Farm Income Situation*, July 1972, pp. 45, 49, 50.

farm population. Many people living on farms receive substantial amounts of income from nonfarm sources, including federal government payments. But it is net income from farming only that is considered at this point. The data are consistent with the observation that income from farming is much more volatile and unstable than income from the aggregate of nonfarming pursuits.

Natural Causes. Some of the instability of farm income results from phenomena of nature or from natural causes. When droughts occur, the wheat, corn, or cotton crop is small. Floods may occur at harvest time, wind and hail can destroy crops, and insects—boll weevils, grasshoppers, chinch bugs, and the like—can invade them. Plant diseases such as corn smut or wheat rust can reduce both the quantities and the qualities of crops.

Economic Causes. Some of the instability of farm income results from recurring periods of expansion and recession in the economy as a whole. During periods of economic expansion like 1945–48 and 1965–66, farm incomes rose farther and faster than average incomes economywide. During periods of recession like 1949 and the middle 1950s, they fell correspondingly farther and faster.

SOME USEFUL ECONOMIC CONCEPTS

Over the years, as Table 2–1 shows, average farm income has risen faster than average nonfarm income. Yet the vast majority of farms are poverty farms. This is the case even though the federal government pours large sums of money annually into the agricultural sector of the economy to alleviate poverty. The government's farm program in recent years has come under increasingly heavy attack. Many questions are being raised: Is farm poverty really different from poverty elsewhere in the economy? Does the farm program really attack the problems of farm poverty and instability of farm incomes? Are there alternative ways of handling the problem that would be better?

To assess the uniqueness and seriousness of farm problems and the impact of the government's farm program on the efficiency and equity of our economic system, we must consider certain economic concepts over and above those developed in the preceding chapter. These include the concepts of demand, supply, and market price determination.

Demand

The demand for a product refers to the quantities of that product that consumers or buyers will purchase. These quantities are expressed in rates per *time period,* like 10,000 bushels of wheat per month. It makes little sense to say that demand is 10,000 bushels unless the time span during which that amount would be taken is specified. Further, the amount taken per month, or per year, or whatever the specified time period is will depend on the price per bushel that buyers will have to pay. It will also depend on (1) the *prices of substitutes* and of *complements* for wheat, (2) the *purchasing power of buyers,* (3) buyers' psychological *states and preferences,* and (4) the *number of buyers* in the group under consideration.

Definition. Demand for a good or service is defined as the set of quantities per time period that buyers are willing to take at various alternative prices of the item, *other things being equal.* We can think in terms of a scientific experiment in which the "other things being equal" are the given conditions of the experiment. These are the factors (other than the price of the good) that were enumerated in the preceding paragraph. When these factors are held constant, how much will consumers take at each of various alternative price levels?

If we could actually consult all consumers of wheat, for example, we could devise a table something like Table 2–5, which is called a

TABLE 2–5
A Demand Schedule for Wheat

Price (dollars)	Quantity (bushels per month)	Price (dollars)	Quantity (bushels per month)
$10	1,000	5	6,000
9	2,000	4	7,000
8	3,000	3	8,000
7	4,000	2	9,000
6	5,000	1	10,000

demand schedule for wheat. This demand schedule is plotted as a demand curve in Figure 2–1. Both illustrate a fundamental characteristic called the *law of demand*—the lower the price of the product, the more consumers will take, and the higher the price, the less they will take.

FIGURE 2–1
A Demand Curve for Wheat

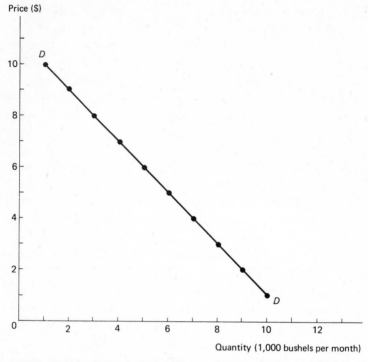

The numbers of Table 2–5 plotted graphically are points forming the demand curve *DD*. The demand curve shows the quantities that all consumers will take at alternative prices, other things being equal.

Changes. Since demand refers to an entire demand schedule or demand curve, a *change in demand* means a shift in the position of the entire curve. This results from a change in one of the "other things equal" which would cause consumers to take more of the product at each possible price or less of the product at each possible price. Suppose, for example, that an increase in consumers' purchasing power causes them to take an additional 1,000 bushels of wheat at each possible price. In Figure 2–2, the demand curve shifts (increases) from *DD* to D_1D_1. An increase or decrease in quantity taken in response to changes in the price of the product, like the movement from *A* to *B* in Figure 2–2, is called a *change in quantity demanded*. It is not called a change in demand.

FIGURE 2–2
A Change in Demand

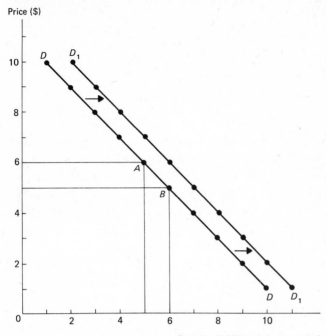

A change in demand means a shift of the entire demand curve from one position to another—say from *DD* to *D₁D₁*. A movement from *A* to *B* is not called a change in demand. Rather, it is called a change in quantity demanded because of a price change.

Supply

Definition. The *supply* of a product refers to the quantities per time period that sellers are willing to place on the market at alternative prices of the item, *other things being equal.* In the case of supply, these "other things" are (1) resource prices, (2) techniques of production, and (3) the number of sellers.

If the suppliers of wheat were asked how much per unit of time they would place on the market at alternative price levels, their answers would provide the information for a *supply schedule* or *supply curve* of the product. These are illustrated in Table 2–6 and

TABLE 2–6
A Supply Schedule for Wheat

Price (dollars)	Quantity (bushels per month)	Price (dollars)	Quantity (bushels per month)
$ 1	2,000	6	7,000
2	3,000	7	8,000
3	4,000	8	9,000
4	5,000	9	10,000
5	6,000	10	11,000

Figure 2–3. Ordinarily, suppliers would be expected to place more on the market at higher prices, so most supply curves slope upward to the right. There are two reasons for this. First, since it is more profitable to produce at the higher prices, each individual supplier is induced to place more on the market. Second, the greater profits

FIGURE 2–3
A Supply Curve

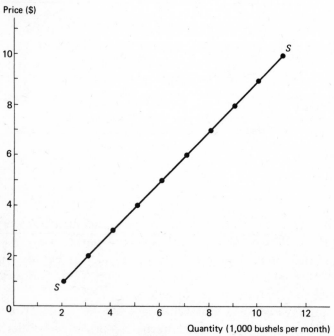

Prices and quantities from Table 2–6 are plotted as points forming the supply curve SS. The supply curve shows the quantities that all suppliers will place on the market at alternative prices, other things being equal.

earned from higher prices induce new producers to enter the market.

Changes. The same distinction is made between a *change in supply* and a *change in the quantity supplied* because of a price change as was made for the corresponding demand concepts. In Figure 2–4 a shift from SS to S_1S_1 is a change in supply, and a move-

FIGURE 2–4
A Change in Supply

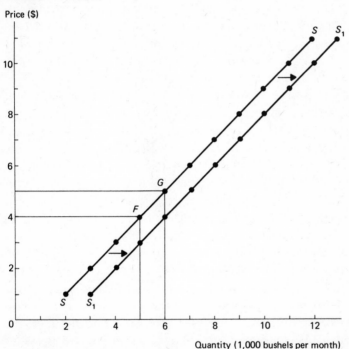

Quantity (1,000 bushels per month)

A shift in the supply curve from SS to S_1S_1 is called a change in supply. A movement along SS from F to G is called a change in quantity supplied because of a price change.

ment from *F* to *G* is a change in quantity supplied. An improvement in techniques of production that makes it possible for each output level to be produced at a lower cost per unit causes an increase in supply, since it also makes it possible to produce more at each possible price level than before.

Markets and Competition

When the buyers and sellers of a product interact with one another and engage in exchange, a *market* exists. The geographic area of any one market is simply the area within which buyers and sellers are able to transfer information and the ownership of whatever is being exchanged. Some markets are local in scope; others are national or international.

The degree of competition that exists in markets is important in economic analysis. At one end of the spectrum, markets fall into the purely competitive classification. At the other they are classified as purely monopolistic. The markets of the world range all the way from one end of the classification system to the other.

Competitive Markets. For a market to be purely competitive it must exhibit three important characteristics. First, there must be enough buyers and sellers of the product so that no one of them acting alone can influence its price. To illustrate this point consider the individual consumer buying a loaf of bread in a supermarket or an individual seller of wheat selling his wheat at a grain elevator. Second, the product price must be free to move up or down with no governmental or other kinds of price fixing impeding its movement. Third, buyers and sellers must be mobile. This means that any buyer is free to move among alternative sellers, and he can buy from whomever will sell to him at the lowest price. Similarly, sellers are free to move among alternative buyers and can sell to whomever will pay the highest price. Few markets are purely competitive in the sense of rigorously fulfilling all three requirements, but some may be almost so. Agriculture provides an example.

Monopolistic Markets. A *purely monopolistic* selling market, by way of contrast, is one in which there is a single seller of a product. The seller is able to manipulate the product price to his own advantage. He is able to block potential competitors out of his market—frequently with governmental help. On the buying side, a situation in which there is only one buyer of a product is termed *pure monopsony*. For the present, competitive markets will be our primary concern.

Competitive Market Price Determination

Equilibrium Price. The price of a product in a competitive market is determined by the interaction of buyers and sellers—or, as economists like to say, by the forces of demand and supply. How this comes about is illustrated in Figure 2–5. The supply curve shows

FIGURE 2–5
Competitive Market Price Determination

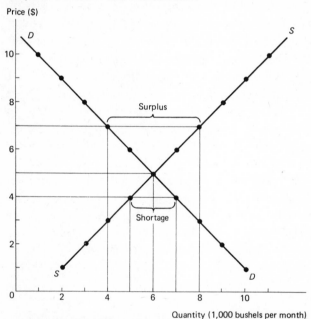

The demand curve and the supply curve together show how the equilibrium price for a product is determined in the market. If the price is above the equilibrium level, surpluses occur, and sellers undercut each other's prices until the equilibrium price is reached. If the price is below the equilibrium level, shortages occur, and buyers bidding against each other for available supplies drive the price up to the equilibrium level. At the equilibrium level there are neither surpluses nor shortages.

that at a price of $5 per bushel sellers want to sell 6,000 bushels of wheat per month. The demand curve shows that at this price, 6,000 bushels per month is what buyers want to buy. The price at which buyers want to buy the same quantity that sellers want to sell is termed the *equilibrium price*.

Effects of a Price above Equilibrium.   If the price is not at the equilibrium level, market forces are set in motion that move it toward that level. Suppose, for example, that the price of wheat in Figure 2–5 were $7 per bushel. Sellers would want to place 8,000 bushels per month on the market, but buyers would be willing to buy only 4,000 bushels. Thus, there would be a *surplus* of 4,000 bushels per month. Any of the many individual sellers who is not able to sell all of his supplies would have an incentive to cut his price a little below that at which the others sell. The price advantage would enable him to dispose of his surplus. As long as surpluses exist, sellers have incentives to undercut one another. When the price has been driven down to $5 per bushel, no seller is caught with a surplus, and the undercutting stops.

Effects of a Price below Equilibrium.   On the other hand, if the price were $4 per bushel, buyers would want 7,000 bushels per month but sellers would be willing to place only 5,000 bushels on the market. A shortage of wheat would exist. Individual buyers wanting more than they can get at that price will bid up the price in the attempt to alleviate their shortages. An incentive exists for them to increase their offering prices as long as shortages occur. When the price reaches the $5 equilibrium level, there are no shortages, and the upward movement of the price will cease.

Elasticity of Demand

A question that comes up frequently in economic analysis is how responsive the quantity taken of a product is to a change in its price, given the demand for the product. The measure of such responsiveness is called the *elasticity of demand*. It is computed by dividing the percentage change in quantity taken by the percentage change in price.

The computation of demand elasticity is illustrated in Figure 2–6. Let *DD* and *SS* be the original demand and supply curves. Now suppose that an improvement in technology shifts the supply curve to the right, to S_1S_1. The equilibrium price was originally $5, but with the increase in supply a surplus exists at that price, causing the equilibrium price level to move downward to $4. The quantity

FIGURE 2–6
A Price Change, Demand Elasticity, and Total Receipts

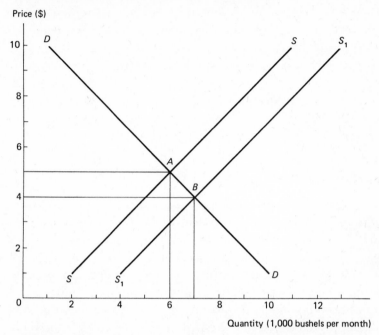

Elasticity of demand for a price change is computed by dividing the percentage change in quantity by the percentage change in price. In this example the percentage increase in quantity is outweighed by the percentage decrease in price. Demand is inelastic, and total receipts fall.

exchanged rises from 6,000 bushels to 7,000 bushels, for a 17 percent increase. Price falls by 20 percent. So elasticity of demand for the price change is 17/20, or 0.85, meaning that a 1 percent change in price generates an 0.85 percent change in quantity taken.

The elasticity measurement may turn out to be greater than 1, less than 1, or equal to 1, depending upon the demand curve under surveillance and on the part of the demand curve for which elasticity is measured. If it is less than 1, as it was in the foregoing example, demand is said to be *inelastic*. If it is greater than 1, it is said to be *elastic*. If it is equal to 1, it has *unitary elasticity*.

The magnitude of elasticity provides information on what will happen to the total receipts of sellers (or the total expenditures of buyers) if the price of a product changes. Consider the original equilibrium situation at point A in Figure 2–6. Total receipts of sellers, found by multiplying the quantity sold by the price, are $30,000. After the increase in supply and the decrease in price, total receipts are $28,000. This will always be the case for a price decrease when demand is inelastic—total receipts of sellers will fall because the percentage increase in quantity taken is less than the percentage decrease in the price. Similar reasoning leads to the conclusion that a price decrease when demand is elastic will cause total receipts of sellers to rise. When demand is of unitary elasticity, a decrease in price leaves the total receipts of sellers unchanged.

ECONOMIC ANALYSIS OF THE FARM PROBLEM

The economic concepts of the previous section are very useful in getting to the core of the farm problem—relatively more poverty in the agricultural sector than in the nonagricultural sector of the economy. There are three major facets to the analysis. These are (1) the growth of the U.S. economy, (2) the changes in demand for agricultural products relative to nonagricultural products, and (3) the changes in supplies of agricultural products as compared with nonagricultural products. All of these will be considered over the time period following World War II.

Growth of the U.S. Economy

The 20th century is appropriately called the century of innovation and invention. Not only has it taken inventions of the 19th century and made them useful to mankind, but it has added a far greater number of its own. Examples abound: the automobile, the airplane, the telephone, radio, television, and the harnessing of electricity and other sources of energy and power.

Innovation and invention go hand in hand with education in generating economic growth. They make it possible to get more output from present supplies of resources and to increase the resource supplies themselves over time. They enable us to improve the qualities of resources and to use resources more efficiently. The net result is a growing gross national product and more income for those who furnish the resources to produce it. In terms of the production possibilities curve described in Chapter 1, a growing GNP is shown by outward shifts of the curve. In terms of the demand and supply concepts of this chapter, it is reflected in increases in product demands stemming from increases in income and increases in product supplies resulting from increases in resource supplies and qualities, as well as from technological improvements.

Changes in Demand Patterns

The increases in demand generated by economic growth are not of the same magnitude for all products. The demands for most agricultural products increase more slowly than do those for most nonagricultural products. The reasons for this are not hard to see. Agriculture produces food and fiber—basic or primary products in the economy. The demand for food is limited by the size of the human stomach, as Adam Smith observed in the 1770s. Once diets reach levels at which the human body can be properly fed, further increases in demand must come from population growth. Although some wardrobes will not demonstrate it, so, too, does the demand for fiber reach levels at which further growth depends upon population growth. But for manufactured goods and services, our demands seem ready to expand without limit as our incomes rise.

Differences in the rate of growth of demands are illustrated in Figure 2–7, in which wheat is illustrative of agricultural products and automobiles represent nonagricultural goods. The initial demand and supply curves for wheat are $D_{w_1}D_{w_1}$ and $S_{w_1}S_{w_1}$, respectively. For automobiles they are $D_{a_1}D_{a_1}$ and $S_{a_1}S_{a_1}$. Wheat is priced at p_{w_1} and automobiles at p_{a_1}. Although these prices are shown at equal distances from their respective diagram origins, they are not equal prices. We have simply scaled the dollar axes of the two diagrams to make the distances the same. Let the price of wheat represented by p_{w_1} be $2.25 per bushel and the price of automobiles represented by p_{a_1} be $4,500 per auto.

Suppose now that economic growth and higher incomes increase the demands for wheat and for autos. Suppose further that the demand for autos increases relatively more than that for wheat. Unless the supply curve for autos is considerably flatter—more elastic— than the one for wheat, the price of autos will increase relatively

FIGURE 2–7

Differences in the Rate of Growth of Demand and Supply for Wheat and Automobiles

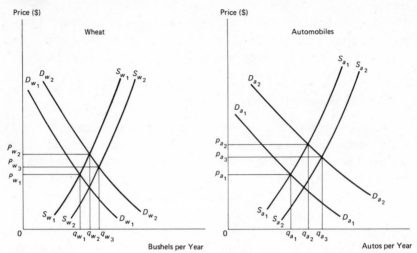

Growth in GNP and income increases demand for all normal goods and services, but the demand for agricultural products such as wheat increases proportionally less than the demand for nonagricultural products such as automobiles. Prices and profits increase relatively more in nonagricultural production, thus raising the incomes of nonagricultural persons relative to those in agriculture and providing an incentive for resource owners to shift some of their resources into nonagricultural production. The shift has not occurred rapidly enough to eliminate the farm-nonfarm per capita income differential.

more than will that for wheat. The effects of the demand increases alone will be new equilibrium prices of p_{w_2} for wheat and p_{a_2} for autos.

Supply Response

The changing demand pattern provides information on how the scarce resources of the economy should be allocated between agricultural and nonagricultural production. The relatively greater increases in nonagricultural prices indicate that nonagricultural goods and services are relatively more valuable to the consumers of the economy. Therefore, relatively greater quantities of the economy's labor and capital should be shifted into nonagricultural pursuits.

What has actually happened is that continuous improvements in the levels of technology, invention, and innovation have occurred in the agricultural as well as the nonagricultural sectors of the economy. In both sectors the effects of the improvements are supply increases—shifts of the supply curves to the right—which in turn would tend to mitigate the product price increases brought about by rising demands. Suppose that agricultural product supply increases in the same proportion as nonagricultural supply, as shown in Figure 2–7. The equilibrium price of wheat at the new demand and supply levels becomes p_{w_3}; that of automobiles becomes p_{a_3}. Thus, when the increases in demand and supply are both considered, the increase in the price of automobiles is relatively greater than that of wheat, because of the proportionally greater increase in the demand for automobiles.

The relatively greater demand and price increases for nonagricultural products over time makes their production more profitable than the production of agricultural products. This is reflected in the differences in incomes of those who live on the farm and those who do not. In more specific economic terms, labor and capital become worth more and are paid better prices in nonagricultural pursuits.

The differences in resource prices and in individual incomes between agricultural and nonagricultural production activities provide incentives for resources to move out of agriculture and into manufacturing and service industries. Even though the population of the United States has been growing rapidly during this century, the farm population has decreased, from some 32.3 million persons in 1934 to 9.4 million in 1971.[1] Diversion of capital resources out of agriculture has not been so dramatic. There has been a consolidation of capital into larger size farms, and these enterprises can compete very effectively with nonagricultural enterprises for the use of capital. The poverty farms are the ones where both labor and capital receive relatively lower rates of return than their counterparts in nonagricultural endeavors.

The supply curves of agricultural products have thus been subjected to two sets of opposing forces. The technological revolution

---

[1] U.S. Department of Agriculture, Economic Research Service, *Farm Income Situation,* July 1972, p. 49.

has served to increase agricultural supply. The exodus of labor and other resources from agriculture has served to reduce it. It appears certain that the former has dominated the latter, however, causing the supply curves in agriculture to shift to the right. This is evidenced by a doubling of farm marketings plus home consumption of agricultural products between 1940 and 1971.[2]

The Farm Problem Summarized

To the extent that there is a farm problem, it is primarily one of lower per capita income plus a highly unequal distribution of that income among farm families. The problem results from economic growth which has left a majority of farm families relatively (though not absolutely) worse off than nonfarm families.

Increases in product demand are generated by economic growth. The demand for agricultural products grows more slowly than does demand for nonagricultural products, so the incomes of the farm population (who own most of the resources used in agriculture) lag behind those of the nonfarm population. The income differentials provide inducements for resource owners to move their resources from the production of agricultural products into the production of nonagricultural ones. The reallocation of resources increases supplies of nonagricultural products relative to those of agricultural products. This situation would be expected to cease when nonfarm prices no longer are sufficiently higher than farm prices to cause nonfarm incomes to exceed farm incomes on the average. In the U.S. economy the reallocation of resources from farm to nonfarm activities has been and is occurring, but it has not been rapid enough and is not yet sufficient to eliminate the income differences.

ECONOMIC ANALYSIS OF GOVERNMENT FARM PROGRAMS

The Great Depression of the 1930s focused governmental attention on farm problems. It is not at all certain that farmers as a group were made worse off by the depression than were nonfarm groups.

---

2 Ibid., p. 7.

They were plagued by falling prices and incomes as well as by un-employment, but so were other sectors of the economy.

In attempting to combat the depression, the Roosevelt adminis-tration seemed preoccupied with prices. Just as the Nixon adminis-tration tried to devise means of holding prices down to stop inflation in the 1970s, the Roosevelt administration tried to devise means of holding prices up to stop the depression. These policies fail to get at the fundamental causes of either inflation or depression. Instead they attack symptoms. This preoccupation with the prices of prod-ucts has permeated the federal government's farm program since its inception. The major facets of the program have been (1) supply restrictions and (2) price supports.

Supply Restrictions

Kill the little pigs and plow up the corn, cotton, and wheat! These were the controversial instructions given to farmers in the initial year following passage of the Agricultural Adjustment Act in 1933. The essence of this act was a set of contracts between farmers and the government to limit the acreages planted to certain basic crops, in return for benefit payments from the government to the co-operating farmers. In addition actions were taken to reduce the size of the hog crop coming on the market by converting pigs into tankage. It was expected that the supply restrictions would raise prices and increase farm incomes, apart from the benefits paid.

The demand-supply analysis of the effects of supply restriction is straightforward. In Figure 2–8, D_1D_1 and S_1S_1 are the demand curve and the supply curve for wheat in the absence of any restric-tions on the number of acres planted. The equilibrium price will be p_1, and the quantity exchanged will be q_1. If farmers are now required to plow under some of their wheat fields, or, alternatively, if the number of acres they can plant is reduced, the supply will de-crease—the supply curve shifts to the left. The price of wheat in-creases from p_1 to p_2, and the quantity produced and sold is reduced from q_1 to q_2.

Does the increase in the price of wheat mean that the incomes of wheat farmers will also increase? Not necessarily. To compute the

FIGURE 2–8
Effects of Supply Restriction

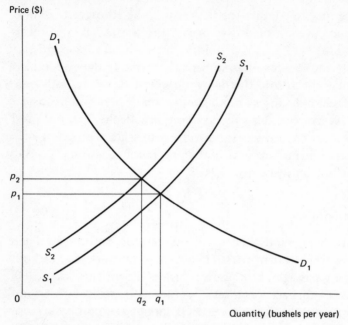

Supply restriction of a product raises the price and decreases
the quantity sold. Only if demand is inelastic for the price increase
will the total receipts of farmers increase.

total receipts (TR) of wheat farmers, the price received, is multiplied by the quantity sold, or

$$TR = q \cdot p.$$

We have noted that, from the law of demand, if p rises, q decreases.
If the percentage decrease in q just equals the percentage increase in
p—that is, if demand elasticity is unity—there will be no change in
TR. If the percentage decrease in q is greater than the percentage *increase* in p—that is, if demand is elastic—then TR will *decrease*
rather than increase. Only in the case of inelastic demand, in which
the percentage decrease in q is less than the percentage increase in p,
will TR increase. The effects of supply restrictions on farmers' total
receipts thus depend upon the elasticity of demand.

Price Supports, Storage, and Loan

The Nature of the Program.   The government's price support activities have been mostly of the storage and loan variety. Under this type of program the government determines a support price level for some product such as wheat. At harvest time any farmer can place his wheat in government-approved storage facilities, obtaining a loan from the government equal to the support price on each bushel stored. When the loan falls due the farmer has the option of paying off or letting the government have the stored wheat in repayment.

Under such a program wheat farmers are given an incentive to store wheat and to borrow from the government whenever the support price exceeds the market price. When repayment is due, if the market price is still below the support price, the farmer lets the government have his wheat. If, however, the market price has risen above the support price, the farmer pays off the loan at the support price, redeems his wheat, and sells it at the market price. In effect, the government guarantees that the farmer can receive a price for his wheat at the support level.

A demand and supply analysis of a storage and loan program is presented in Figure 2–9. Suppose that the equilibrium price p is less than the support price level p_1 set by the government. At the support price level p_1, consumers will buy only q_1 bushels, but farmers want to place q_2 bushels on the market. But if they do so—if they sell more than q^1 bushels—the sales price will necessarily be less than p^1. Rather than sell the excess over q_1 they will store the surplus wheat—quantity $q_1 q_2$—obtaining loans for it. Unless the market price exceeds p_1 when the loan is due, farmers will let the government have the wheat in repayment of the loans. In effect, then, when the government sets a support price above the equilibrium price level, consumers buy the quantity they want at that price, and the government buys the surplus wheat.

Economic Effects of the Program.   Since storage and loan programs are still used to support farm prices, it is important to be aware of their consequences. Like most social and economic policies, they have repercussions that go beyond their immediate objectives of raising farm prices and incomes.

FIGURE 2–9
Effects of Price Supports, Storage and Loan

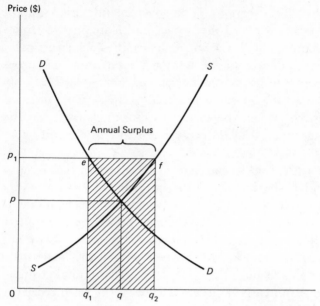

The support price p_1 is above the equilibrium price p. Consumers will purchase quantity q_1 at the support price, but farmers produce quantity q_2. The government purchases the surplus, making total payments to farmers equal to the shaded area q_1efq_2.

A most obvious result is that if the support for a product is effective it must result in the accumulation of the product by the government. If a support price is set at or below the equilibrium price level, the equilibrium price level will prevail and the support price will not be effective. To be effective the support price must exceed the equilibrium price, and when this is the case the accumulation of surpluses of the product is inevitable. This is exactly what has happened but, instead of being expected, it has been taken by many to mean that the program is in some way not being operated properly.

As the government accumulates surpluses of the product, pressure builds for the establishment of special surplus disposal programs. These take several forms. Surpluses may be sold abroad by the government at less than support prices. They may also be used to provide low-cost school lunches. They can be left to deteriorate in storage. All of these have been used to some extent.

Probably the most important consequence of surplus accumulations is that they provide additional incentives for supply or acreage restriction programs to be established by the government. To qualify for price supports, individual farmers are required to restrict their planting. The supply curve is shifted to the left, and the annual surplus is reduced. But the cost of this to consumers in the economy is that some quantities of the economy's scarce resources —land—are left idle, with a consequent reduction in gross national product and living standards.

In addition to the surplus disposal problem, consumers are harmed directly by a storage and loan price support program. It causes them to buy less of the price-supported product than they would otherwise choose to buy and to pay a higher price for it than would be the case under free market conditions. In Figure 2–9, without price supports consumers get q bushels at price p per bushel. The imposition of the support price raises the price to p_1 and reduces the amount they purchase to q_1. This makes consumers worse off than they would be in the absence of the support.

Finally, the direct costs of a storage and loan program must be met by taxpayers. These direct costs are of three kinds. The first is the cost of governmental purchase of the surplus; it amounts to the number of bushels of surplus product multiplied by the support price. In Figure 2–9 this amount is q_1q_2 multiplied by p_1, or it is the area of the shaded rectangle q_1efq_2. It represents a shift of purchasing power from taxpayers to the farmers who receive the support-price payments. The second is the costs of storage, handling, and disposal of surpluses. These costs, too, are incurred by the government and paid by taxpayers. Third, in addition to the acreage restriction required for participation in a storage and loan plan, further reductions in planting have been sought through direct payments to farmers for leaving additional land idle. Again transfers of purchasing power from taxpayers to farmers are involved.

Price Supports, Direct Subsidy

The Nature of the Program. Direct subsidies provide an alternative to storage and loan as a means of supporting prices of farm products. Under a direct-subsidy program, the support price level for a product would be determined in the same way as in the storage and loan case. Farmers would be permitted to produce as much as they desire to produce at the supported price. The direct-subsidy program differs, however, in that the quantity produced would be sold to consumers for whatever they are willing to pay. Sellers would then be paid a subsidy per unit of product equal to the difference between the support price and the price at which the product is sold to consumers.

The mechanics of the direct-subsidy program are shown in Figure 2–10. The equilibrium price and quantity are p and q, respectively. The supported price is p_1; at that price, farmers produce q_2 bushels. For q_2 bushels consumers will pay a price of only p_2 per bushel. The government makes up the difference by paying a subsidy to farmers of p_2p_1 per bushel for each bushel they produce and sell. The total money amount of the subsidy is represented by the shaded area p_2p_1gh.

The Economic Effects of the Program. What are the consequences of a direct-subsidy program? First, there is a transfer of purchasing power from taxpayers to farmers amounting to p_2p_1gh dollars. But note that there is no surplus problem and, therefore, no storage, handling, and disposal costs.

Second, consumers buy a larger amount of the product, q_2, and pay a lower price, p_2, than would be the case without the support price and the subsidy. This is not in the consumers' interest, however. At output and consumption level q_2, consumers pay a price of p_2 or q_2h per bushel, but production costs are q_2g per bushel. A per bushel cost level that exceeds what consumers are willing to pay means that too much of the product is produced. Consumers would rather have the resources needed to produce the extra amount of qq_2 bushels used to produce other products.

Third, the subsidy system has the virtue of bringing the amount of subsidization of farmers out in the open. It is easy to see that the subsidy is the difference between the support price and what con-

FIGURE 2–10
Effects of Price Supports, Direct Subsidy

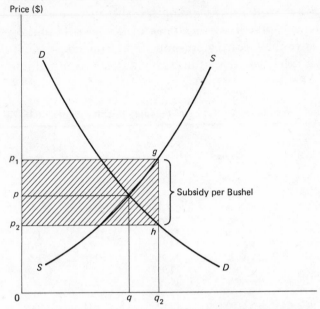

Quantity of Wheat (bushels per year)

The support price p_1 is above the equilibrium price p. Farmers will produce quantity q_2 at the support price and sell it for whatever it will bring in the market. Consumers are willing to pay price p_2 for that quantity. The government pays a subsidy to producers equal to the difference between the support price and the price that consumers will pay. Total payments made to farmers by the government are equal to the shaded area p_2p_1gh.

sumers pay for the product. In the storage and loan case, the amount of the subsidy is obscured.

Evaluation of Government Programs

What has been the impact of the federal government's agricultural program on farm problems? The available data do not provide us with conclusive answers, but we can draw inferences from the evidence they present.

The Poverty Problem. Has the government's farm program made progress in combating farm poverty? This is a difficult question to answer because we do not have reliable information on what farm incomes would have been had there been no subsidies. The data of Table 2–1 show that per capita disposable income as a per cent of nonfarm per capita disposable income has risen substantially over the years since the Great Depression. If we compare the data of Table 2–7 with those presented in Table 2–1 it becomes imme-

TABLE 2–7
Government Payments in Relation to Net Farm Income, Selected Years, 1935–72

Year	(1) Total Gross Farm Income (000,000 omitted)	(2) Production Expenses (000,000 omitted)	(3) Total Net Farm Income (000,000 omitted)	(4) Government Payments* (000,000 omitted)	(5) (4) as a Percent of (3)
1935	$10,394	$ 5,116	$ 5,278	N.A.	
1940	11,340	6,858	4,482	N.A.	
1945	25,374	13,062	12,312	$1,470	11.9%
1950	33,083	19,410	13,673	1,844	13.5
1955	33,353	21,889	11,464	3,508	30.6
1960	38,431	26,352	12,079	2,370	19.6
1965	45,920	30,933	14,987	3,438	23.0
1970	57,916	41,091	16,825	3,651	21.7
1971	61,403	44,006	17,397	5,501	31.6
1972	67,020	47,200	19,820	5,011	25.3

* Direct payments plus net price support payments.
Source: U.S. Department of Agriculture, Economic Research Service, *Farm Income Situation*, July 1972, pp. 45, 52, and February 1973, p. 7; *The Budget of the United States Government*, 1947, 1953, 1957, 1967, 1973.

diately apparent that the large relative increases in farm incomes in 1965 and the following years coincide with large increases in government payments to farmers in those years. This, together with the fact that in 1972 government payments were equal to some 7 percent of total gross farm income and over 25 percent of net farm income, implies strongly that government payments have played a substantial role in raising farm per capita income as compared with nonfarm per capita income.

Though government payments to farmers undoubtedly have in creased per capita farm income, however, it is by no means certain that they have eased the farm poverty problem to any significant degree. Government payments to farmers are directly related to income. The smaller the output of a farmer—the poorer he is—the less is the amount of government payments that he receives. The greater his output—the richer he is—the larger is the amount of subsidies received. In 1972, for example, some $656 million was paid to farmers receiving $20,000 or more in subsidies; subsidies of these magnitudes go to farmers already in the upper income brackets. This is the direct result of supporting the prices of particular products rather than the incomes of poor farmers. As a means of combating poverty, the price support program is an upside-down welfare program doing much for rich farmers and little for poor ones.

The Instability Problem. There is little evidence indicating that government payments to farmers have brought about greater stability over time in farm incomes. During periods of economic recession when farm prices and farm incomes drop, government payments have declined also. During the prosperous 1960s when farm incomes along with incomes in other sectors of the economy were rising rapidly, government payments to farmers reached record levels.

Instability in farm incomes arising from natural causes has been reduced by the government in various other ways. It has established comprehensive crop insurance programs to lessen the impact of the forces of nature on farm incomes. The research efforts that it has sponsored and supported have brought about improvements in pest and insect control. They have also substantially improved irrigation techniques, thus decreasing the dependence of farmers on the timeliness of rainfall in areas where irrigation is possible.

Economic Efficiency. Farm price support programs have probably reduced in some measure the overall efficiency of the U.S. economy. Supply restrictions, inducing farmers to leave some of their land idle, mean that the total output of the economy is kept below its potential level, so the population as a whole has less to consume than it would otherwise have. Also, to the extent that government payments to farmers increase farm incomes relative to nonfarm incomes, incentives for labor and capital resources to move from the agricultural sector into the industrial and service sectors of the economic system are reduced. In the absence of government payments to farmers, higher earnings available in the nonfarm sectors would indicate that in those sectors resources are more productive or are more efficiently utilized in producing what people want produced.

The adverse effects of price supports and supply restrictions on the efficiency of the economy may be partly offset by their effects on farm size. Inasmuch as government payments to farmers favor those that produce much and discriminate against those that produce little, they encourage increases in farm size. Referring again to Table 2–3, it can be seen that average farm size increased from 155 acres per farm in 1935 to 389 in 1971. As we noted earlier, larger farms are better managed and are better able to make use of advanced technology.

ALTERNATIVES TO PAYMENTS TO FARMERS

The general program of government payments to farmers appears vulnerable from several angles. As an antipoverty program it is highly inequitable, paying much to rich farmers and little to poor ones. In practice it seems to have made no significant contributions to the stability of farm incomes. It reduces economic efficiency by idling some of the economy's scarce resources.

In considering whether there could be a better way to provide assistance to the rural poor, an important question that should be raised is whether or not farm poverty should be singled out for special attention. Is it any different from nonfarm poverty in its effects? If government payments are made to alleviate poverty, should they not go to the nonfarm poor as well as to those who live on farms?

An alternative to the complex government payments program for agriculture is a simple but comprehensive antipoverty program for the entire economy that makes no distinction among the places of residence of the poor or the special interest groups to which they belong. Such a program will be developed in detail in Chapter 7; at this point we shall simply point out some of its underlying features. It would (1) increase the capacities of the poor to earn income wherever this can be done and (2) provide income supplements for those unable to earn an income level arbitrarily defined as poverty-line. Income supplements would be sufficient to raise everyone's income to the poverty-line level, and they should interfere as little as possible with incentives of the poor to earn income.

The instability of farm incomes need not be a serious problem. Much has been accomplished since the days of the Great Depression in the control of economic fluctuations. If the economy as a whole can be made reasonably free from large fluctuations, much of the instability of farm incomes will disappear.

SUMMARY

The agricultural "problem" is generally thought to be a low-income problem—per capita farm income is lower than per capita nonfarm income. Secondarily, the problem is one of instability of farm incomes over time.

Sound analysis of the agricultural problem rests heavily on the fundamental economic concepts of demand and supply. The interactions of the forces underlying the demand for and the supply of a product determine its price. The concept of elasticity of demand is important in the formulation of sound economic policies.

Per capita farm incomes lower than per capita nonfarm incomes are primarily the result of economic growth processes. As growth has occurred, demand for the outputs of the nonagricultural sector of the economy has expanded more rapidly than that for the outputs of the agricultural sector, generating differences in incomes. Resources have not been shifted rapidly enough out of agricultural production into nonagricultural production to eliminate the differences.

Government farm programs received their initial impetus in the Great Depression of the 1930s and have snowballed since that time. Supply restrictions and price supports have been the principal devices used to bolster farm incomes. The ways in which they have been used have produced perverse results—the greater the productive capacities and the outputs of individual farmers (the richer they are), the larger the payments they receive from the government. Poor farmers with small capacities and outputs receive very little. In addition, farm programs result in the waste or idleness of some of the economy's scarce resources.

Economic analysis of the agricultural problem indicates that present programs are not likely to solve it. It would appear that farm poverty differs in no significant way from nonfarm poverty and that an economywide antipoverty program may be the appropriate attack.

APPENDIX

THE MEAT BOYCOTT OF 1973

Only consumer blood pressure seemed to be rising faster than the food prices during the first quarter of 1973. Retail food prices in general were 8 percent above the same quarter of the previous year. Red meat—beef and pork—prices were 15.8 percent above the first quarter of 1972, and they rose 9.5 percent above those of the immediately preceding quarter. Alarmed consumers all over the country rumbled into one of the few spontaneous grass-roots protests in this country's history—the April 2–9 boycott against red meat.

The consumers' alarm is understandable, but the effectiveness of a boycott in doing more than venting their frustrations depends upon the economic foundations of the frustrating situation itself. The thoughtful consumer would ask a number of questions, the answers to which would guide his protest against high prices for agricultural products in the most useful direction: Why are prices so high? Is it because farmers are greedy? Or middlemen? Or packers? Is there some kind of ganging up on consumers? Will it help if consumers take organized actions? Is a boycott an effective means of obtaining lower prices?

DEMAND, SUPPLY AND MEAT PRICES

Could it be that there were no real villains in the meat price situation? Is it possible that the rise in prices can be explained with the demand and supply tools developed in this chapter? Suppose we examine the evidence and see what it indicates.

Demand for Meat

The available data seem to show that demand for meat as well as for other goods and services has been increasing over the years. Table 2–8 shows that consumers' incomes were increasing steadily from 1969 through 1973. The upward trend predates 1969, but we are interested primarily in recent years. We would expect increases in income or purchasing power—one of the "other things being

TABLE 2–8
Per Capita Disposable Personal Income, 1969–73

Year	Current Dollars	Annual Percentage Change
1969	$3,130	——
1970	3,376	7.8%
1971	3,603	6.7
1972	3,816	5.8
1973*	4,140	7.8

° Second quarter at an annual rate.
Source: U.S. Department of Commerce, Bureau of Business Analysis, *Survey of Current Business*, July 1973, pp. 12, 27.

equal" in the explanation of demand—to cause demand to increase.

Additional evidence to show that demand for meat was indeed increasing is contained in Table 2–9, which puts together prices and

TABLE 2–9
Prices and Consumption of Beef and Pork, 1968–73

Year	Beef and Veal		Pork	
	Price Per Pound of Choice Beef (dollars)	Per Capita Annual Consumption (pounds)	Price Per Pound (dollars)	Per Capita Annual Consumption (pounds)
1968	$0.866	113.3	$0.674	66.2
1969	0.962	114.1	0.743	65.0
1970	0.98.6	116.6	0.780	66.4
1971	1.04.3	115.7	0.70.3	73.0
1972	1.14.6*	117.7	0.88.5*	66.8
1973	1.22.1†		0.94.1†	

° December
† January
Sources: U.S. Department of Agriculture, Economic Research Service, *Livestock and Meat Situation*, August 1973, pp. 16, 18.

per capita annual consumption of beef and pork. Looking first at beef, note that even though prices were increasing, per capita consumption was increasing, too, except for 1971. The same thing holds for pork, except for the years 1969 and 1972. Unless supply is decreasing, rising per capita consumption coupled with rising prices can come about only if the demand curve for meat is increasing. Such an increase is illustrated in Figure 2–11 by a shift in the demand curve from D_1D_1 to D_2D_2.

TABLE 2–10
Supplies of Beef and Pork, 1967–72

Year	Beef (pounds; 000,000 omitted)			Pork (pounds; 000,000 omitted)		
	Production	Net Imports	Total	Production	Net Imports	Total
1967	21,011	1,285.5	22,296.5	12,581	334.6	12,915.6
1968	21,614	1,479.8	23,093.8	13,063	322.8	13,385.8
1969	21,831	1,603.8	23,434.8	12,953	255.0	13,208.0
1970	22,273	1,775.9	24,048.9	13,434	380.0	13,814.0
1971	22,446	1,702.7	24,148.7	14,793	386.2	15,179.2
1972	22,871	1,934.2	24,805.2	13,626	401.8	14,027.8

Source: U.S. Department of Agriculture, Economic Research Service, *Livestock and Meat Situation*, May 1972, p. 21, and August 1973, p. 22.

Supply of Meat

It appears that the supply of meat has also been increasing over time. Table 2–10 shows substantial increases in the quantities of beef placed on the market between 1967 and 1972. Both domestic production and net imports have been rising. The total quantities of pork, both domestic and imported, have also been increasing, except for the year 1969.

We cannot be sure whether the larger quantities supplied reflect movements up a supply curve or shifts to the right of the supply curve. Probably some of both have been occurring. This is shown in Figure 2–11 by a shift in the supply curve from S_1S_1 to S_2S_2.

Equilibrium Price

The rising prices of beef and pork listed in Table 2–9 indicate that demand for meat has been increasing faster than has supply. This is represented in Figure 2–11 by the shifts noted in the demand curve from D_1D_1 to D_2D_2 and in the supply curve from S_1S_1 to S_2S_2, the consequent rise in price from p_1 to p_2, and the increase in quantity exchanged and consumed from q_1 to q_2.

What happened in 1973 to make consumers so unhappy with meat prices? Much of the answer is contained in Table 2–9. The prices of beef and pork were rising, but the rate of increase was slow enough to be acceptable from 1967 through 1970. The price increases for beef accelerated rapidly in 1971, 1972, and 1973, with particularly large increases occurring in early 1973. Very large price increases were also registered for pork in early 1973. Buyers of meat were astonished by the increases and began to look for scapegoats.

What were the economic causes? Actually, as Table 2–11 shows,

TABLE 2–11
Supplies of Beef and Pork, First Quarter, 1972 and 1973

First Quarter	Beef (million pounds)			Pork (million pounds)		
	Production	Net Imports	Total	Production	Net Imports	Total
1972	5491	360	5851	3500	165	3615
1973	5482	410	5892	3262	45	3307

Source: U.S. Department of Agriculture, Economic Research Service, *Livestock and Meat Situation*, August 1973, p. 22.

FIGURE 2–11
Demand, Supply and Equilibrium Price of Meat

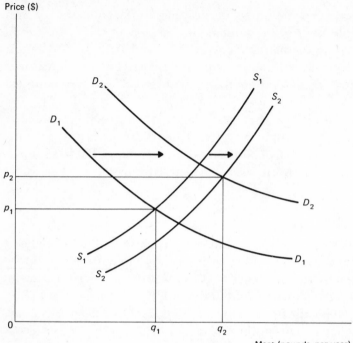

The initial demand and supply curves for meat are represented by D_1D_1 and S_1S_1, and the consequent equilibrium price and quantity are p_1 and q_1. An increase in demand for meat is shown by a shift in the demand curve to D_2D_2 while an increase in supply is indicated by a shift in the supply to S_2S_2. Since demand has increased more than has supply, the price increases to p_2 while the quantity exchanged increases to q_2.

total quantities of meat supplied decreased in the first quarter of 1973 as compared with the first quarter of 1972, but demand continued to grow. Due to bad weather in the summer of 1972, grain harvests were smaller than usual. Grain exports were up. The decreased grain supplies sent grain prices and the costs of feeding livestock soaring. Severe weather in the winter of late 1972 and early 1973 took its toll on livestock and, in addition, the growth stimulant DES for cattle was banned from use. The continuing increase in demand, coupled with a decrease rather than the usual increase in supply, simply boosted meat prices higher than consumers would quietly accept.

FIGURE 2-12
Effects of the Demand Increase and the Supply Decrease in Early 1973

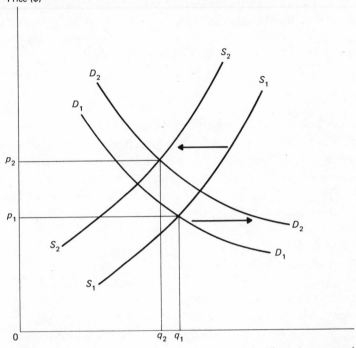

An increase in demand for meat coupled with a decrease in supply
caused a large increase in price and a decrease in quantity exchanged.

The meat situation for the first quarter of 1973 as compared with
the first quarter of 1972 is illustrated in Figure 2–12. Let D_1D_1 represent demand for meat in the first quarter of 1972 and S_1S_1 represent supply. The equilibrium price and quantity exchanged are p_1
and q_1, respectively. By the first quarter of 1973 demand had increased to D_2D_2 but supply had decreased to S_2S_2. The result was
a very large increase in price to p_2, while quantity exchanged fell
to q_2.

THE BOYCOTT

That the forces of demand and supply had pushed meat prices
toward the stratosphere would have given customers small comfort

even if they had known such forces were working—which they did not. According to news stories, consumers were hopping mad (at sellers?), and their anger gave rise to boycotting activities. Participants appear to have sought to "break" demand—whatever that means—in order to force prices down, thereby punishing sellers for charging high prices. What effects did the boycott have?

Short-Run Effects

During the boycott some consumers dropped out of the market altogether, while others curtailed their purchases. The expected effect is a shift in the demand curve to the left because of a change in consumers' tastes and preferences. Such a decrease in demand is shown in Figure 2–13 by the shift of the demand curve from D_1D_1 to D_2D_2. If the supply were S_1S_1 this would cause a drop in price from p_1 to p_2 and in quantity consumed from q_1 to q_2. The more people who joined the boycott, the more effective it would be in shifting the demand curve and decreasing the price.

But the world does not stand still while consumers do their thing. Retailers hold supplies off the market waiting for the boycott to end. They also cut back their orders from packers, and packers reduce their purchases from meat producers. So supply also shifted to the left, toward S_2S_2, cutting quantity exchanged to q_3 and raising the price to p_3, thereby mitigating to some extent the impact of the boycott on prices. Nevertheless, according to news reports, prices in some places dropped by 15 to 25 percent. These lower meat prices were offset to some extent, however, by increases in the demand for and in the prices of meat substitutes such as chicken and fish.

There is no doubt that economic punishment was administered to sellers—whether it was justifiable or not. Boycotters also punished themselves to some degree by doing without meat and by purchasing substitutes that in some instances were even higher in price. The main beneficiaries of the boycott were those consumers who did not observe it and who were able to buy meat at lower prices because of it.

Long-Run Effects

The long-run effects of a short period of boycotting are likely to be negligible. Demand cannot be "broken"; the demand curve can

FIGURE 2–13
**Effects of a Boycott on Demand, Supply, Price,
and Quantity Exchanged**

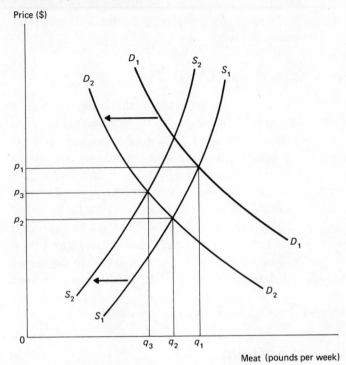

A boycott shifts the demand curve from D_1D_1 to D_2D_2. Suppliers respond by cutting supply to S_2S_2. The overall effect of the boycott is to reduce the price from p_1 to p_3, while quantity exchanged is decreased from q_1 to q_3.

only be shifted to the left, through an alteration in consumers' tastes and preferences. Though a temporary alteration may be rather easily achieved, the maintenance of a spirit of outrage and self-denial over time is a very different matter. Tastes and preferences for meat versus other food products are unlikely to be significantly changed in the long run.

Still, the boycott may have resulted in an expansion of consumers' knowledge that would affect tastes and preferences in a small marginal way. Many housewives may have tried new recipes using chicken, fish, and cheese, discovering in the process that their families liked them as permanent additions to their menus. They also may have taken advantage of an opportunity to introduce menus with lower cholesterol content. But most of the evidence indicates that following the week of the boycott, demand for beef and pork failed to stay permanently lower.

CONCLUSIONS ABOUT BOYCOTTS

However uncomfortable consumers are with rising prices of a product, they are not likely to dispense with it permanently through boycotting. Nor should they, in most cases. Rising prices ration the existing supply when demand is rising and provide incentives for increasing future supplies. Problems of equity—fears that sellers gouge consumers and that only the rich will be able to afford the high-priced items—can be dealt with more effectively by other means, through governmental antimonopoly policies and through transfer payments to the poor, for example. Consumers should understand that market forces continue to operate even in a regulated economy. Properly understood and used, these forces can be used to make our economy a more stable, more equitable one. Improperly understood or ignored, they can wreak havoc.

SUPPLEMENTARY READING

Heady, Earl O.; Haroldsen, Ervin O.; Mayer, Leo V.; and Tweeten, Luther G. *Roots of the Farm Problem,* Ames: Iowa State University Press, 1965, chap. 1–3.

Provides an excellent discussion of U.S. agricultural problems, with emphasis on the supply side, and traces out the historical development of agriculture in the United States.

Higbee, Edward. *Farms and Farmers in an Urban Age.* New York: Twentieth Century Fund, 1963.

Provides a highly competent, well-reasoned criticism of post World War II farm policies.

Paarlberg, Don. *American Farm Policy.* New York: John Wiley & Sons, 1964.

Paarlberg is an economist with long experience as a teacher, researcher, and advisor to U.S. presidents on farm policies. His critique of government programs is somewhat different from that of most agricultural economists and is well worth study.

Tweeten, Luther G. *Foundations of Farm Policy,* chap. 6. Lincoln: University of Nebraska Press, 1970.

This well-balanced presentation of the nature and causes of farm problems is somewhat advanced for beginning students, but there is much in it that can be readily grasped by all. Tweeten is a recognized expert in this field.

Chapter 3

ECONOMICS OF HIGHER EDUCATION

CHECKLIST OF ECONOMIC CONCEPTS

Investment in Human Capital
Social Spillover Benefits
Social Spillover Costs
Alternative-Cost Principle
Production Possibilities Curve
Explicit Costs
Implicit Costs

3

ECONOMICS OF
HIGHER EDUCATION
Who Benefits and
Who Pays the Bills?

THE ATMOSPHERE was tense in the Wilson household, but young Doug stood his ground. The problem was not new; it had been brewing all through his senior year in high school. Now that the year was almost over and decisions must be made about where he would go to college, the problem had come to a head.

Doug's parents wanted him to attend State University. It would be much less expensive than Private University where Doug had been accepted and where he desired to go. Tuition at S.U. for in-state students was only $500 per year, and at P.U. it was $3,000. With three kids to put through college, the Wilsons considered Doug's desire to go to P.U. unreasonable.

There were some intangibles, too, in the Wilsons' thinking. They would be more comfortable with Doug at S.U. It offered good, solid academic work, even though it was overcrowded with students and despite the fact that the legislature never seemed to appropriate quite enough money for its operation. They would feel a little better, too, knowing that the legislature sort of kept on eye on things at S.U. so that nothing very far out—like the operation of coed dorms—was likely to occur.

Doug thought the academic challenge would be greater at P.U. It had a reputation for academic excellence and for flexibility in the programs that students could pursue. Many of its faculty had na-

tional and even international reputations in their fields. Doug
had been a Merit Finalist in high school and had done exceptionally
well on his Standard Achievement Tests. He wasn't sure what major
field of study to pursue—he wanted to sample several before
making up his mind. At P.U. he could major in about anything he
wanted to—ethnomusicology, for example. If it were not a standard
major, they would help him build a nonstandard one. Doug was
ready for P.U.

In addition to the appeal of P.U.'s program, Doug thought college life would be much more enjoyable if he were far enough from
home to be relatively independent of his family. There comes a time
in one's life to cut the apron strings, and this seemed to Doug to be
it. He believed that he was quite capable of making sound decisions
on his own.

PROBLEMS IN HIGHER EDUCATION

While students like Doug wrestle with their problems of choice,
colleges and universities themselves are going through troubled
times. Enrollments increased rapidly immediately following World
War II, although the increase has now slowed considerably. The
riots, strikes, boycotts, and other disruptions of the academic
processes that were commonplace in the sixties remain as a threat
to administrators. Most institutions also face serious financial problems. Some say too many degrees are being granted—there is no
room for new college and university graduates to work in the fields
of their choice. Others say that colleges and universities are too
tradition-bound and do not respond to the needs of society.

All of these issues—and more—call for systematic analysis of the
higher education system. Such an analysis must center around three
interrelated primary problems: (1) what kinds of higher educational
services should be provided and what institutional structure is
appropriate for providing them, (2) how much should be provided,
and (3) who should pay for them.

What Kinds of Services?

We expect higher educational institutions to provide both general education and training for professions. They are expected to

transmit to students knowledge that has been accumulated in the past, to engage in research and other creative activities that advance the frontiers of knowledge, and to be at the cutting edge of the intellectual, cultural, social, and technological developments of mankind. Are these expectations realistic? If not, in what ways should they be modified? What should be the structure of the system that provides these services?

The present system is a dual one in which public as well as private colleges and universities operate. Both the public and the private components of the system contain three types of institutions: (1) junior colleges, (2) four-year colleges, and (3) universities. The public institutions are state-owned and operated, except for a few municipal and community colleges.

How Much Service?

The question of how much college and university educational service the society should provide is a very live issue today. Another name for this problem is "the financial crisis" of higher education. Most administrators, faculty members, and students are convinced that a financial crisis exists—that not enough is being spent for educational services.

Over the years legislative appropriations to public institutions have not kept pace with growing enrollments and rising costs. Tuitions have been increasing in both public and private schools. Many private schools have been operating with deficits, and a number face the possibility of shutting down their operations. Is all this an indication that the society believes relatively too much is being spent for higher educational services? Or do our methods of paying for higher education obscure the real demand for it?

Who Should Pay?

A related question concerns the extent to which governments (taxpayers) should bear the costs of producing the services of higher education and to what extent the costs should be borne by students and their families. If the government is to bear a substantial part of the cost, how should it go about doing so? Is the state university, with state appropriations for its capital and operating costs, the best way? Or should the state, instead of making appropriations to institutions, make funds available to students themselves, letting them choose their schools and pay tuition and fees sufficient to meet the costs of their educations? Should government payments of the costs of higher education favor poor families? These are some of the questions that bother us.

The Economic Basis of the Problems

The basic issues outlined above are largely economic problems. The economics of providing higher education services was largely ignored until the 1960s because such services comprised a relatively small part of the group national product and used small proportions of the nation's resources. In addition, it was somehow thought that education was above mundane things like economic benefits and costs.

The burgeoning enrollments since World War II have changed all that. Those responsible for decision making with regard to higher education—legislators, administrators, faculties, students, and concerned citizens—can no longer ignore the economic consequences of their decisions. The provision of higher educational services requires the use of large quantities of resources, and resources so used are not available to produce other goods and services. Higher educational services represent one of a great many competing uses for resources.

In this chapter we shall consider an economic framework of the higher education "industry" that should be useful in the decision-making processes concerning it. The present system of higher education will be evaluated within the context of that framework.

THE "PRODUCT" OF HIGHER EDUCATION

Like other producing units in the economy, institutions of higher education use resources and technology to turn out something of benefit to individuals and to society. This "something" can probably best be characterized as *educational services*. To get at what comprises educational services, we can pose the question, "Why are you attending a college or university?" There are at least three answers to the question. First, you expect higher education to improve your capacity to produce and to earn income, that is, to augment the quality of your labor resources. Second, the act of attending a college or university, quite apart from improving your labor resources, adds to your sense of well-being—there are benefits to you from the act of consuming educational services. Third, the society expects to get some social spillover benefits from your education over and above the benefits that accrue directly to you.

Investment in Human Capital

A large part of educational services consists of the development of the human or labor resource. This is called an investment in human capital because in an economic sense it is very much the same thing as investing in machines, buildings, and other material capital. We invest in nonhuman capital whenever we think that the increase will generate enough additional product output to more than repay the investment costs. Similarly, it pays to invest in human capital—additional education—if the increase in education increases the earning power of the person being educated by more than the cost of the additional education. Just as we invest in nonhuman capital to increase and expand the capacity of capital resources to produce, so is a large part of the investment in human capital expected to augment the capacity of labor resources to contribute to gross national product.

Investment in human capital is in no sense restricted to the provision of vocational education. Classical education—language and literature, the humanities, the fine arts, philosophy, and the like— broadens and deepens people's capacities to think, act, and enjoy and thereby increases their productivity in an economic sense. In many cases employers of college graduates are as interested in hiring students with broad liberal arts degrees as they are those trained in specific vocational majors. What they want are bright young people who know how to think and how to accept responsibility.

Direct Consumption

Some part of the educational services produced by colleges and universities consists of direct consumption benefits. The process of participating in the activities of the institution and of interacting with other students in university life yields direct satisfaction to many. Students at odds with the establishment who have no intention of making their education pay off through increased earning power are prime examples of direct consumers of educational services.

By way of contrast, there are students whose sole purpose in attending college is to enhance their capacities for earning income. Sometimes these are part-time students who are employed by business enterprises. Sometimes they are commuters who attend classes only and do not participate in other aspects of university life. Direct consumption benefits are zero for them.

For most students the consumption benefits are inextricably mixed with the human investment elements of educational services. Classes, discussions, and social life combine to provide personal satisfaction as well as to increase the capacities of the human resource to produce goods and services.

Social Spillovers

Sometimes the production or the consumption of a product yields benefits to people who neither produce nor consume it. For example, suppose my wealthy neighbor hires an orchestra to play at her garden party and I am not invited. She pays for the pleasure of her guests. But who is to stop me, a lover of beautiful music, from listening to its strains from my own side of the property line? The production and consumption of the music yields *social spillover benefits.*

Production or consumption of a product can yield *social spillover costs,* too. These are costs imposed on people not involved in the production or consumption of the good. If one of my neighbors opened a beauty shop in her home, there would be a noticeable increase in traffic on our street. It would be necessary to supervise the kids more closely to keep them from being run over. This nuisance is a social spillover cost.

The widespread provision of educational services is generally thought to have social spillover benefits. It is believed by many that over and above the direct benefits to the individuals who receive them—greater productivity, earning power, and direct consumption benefits—there are additional benefits to the society as a whole.

Some of the spillovers commonly cited are reduced fire hazards, reduced crime rates, improved community sanitation techniques and
facilities, better governmental services to the commuity, more en-
lightened citizens who make the society a more pleasant place in
which to live, and a better functioning democratic process stemming
from greater voter literacy.

The Incidence of the Benefits

When an individual obtains a college or university education, to
whom do the foregoing benefits accrue? Suppose we look again at
the nature of the "product." The direct consumption benefits are
easiest to assign. They very clearly add to the level of well-being of
the individual himself. There are no obvious widespread spillovers
of these to others as the student works his way through the usual four
years of undergraduate study.

The development of human capital also provides first-order
benefits to the individual and his family. An individual who develops engineering skills, or medical skills, or legal skills, or specialized knowledge and teaching skills increases his capacities to contribute to gross national product; however, he is at the same time
increasing his ability to earn income. The extra income that he can
earn will be approximately equal to the value of his additional
on-the-job productivity. Society as a whole benefits from his additional productivity—it makes greater supplies of certain goods and
services available for consumption, or it may make some available
that were previously not available, penicillin, for example. But
these are not really social spillover benefits. They represent the
same kind of increase in the productivity of the economy's resources
that occurs when someone invests in a new, more productive machine. The resource owner is paid for the first-order increases in his
productivity. Then society receives a second-order benefit in the
form of a greater gross national product.

To the extent that true social spillover benefits occur from higher
education, the society, apart from the individual and his family,
must receive them. It is very difficult to identify, quantify, and measure such benefits. Consequently, there is much debate and con-
jecture about whether they exist and the extent to which they exist
for higher education.

Many people argue that the additional social spillover benefits associated with each additional year of education tend to decrease as an individual moves up through the educational system. They believe that the greatest spillovers come from the achievement of literacy—learning to read, write, and do arithmetic. These are associated with primary education. They expect secondary education to develop skills of interacting with others in the society and to provide some measure of sophistication in the administration of the joint affairs of those comprising the society. They do not believe that higher education provides much more in social spillovers. They believe that it benefits society mostly through the benefits it provides to those who obtain its services.

In summary, then, the benefits of higher educational services seem to accrue mostly to the individuals who obtain those services. Society may receive some social spillover benefits, but the magnitude of these is debatable.

ECONOMIC CONCEPT OF COSTS

One of the most important principles of economics is summed up in the statement, "There ain't no such thing as a free lunch." We speak glibly of such things as free medical care, free housing, free food, and free education. What we mean is that those who use the "free" goods and services do not have to pay money for them. All too often our chain of reasoning stops right there. But if we really think that these are free to the society as a whole, we delude ourselves. The production of the "free goods" is costly to someone— perhaps even to their users.

The economic costs of a product may or may not be reflected in the direct money outlays that must be made in producing it. The basic concept underlying economic costs is the *alternative-cost principle*. In considering the costs of producing any given product, it is useful to classify its costs into two categories: (1) *explicit costs* and (2) *implicit costs*.

The Alternative-Cost Principle

According to the alternative-cost principle, the cost of producing a unit of any good or service is the value to the economy of the alter-

native goods or services that must be foregone in order to produce it. This notion is not really new in our discussion—it was suggested in Chapter 1 in the discussion of the nature of economic activity. We must develop and clarify it at this point, however.

We can start with the production possibilities curve or transformation curve of Figure 3–1, which measures units of educational services along the horizontal axis and composite units of all other goods and services along the vertical axis. The transformation curve TT_1 shows all alternative combinations of other goods and services

FIGURE 3–1
The Costs of Education

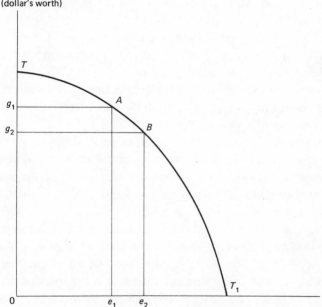

In Figure 3–1, transformation curve TT_1 shows all alternative combinations of other goods and services and education that the economy's resources and technology can produce per year. Two possible alternative combinations are represented by *A* and *B*. If the economy is initially producing combination *B*, it is obtaining g_2 units of other goods and services and e_2 units of education. If e_1e_2 represents one unit of education per year, it becomes apparent that g_2g_1 units of other goods and services must have been sacrificed to obtain it. The value of the g_2g_1 units thus measures the cost of a unit of education at the e_2 level of production.

and education that the economy's given resources can produce per
year. Suppose that initially combination B, made up of e_2 units of
education and g_2 units of other goods and services, is being produced
and the economy's resources are fully employed.

What is the cost to the society of a unit of education when B represents the economy's output mix? *It is the value of the alternative
goods and services that must be foregone to produce it.* Let the distance e_1e_2 represent one unit of education. If this unit had not been
produced, the society could have had more of other goods and services, equal to the amount g_2g_1. Thus the society had to sacrifice g_2g_1
of other goods and services to produce the one-unit of education.
The sacrifice of the other goods and services releases just enough
resources to produce the additional unit of education. We call the
amounts of other goods and services sacrificed the *real cost* of producing the unit of education. The value that consumers attach to
the goods and services given up is the true *economic money cost*.

Stated in a slightly different way, *the cost of producing a unit of
any one good or service is the value of the resources used in producing it in their best alternative use.* A little reflection will show that
this statement of the alternative-cost principle is identical to the one
developed in the preceding paragraph.

The alternative-cost principle is capable of general application.
In an economy in which resources are fully employed, an increase
in the amount of medical services provided draws resources from the
production of other goods and services. The value of the goods and
services foregone (that is, the value of resources that would be used
in their production) is the cost of the increase in medical services.
The cost of a bushel of wheat is the value of the corn that must be
foregone in order to produce it, if corn production is the best
alternative to use to which the resources used in wheat production
could be put. The cost of a soldier in the society's army is the value
of what he could have produced as a civilian. Thousands of such
examples could be cited.

Explicit and Implicit Costs

The economic costs to a society of producing a good or service do
not necessarily coincide with its accounting costs. As an example,
consider a small family-owned grocery store for which the labor is

provided by the owner and his family. A large part of the costs of resources used by the store to put groceries in the hands of consumers—costs of grocery stocks, utilities, and the like—are indeed accounting costs, but some will be omitted from the accounting records. The costs of labor are not likely to be listed. Amortization and depreciation costs on the land, building, furniture, and fixtures also may be omitted. The owner and his family may simply "take what is left" after the out-of-pocket expenses are paid, calling this remainder their "profits."

The costs of resources bought and hired for carrying on the business are called *explicit costs of production*. These are the economic costs that are most likely to be taken into account by the business, since they are usually actual cost outlays.

The costs of self-owned, self-employed resources (like the labor of the owner's family in the example) are called *implicit costs of production*. They tend to be hidden or ignored as costs. Implicit costs of a resource can be identified by using the alternative-cost principle. What the resource would be worth in its best alternative use is determined; this is its cost to the owner-user. Had the store owner used his labor working for someone else, his labor would have produced other goods and services and would have earned him income about equal to the value of those other goods and services. So the cost of his self-employed labor is what he could have earned in his best alternative employment.

THE COSTS OF HIGHER EDUCATIONAL SERVICES

From the point of view of the society as a whole, the services of higher education are not free. Resources used in their production could have been used to produce other goods and services, and the value of those foregone goods and services is the economic cost of higher education. In this section we shall try to pin down the nature of those costs and identify who pays them.

The Explicit Costs

The explicit costs of the services provided by a college or university are the costs of the resources that it buys and hires to provide those services. These may be costs of capital resources or of labor resources. The university uses land, buildings, equipment, and supplies. It also uses professors, maintenance personnel, administrators, secretaries, and clerks.

The institution's annual budget provides a first approximation of the annual explicit costs of its services. The budget will include amortization costs of major capital outlays, depreciation costs, small-equipment costs, maintenance costs, and the costs of hundreds of kinds of supplies. It will also include the wages and salaries of labor resources used.

The true explicit costs are the values of the resources used by the institution in their best alternative uses. This should be interpreted with some degree of caution. The economic cost of a university's buildings is not what the value of the building would be if the university were to close its doors. Rather it is the value of the goods and services that were foregone in order to build and maintain the building. Whether or not the institution's explicit economic costs are reflected accurately by its accounting records depends upon the accounting procedures it uses.

The Implicit Costs

The most important implicit costs of the services produced by a college or university are the costs of resources owned by its customers—the students. Most students would be working if they were not in school, producing goods and services that comprise a part of the gross national product. In order for them to be students, they sacrifice what they could have earned as workers, and the society sacrifices the value of the goods and services they would have produced had they been working. These foregone earnings, or the equivalent foregone GNP, is a cost to the student and to society of the educational services obtained by the student. They do not show up in the institution's budget or books of account.

Another category of implicit costs of educational services consists of the costs of books and various other miscellaneous items incidental to attending a college or university. The test of whether or not units of some specific good belong to this category of costs is whether they would have been purchased if the users were not in school. Units of textbooks, pencils, paper, some items of clothing, and some forms of recreation or entertainment will pass this test and will be considered implicit costs. Ordinarily these are not a part of the institution's budget or expense accounts.

Sources of Support

One of the unique economic features in the production and sale of higher educational services in the United States is the diversity of the sources tapped to pay the costs. Those who have taken on the responsibility of providing higher educational services have traditionally not been willing—or able—to leave them subject to market forces. Neither public nor private university officials charge their customers the full explicit costs of the educational services provided, but the extent to which they approach full costing of those services is a key difference between the two types of institutions.

Public Institutions. Public colleges and universities depend heavily on *state appropriations* to meet their explicit costs. In addition, land grant universities receive substantial funds from the federal government. Governmental units also provide loan funds, work-study funds, scholarships, and other kinds of support for students of public institutions.

Tuition and fees as a means of meeting explicit costs are relatively low at most educational institutions. In some—those of the state of California, for example—they approach zero. Usually state colleges and universities charge higher tuition rates for out-of-state than for in-state students, recognizing that state appropriations are a substitute for tuition to which they believe only the citizens of the state are entitled.

To a relatively small extent public institutions depend on *donors* to help meet their explicit costs. Funds are received from donors as endowment funds, unrestricted cash grants, scholarship funds, and the like. The donors include foundations, corporations, philanthropists, and alumni who can be convinced that they are contributing to a worthwhile cause. To the public institution, funds from donors, rather than being a primary source of support, tend to be the frosting on the cake that enables it to engage in some activities that nononsense legislative appropriations will not permit.

Even at public colleges and universities students and their families must pay the implicit costs of educational services. If a student does not work at all, his foregone earnings or foregone goods and services for the society as a whole are implicit costs. If he works part time, the implicit costs are the difference between what he could have earned and what he actually earns. If the wife or husband of a student is forced to accept unemployment or less remunerative employment than could have been obtained elsewhere at the college or university site, foregone earnings will be larger than those for the student alone. In addition to foregone earnings, implicit costs at the public institution include the costs of books and miscellaneous expenses incidental to the generation of educational services.

Private Institutions.   Private colleges and universities, since they do not receive state appropriations, must meet the bulk of their explicit costs from the payment of *tuition* and *fees*. Contributions from *donors* is also an important source of support—the more they can secure from this source, the less pressure there is to rely on tuition and the better able they are to compete with the low tuition rates of public institutions. Seeking funds from donors is always a major activity of private institutions.

Federal grants to private educational institutions vary widely from school to school. Those that are research oriented have secured sizable research grants. Many schools receive very little from federal sources.

The implicit costs of educational services are the same for private as for public institutions. They amount to foregone earnings, plus the cost of books and other miscellaneous items.

The Incidence of the Costs

Where do the costs of producing the services of higher education finally rest? Table 3–1 is a rough estimate of the incidence of costs for a typical public institution and a typical private institution. We assume that the kinds and qualities of services provided are the same for each institution and that each is equally efficient in providing them. Three features of the incidence of costs are significant.

First, the implicit costs are a very large part of the total costs of the educational services provided a student. They amount to a little over 70 percent of the total costs. Note that they are the same whether the student attends a public or a private institution. They are borne by students and their families.

Second, the major source of support for the explicit costs of public institutions is state appropriations, while that for private insti-

TABLE 3–1
Typical Annual Per Student Cost of Higher Education by Type of Institution and Source of Support

Source of Support	Amount of Support by Type of Institution	
	Private	Public
For explicit costs		
Donors	$ 800	$ 25
Federal grants	50	75
State appropriations	—	2,400
Tuition and fees (student and his family) ..	2,200	550
Total explicit costs	$ 3,050	$ 3,050
For implicit costs (student and his family)		
Books and miscellaneous expenses	$ 1,000	$ 1,000
Foregone earnings	7,000	7,000
Total implicit costs	$ 8,000	$ 8,000
Total costs	$11,050	$11,050

This table is an approximation of components for a "typical" public university and a "typical" private university. Size of the institutions and quality of educational services provided are assumed to be the same.

tutions is tuition and fees. Except for a few scholarship holders, tuition and fees in private institutions rest on students and their families. State appropriations are made from general revenue funds in any given state and consist of money collected from taxpayers of the state; consequently, the incidence of this large part (a little over two-thirds) of the explicit costs of public institutions rests on taxpayers rather than on students and their families. Public institutions, then, bring about a shift in the incidence of some two thirds of the explicit costs of higher educational services from students and their families to taxpayers.

Third, private institutions rely more heavily on donors as a source of support than do public institutions. To the extent that funds can be obtained from donors and substituted for tuition, the incidence of explicit costs is shifted from students and their families to donors. About one fourth of the incidence of explicit costs of private institutions is shifted from students and their families to donors.

ECONOMIC EVALUATION OF THE PROBLEMS

While the economic framework established in the preceding sections permits the problems of higher education to be approached in a systematic and logical way, it does not always provide clear-cut, correct solutions. Economic analysis helps determine what causes what, and why. It helps determine, once goals have been set, the most efficient way of reaching those goals. However, economic analysis cannot always provide answers as to what the goals or objectives in higher education or any other activity should be. Equally intelligent people often disagree on the goals that should be sought by a particular society.

What Kinds of Services?

Are our expectations with respect to the kinds of services higher education should produce realistic? Of course they are! The industry can produce whatever mix of services we as a society want it to produce. The important economic problem is concerned with how well institutions respond to the society's desires or demands for those services. The "relevancy" issue in education during the late 1960s and early 1970s is a manifestation of this problem.

Economic analysis leads to questions as to how responsive the current structure of higher educational institutions permits them to be in meeting societal demands. By and large, throughout the economic system consumers register their demands for goods and services by the ways in which they dispose of or spend their purchasing power. Suppliers respond to the demands of the spenders. In the case of higher education, colleges and universities would be expected to be most responsive to the demands of those who provide the funds to meet their explicit costs. This suggests that public institutions will be primarily responsive to the desires or demands of the legislatures from which they receive their appropriations. Private institutions will be primarily responsive to the desires and demands of students and their families and secondarily responsive to those of their donors.

Since almost 65 percent of degree-credit college and university students in the United States attend public institutions,[1] we find ourselves with a system in which large numbers of those who receive the services—students—are not the ones who pay the explicit costs

---

[1] U.S. Department of Commerce, Bureau of the Census, *Statistical Abstract, 1972*, p. 129.

of the services. Legislatures rather than students and their families heavily influence decisions as to what services are to be provided. If legislatures are in turn responsive to students and their families, the divergence between legislative demands and student demands may be small. But students and their families are a small part of the constituencies of legislators. In many cases, public institutions are subjected to legislative demands that diverge from the demands of those who receive their services.

Experience suggests that public colleges and universities will be more inclined to maintain the status quo than will private ones. Legislatures move slowly, and many functions other than education occupy their time and attention. Yet they are not inclined to give the regents, administrations, and faculties of colleges and universities under their control a free hand, since the legislatures remain "accountable" to the general public for how appropriations are spent. The programs of private colleges and universities are likely to be more flexible over time.

How Much Service?

Economic analysis provides a conceptual answer to how much educational service the economy should produce relative to other goods and services. The resources used in producing educational services can be used to produce other goods and services, and, from the alternative-cost principle, the costs of educational services are the values of those resources in their alternative uses. Consequently, if the value to society of a unit of educational services is greater than its costs—the resources used in producing it are more valuable in the production of education than in alternative ones—then the output of educational services should be expanded. On the other hand, if the value of a unit of educational services is worth less to the society than it costs to produce it, the output should be reduced.

The value of higher educational services in relation to their costs is obscured by the way they are provided. Higher educational services are not priced in the marketplace in a way that will cause the quantity supplied to be adjusted to the quantity demanded. On the demand side it is difficult, if not impossible, for students in the present system to make known how they value educational services. The combination of public and private sources of support on the supply side compounds the difficulties of valuing educational services and of determining how much should be produced.

On the demand side, consider potential students who want educational services in some specific field—say medical training. In medical schools throughout the country, the annual number of openings for students is limited. At current levels of costs to students, many more want training than can be accepted—that is, there is a shortage of medical training services. This is the same thing as saying that potential medical students would be willing to pay more for the services of medical schools than they are now required to pay. However, students are not permitted to bid up the price at which these educational services are offered, and hence the price system cannot express their valuations of them. The same kind of analysis holds true for a great many other fields of specialization.

The supply of educational services made available by public higher education institutions is not a direct response to student demands. The amounts supplied are determined primarily by the appropriations public institutions receive from the state legislatures rather than by what students are willing to pay. Colleges and universities compete with a number of other state-supported activities for the dollars that legislatures have available to appropriate and, since state revenues are limited, they will never receive as much as educational administrators think they ought to have. At the same time, public institutions are reluctant to supplement the funds received from the state with tuition receipts. Tuition is supposed to be kept low because of state appropriations—this is the purpose of the state-allocated funds. The higher tuition rates are set, the less will be the baragining power of the public institutions for state funds.

State colleges and universities will encounter a continuous financial crisis. The services they can provide are limited by the always inadequate appropriations received from the state and by pressure to keep their tuition rates low.

At the same time, the relatively lower tuition rates of the public institutions enable them to draw students away from private institutions. The competition of public institutions limits the services that can be provided by private institutions. It also sets upper limits on the tuition rates that private institutions can charge and still remain in business. Pressure on private institutions to obtain gifts, grants, and the like is increased. Competition from public institutions makes it very difficult for private colleges and universities to stay solvent.

Who Should Pay?

The controversy over who should pay for higher educational services is undoubtedly the key problem faced by higher education. If this problem could be resolved, answers to "what kind" and "how much" would be much easier to determine. At one extreme of the controversy are those who maintain that educational services should be above market forces. Education is seen as the great equalizer, providing opportunities for self-development and self-realization. Everyone is entitled to as much education as he is able to absorb, and consequently, educational services should be free. At the other extreme are those who believe that each student and his family should bear the full costs of his own education.

"Free" Education. What is meant by "free" education? The economic aspects of higher education discussed in this chapter make it clear that there is no such thing from society's point of view. Neither is education free from the individual student's point of view—unless, of course, both explicit and implicit costs are covered by scholarships. Ordinarily education is said to be free if state appropriations to state colleges and universities are large enough so that no tuition is charged. This has been the case in the California system of higher education. In most states public colleges and universities are not tuition-free; state appropriations simply permit them to charge substantially lower tuitions than do private institutions.

The differences in costs between what is generally called a free education in a state college or university and what is called a full-cost education in a private college or university is nowhere near as great as tuition differentials would lead us to believe. In the example in Table 3–1, the annual costs borne by the student and his family in a public institution would be about $8,550, while in the private institution they would be about $10,200.

State Support of Higher Education. In terms of economic analysis, state support of higher education means that some part of the costs of obtaining educational services is shifted from the student

who receives the services to taxpayers. State appropriations to
the college or university decrease the tuition that students are required to pay. Funds appropriated to the institution by the state are
obtained from taxpayers. Thus state support constitutes a transfer
of purchasing power from taxpayers to college and university
students.

Under what circumstances do such transfers seem to be in order?
It appears that they are defensible: (1) to the extent that social spillover benefits are generated by higher education and (2) as a means
of enabling children of the poor to develop their human resources.

When the consumption or utilization of some good or service by
one or more people results in spillover benefits to others, those who
receive the spillover benefits are in a good position to be *free riders*.
Direct consumers of an item pay for the direct benefits they receive;
otherwise, they will not be able to obtain whatever it is they want
to consume. Those who receive the spillover benefits receive them
whether they pay anything or not; their tendency is to be "free
riders." Direct consumers are in no position to force the free riders
to pay, but what they cannot do as individual private citizens they
may be able to accomplish collectively through their government.
The government can levy taxes on the free riders, thus coercing
them to pay for the spillover benefits they receive. The government
is a unique and logical agency for this purpose.

If social spillover benefits from higher educational services exist,
the use of state taxing powers and state support of higher education
sufficient to pay for those benefits would seem to be reasonable.
Several questions arise. The most important one is whether or not
significant social spillover benefits are generated in the provision
of higher educational services. If they are, they have never been
unambiguously identified, much less measured in value terms. Further, if they do exist, they are generated by private colleges and
universities as well as by public institutions. On these grounds,
should not the higher education provided by private universities be
subsidized to about the same extent as is provided by state
universities?

The other major argument for state support of higher education
is that it enables capable but poor students to obtain a college or
university education. Education serves to increase the capacities of
human resources to produce and to earn income. Since poor families

do not have the means of paying for higher education for their children, and this is not the fault of the children, the state can do much to enable them to escape from poverty by providing them with the same kind of educational opportunities that are still available to the children of middle and higher income families.

The case has much merit. One of the generally recognized functions of government in the modern world is that of mitigating poverty. In the United States a very substantial part of both state and federal budgets is for this purpose. Welfare programs, farm programs, and income taxes that are intended to take larger proportions of the incomes of the rich than of the poor provide examples. It seems reasonable that state support of higher education for the poor should be an integral and important part of any antipoverty program.

However, though state support looms large in meeting the explicit costs of educational services, the implicit costs that still must be met by the student and his family are a very substantial part of the total costs. The inability of a poor family to meet the implicit costs—the need for children to go to work and earn income—discourages the children of the poor from attending *any* college or university, public or private. State support of public institutions does not really transfer purchasing power from taxpayers to the children of the poor. It transfers purchasing power from taxpayers to those able to meet the implicit costs of higher education, and most of such students are from the middle and upper income groups.

The foregoing statement is substantiated by 1972 data on entering freshmen in the United States as a whole. For public and private institutions combined, about 80 percent of the entering freshmen came from families earning over $10,000 per year. Only 3.4 percent came from families with income levels below $4,000 per year. At a typical state-supported land-grant university in a state with per capita income substantially below the average for the United States, about 75 percent of the entering freshmen came from families with income levels above $10,000 per year, and about 5.1 percent came from families with income less than $4,000 per year.[2]

Student Self-Support. Many people believe that students and

---

[2] American Council on Education, Office of Research, *Summary of Data on Entering Freshmen, Fall, 1972.*

their families rather than the state should bear the costs of higher education. This does not necessarily mean that there should be no such institutions owned and operated by the state. A state-owned college or university can recover the full costs of education through tuition and fees levied on students as easily as a private one can. There are two main arguments why students should pay for their own education. These are that (1) those who benefit are the ones who should pay, and (2) economic resources would be used more efficiently, that is, some waste would be avoided.

The argument that those who benefit should pay is rooted in equity grounds. It asks why one group of persons—taxpayers—should be forced to pay a part of the educational costs of another group—students and their families. To be sure, there will be over-lapping of the two groups; students and their families are taxpayers. However, a much larger proportion of taxpayers are not college and university students, and neither are their children. Many of these are poor families; as indicated above, three fourths of the freshmen entering a typical state-supported institution in 1972 came from families with incomes above $10,000 per year. Is it equitable for the state to levy taxes that rest partly on poor nonstudent families to help pay for the education of children from middle-income and wealthy families?

The argument maintains further that investment in human capital is essentially comparable to investment in material capital. Suppose a high school graduate has a choice of investing in an education or investing in a business. He considers the payoff of each in terms of his future well-being and chooses the one that he (and his family) thinks will yield the highest return on the investment. This is the way that intelligent economic decision making should be accomplished. Ordinarily we do not expect taxpayers to bear a part of the investments of high school graduates in businesses. Why should we expect them to bear a part of such investments in higher education?

Another argument for student self-support is that people tend to waste whatever is free to them and to economize or conserve what-ever they have to pay for. The greater the cost of a purchase relative to one's income, the more incentive one has to use the item care-fully in order to increase the possible returns from it. This is said to be the premise underlying high charges made by psychiatrists for their services. The argument is used extensively by those who think students should pay for their own education.

If higher educational services are provided at reduced or free tuition costs to students, the incentive to economize on or make the best possible use of the resources providing those services is weakened—so the argument runs. Low tuition induces students who have no interest in learning to attend the university, whereas higher tuition charges would make them think more carefully about whether or not they should do so. Further, those who do attend would be inclined to make more of their opportunities if they cost more. There would be less inclination to waste professors' time or to destroy property.

Which Way? Which of the arguments is correct? If the student and his family reap the benefits of higher education—that is, if the benefits of higher education are primarily private human capital development—then a strong case can be made that the student and his family should pay its full costs. If substantial social spillover benefits result from putting some part of the population through the processes of higher education, or if it is used effectively as a campaign against poverty, a strong case can be made for shifting a part of its costs to taxpayers.

An Alternative Institutional Structure

When an activity such as higher education has been pursued over a long period of time, a set of institutions is developed to carry on the activity. The structure of the set that evolves becomes very difficult to change. First, people think in terms of the structure to which they have become accustomed and find it hard to think of terms of alternatives. Second, the present structure is the known here and now; the alternative might not work. Third, many people build up vested interests in the existing structure and can be expected to resist changes that would affect them.

It appears that higher education may be saddled with just such an outmoded institutional structure. Some 65 percent of college and university students in the United States are enrolled in public institutions that receive the bulk of their support from legislative appropriations. The rationale for the state-supported system is that (1) it makes higher education available to the children of poor families and (2) it encourages large enrollments, to increase the social spill-over benefits of higher education. As we have seen, it does not appear to serve either of these purposes very well. The implicit costs of higher education are so great that even with the low tuition rates of public institutions, few children of the poor find it possible to attend. It appears that the most important effect of the low tuition rates of public institutions is to divert students from private to public institutions rather than to bring about any substantial increase in enrollment in all institutions. In addition, the present system does not enable the society to place accurate demand values on the services being provided, nor does it provide the mechanism for colleges and universities to be responsive to the demands of the society.

The alternative to the present higher education institutional structure is one that would make greater use of the price system in the production of higher educational services. The key feature of the alternative is that students obtaining educational services would pay tuition to the colleges and universities they attend sufficient to cover the full explicit costs of the services obtained. There would be no differentiation between private and public institutions in this respect. If public institutions were to remain public, they would be required to pay their own way without obtaining direct appropriations from legislatures.

If the society desires to help the children of the poor to obtain educational services, it can do so easily and directly. Instead of allocating money to public colleges and universities, legislatures can make grants directly to the children of the poor, letting them choose for themselves which institution they will attend. Presumably each will attend the institution that best meets his needs. Thus, the anti-poverty aspects of state support will be realized directly and efficiently. The state will not be supporting those who are not in need; with the present system, most of those it supports are not in need.

If, because of spillover benefits, the state desires to encourage larger enrollments than would occur if all students were required to pay the full costs of the services they obtain, this can be done easily and directly. By raising the minimum income standards used to define what constitutes a poor family, the state can increase the number of students eligible for state support. In addition to tuition scholarships to meet explicit costs, various devices now in use can continue to assist students from low-income families in meeting their implicit costs. These include access to loan funds, part-time employment, and the like.

Such an institutional structure should go far toward solving the problems that confront higher education. It would attack the problem of who should pay, moving toward a structure in which those who receive the benefits are the ones who pay the costs. But note that this *does not* preclude using the system of higher education as a part of an antipoverty program, nor does it preclude government (taxpayer) support of higher education. Government support would contribute more directly and more efficiently to making higher education available to the children of the poor.

Such a structure would also move toward a solution of the perpetual financial crisis of higher education. Government support of higher educational services—whatever the amount of such support the society desires—would be provided to students and not to institutions. This would eliminate the primary cause of the crisis—the support of public institutions by the state, which, though usually thought to be inadequate, entails low-tuition competition and attendant financial problems for private institutions.

Further, it would tend to induce the education industry to supply the quantity of educational services the society wants relative to the quantities of other goods and services produced in the economy. Tuition would be the main source of revenue for institutions; it would cover the full explicit costs of services supplied. Colleges and universities would supply services to as many persons as are willing to pay that tuition. Persons not willing to pay the full tuition are saying in effect that alternative ways of spending that amount of money yield greater satisfaction to them.

Finally, the proposed institutional structure should be responsive to its clientele—students and their families. Institutions not responsive to the wants of students and their families would lose students to those that are. Competition among institutions for students' tuition should generate greater efficiency and a variety of innovations in programs and in the techniques of providing educational services.

SUMMARY

Colleges and universities face many problems, most of them stemming from three fundamental issues: (1) what kinds of services they should provide, (2) how much service should be provided, and (3) who should pay for it. These are issues about which economic analysis has much to say.

Institutions of higher education use resources to produce educational services. These services provide (1) investment in human capital, (2) direct consumption benefits, and (3) social spillover benefits. By far, the greater part of educational services is composed of investment in human capital. There is controversy over the extent to which social spillover benefits exist, but these are not likely to be a large part of the total. The first-order benefits of educational services accrue mainly to the student who obtains them, although society gains from secondary benefits just as it does from investment in material capital.

Higher educational services, like other goods and services, have economic costs. All economic costs are measured by the alternative-cost principle. Some costs are explicit in nature, while others are implicit. The explicit costs of higher education services are the costs of the capital and labor resources used by colleges and universities. Most people view these as the total costs. However, to students and their families there are implicit costs that are greater in amount than the explicit costs. Most important of these are the foregone earnings of students and their families.

Sources of support (payment of explicit costs) for higher educational institutions in the United States are different for public and for private institutions. Structurally, the system of institutions consists of public institutions, which receive the bulk of their revenues in the form of state legislative appropriations, and private institutions, which receive the bulk of their revenues from tuition. The implicit costs to students do not enter into college and university budgets and are the same whether they attend public or private institutions. The incidence of the costs of higher educational services rests most heavily on the student and his family, even in public institutions, with their relatively low tuition levels.

An economic evaluation of the fundamental problems involved in the provision of higher educational services highlights several shortcomings of the present institutional structure of higher educational facilities. Public institutions, supported primarily by legislative appropriations, are likely to be more responsive to the demands of legislators than to the demands of students in the determination of what kinds of services should be provided. The amounts of services provided also are determined by legislative appropriations rather than by the economic factors of demand and costs. As a device for making educational opportunities available to the children of the poor, public institutions leave much to be desired.

An alternative structure for higher educational institutions that appears worthy of serious consideration is one in which the tuition rates charged are sufficient to cover all of the explicit costs of providing educational services. This would tend to make institutions more responsive to the demands of students and their families. It would tend toward the production of the "correct" amounts of higher educational services, as compared with other goods and services. It would also provide a structure in which state (taxpayer) support of the educational costs of the children of the poor could be met directly and efficiently.

SUPPLEMENTARY READING

Alchian, Armen A. "The Economic and Social Impact of Free Tuition." *New Individualist Review,* Winter 1968, pp. 42–52.

Discusses the economic and social impacts of a low or zero-tuition method of providing higher educational opportunities. It is asserted that a system of full tuition will yield a greater variety of educational opportunities and a higher quality of education.

Bowen, Howard R. "Who Pays the Higher Education Bill?" in M. D. Orwig (ed.), *Financing Higher Education: Alternatives for the Federal Government,* Iowa City: The American College Testing Program, 1971. pp. 281–298.

Discusses the incidence of higher education costs and concludes that the student and his family now bear the major costs. Bowen proposes a grant-loan plan to students combined with grants to educational institutions. The grant-loan plan is designed to help students from low-income families, while grants to institutions are intended to help institutions meet rising costs of education.

Buchanan, James M., and Devletoglou, Nicos E. *Academia in Anarchy,* Part 1, pp. 3–62. New York: Basic Books, 1970.

A good, provocative summary of the characteristics of public higher education. Points out that to a large extent the students who consume it are not the ones who pay for it; the faculties that produce it do not sell it; and the taxpayers who own it do not control it.

Hansen, W. Lee, and Weisbrod, Burton A. *Benefits, Costs, and Finance of Public Higher Education,* chaps. 1–4, pp. 7–77. Chicago: Markham Publishing Co., 1969.

Adopts a benefit-cost approach to higher education, with particular reference to the state of California. Study identifies the forms of benefits and costs associated with higher education and attempts to assess the incidence of each.

Windham, Douglas M. "The Economics of Education: A Survey." In Neil W. Chamberlain (ed.), *Contemporary Economic Issues,* pp. 159–217. Rev. ed. Homewood, Ill.: Richard D. Irwin, 1973.

A good general reference. The nature of education as an economic good is elaborated on, and the present means of financing higher education and some possible alternatives are presented.

Chapter 4

ECONOMICS OF CRIME AND ITS PREVENTION

CHECKLIST OF ECONOMIC CONCEPTS

Individually Consumed Goods and Services
Collectively Consumed Goods and Services
Semicollectively Consumed Goods and Services
Social Spillover Benefits
Social Spillover Costs
Economic Costs
Marginal Benefits
Marginal Costs
Equimarginal Principle
Alternative-Cost Principle
"Free Rider" Problem

4

ECONOMICS OF CRIME AND ITS PREVENTION
How Much Is Too Much?

It seemed to Linda that somehow, somewhere, things were all mixed up. The police had swarmed in on the students in her apartment last night, and three of her friends were in jail on pot possession charges. Fortunately, Linda was clean. Sure, the three who were arrested were smoking the stuff, but whom were they hurting? It was a relatively quiet, peaceful gathering. They listened to a few records that may have been a little loud for the neighbors, but mostly there was just talk. A little pot never hurt anyone—why do people get all uptight about it? Everyone knows that smoking pot, if it leads to any problems at all, has much less serious consequences than the use of alcohol, and in most places it is no crime to drink.

Why didn't the police go after the real criminals and leave the young people alone? Why didn't they spend their time fruitfully, tracking down and apprehending murderers, rapists, muggers, thieves, and the like? Just last week two men had followed her friend, Jim, into his apartment house and pulled a gun on him, taking his watch and the little bit of money he had in his billfold. Why didn't law enforcement officials do something about such serious crime problems as the Mafia and other organized crime? It seemed to Linda that the police spent their time picking on young people and let the real criminals get by with—murder.

Criminal activities create an important set of social problems in the United States. They affect our general well-being by threatening the loss of money and property and generating concern for physical safety. Yet, for most of us, crime is something we read about in the papers—something which usually affects other people but always has the potential of affecting us. We seldom look at crime from a systematic analytical point of view, but if we are to do anything about the problem this is what we must do.

WHAT IS CRIME?

It seems almost silly to raise such a question as "What is crime?" However, if we are to look at crime analytically, we must have a common base from which to work. The concept of what constitutes criminal activity is often not clear in the mind of any one person and may be ambiguous from one person to another. Some people think of crime in terms of that which is immoral; others think of it in terms of that which is illegal.

Immorality?

Are immoral acts criminal? The answer to this question is not easy. In the first place, many acts do not fall clearly into a moral-immoral classification. In modern societies some acts are generally considered to be immoral—murder, and most kinds of theft, for example. But there are many other acts, the morality of which depends upon what group in the society is evaluating them. Examples include pot smoking, drinking alcoholic beverages, betting on horse races, homosexual activities, and many more. It appears that morality versus immorality does not provide a clear basis for defining whether or not specific acts are criminal.

Illegality?

A definition that seems to be meaningful and useful analytically is that a criminal act is one the society (or one of its subdivisions) has decided it is better off without and which it has therefore made illegal through laws, ordinances, and the like. It may or may not be immoral. For example, is it immoral to inadvertently drive 30 miles an hour along a deserted street that is posted for 20 miles an hour, or to accidentally run a stop sign at an intersection where there are no other cars, or to catch a fish in a mountain stream before you have obtained a fishing license? As you quickly discover when you are caught, these acts may very well be criminal in nature. On the other hand, if gambling, drinking, and prostitution are immoral, there are many places where they are not illegal and are, therefore, not criminal.

Acts that are illegal or criminal are designated as such by legislative bodies, such as city councils, state legislatures, and Congress. There are a number of reasons for making certain acts illegal. Some acts may indeed be offensive to the moral standards of a majority of legislators and their constituents. Murder, rape, and theft are cases in point. Others may lead to consequences (in the minds of legislators, at least) of which the doer is ignorant. The consumption of alcohol, or pot, or heroin thus may be illegal because legislators fear that those who try them may become hooked, with disastrous consequences to themselves. Still other acts are designated illegal in order to prevent chaos or to promote order—violation of established traffic rules, for example. Further, some acts may carry no taint of immorality but may be made illegal because they are considered contrary to the general welfare of the society. Acts of pollution like burning your trash within the city limits illustrate the point.

Classification of Criminal Acts

Criminal acts are usually classified as (1) crimes against persons, (2) crimes against property, (3) traffic in illegal goods and services, and (4) other crimes. Crimes against persons are violent crimes. They include murder, rape, and aggravated assault. The latter is in many instances associated with robbery. Crimes against property include such things as fraud, armed robbery, theft, embezzlement, forgery, arson, vandalism, and the like. Traffic in illegal goods and services is made up of such things as gambling, narcotics, loan-sharking, prostitution, and alcohol. The "other crimes" classification is, of course, a catchall for everything from nonpayment of alimony to speeding.

Crime is generally thought to be a very serious problem in the United States. In every large city and in many small ones people are reluctant to go out at night for fear of being robbed, raped, beaten, or even murdered. And there is no evidence of improvement in the situation. From 1966 to 1971 the overall crime rate—the number of reported offenses per 100,000 persons—rose by 74 percent. During the same period crimes of violence—crimes against persons —showed an 80 percent increase in the number of offenses per 100,000 persons, and the rate of crimes against property evidenced a 73 percent rise.[1]

Causes of Crime

Criminal activity stems from many sources. Some are economic in nature and others are not. Different kinds of crime may have their roots in different sources. The problem of the causes of crime is a hard one to attack—like asking what causes a society to be what it is. We can, however, identify some of the broad factors that tend to result in criminal activities.

Unrestrained passions or emotions are an important factor in many violent crimes. Most murders, for example, result from deep-seated, intense feelings of some sort between the murderer and the victim. The victim may be a wife, a husband, a girlfriend, or the guy who cheats in a poker game. The level of the murderer's emotion pushes aside the constraints of conscience and law that the society has established. Murders in which the victim is unknown to the murderer are the least common type.

When poverty is coupled with *high levels of economic and social aspirations,* the stage is set for criminal activities—particularly robbery and dealing in illegal goods and services. People who are thwarted in obtaining desired social and economic goals legally seek to obtain them illegally. Thus we find that ghettos of large cities produce a disproportionate share of criminals. The incidence of robbery and traffic in illegal goods tends to be high among minority groups who feel the burden of both economic and social discrimination.

The standards of social values of a society are an important determinant of criminal activities. Society's attitudes toward cheating on one's income tax, stealing from one's employer, embezzlement,

---

[1] U.S. Department of Justice, Federal Bureau of Investigation, *Uniform Crime Reports for the United States, 1971,* pp. 1–4.

wiretapping and other interferences with the right to privacy help set the stage for acts which may be considered criminal. The real tragedy of Watergate is not so much what the bugging did to the Democrats, but the low level of social values shown to be held by people in positions of public trust.

THE COSTS OF CRIME

That crime has economic costs is certain. The measurement of those costs, however, is very inaccurate. In the first place, many criminal activities go unreported. In the second place, an accurate dollar value cannot be attached to the cost of those crimes that do occur. Nevertheless, estimates of the costs of crime are necessary if decision making regarding the level of crime prevention activities is to have any degree of soundness. The better the estimates, the better the decisions that can be made.

The basis of measuring the cost of crime is the alternative-cost principle. The economic cost of crime is thus the difference between what gross national product would be if there were neither criminal nor crime prevention activities and what GNP currently is, given present criminal and crime prevention activities.

Some estimates of the costs of crime are presented in Table 4–1, but these estimates are a mixed bag. Crimes against persons, if correctly estimated, are an authentic part of economic costs, since they attempt to measure the loss of earnings of the victims of the crimes. So, too, are the costs of prevention, apprehension, and correction, since resources used for these purposes could have been used to produce alternative goods and services valuable to consumers. Many of the other items listed as costs are really transfers of purchasing power to the perpetrators of the crimes from their victims. In the case of theft, the thief is made better off at the same time that the person from whom he steals is made worse off. Reprehensible as theft may be, it is difficult to conclude that it represents a large net economic cost to society. It may, however, represent sizable costs to the individual victims. The prime purpose of the table is to provide some idea of the relative money magnitudes involved in different types of criminal activities.

Since criminal activities in the aggregate lower GNP below what it would be without them, it follows that crime prevention activities

TABLE 4–1
Estimated Costs of Crime by Type of Crime and of Crime Prevention, 1965

Crime		*Crime Prevention*	
Type of Crime	*Cost (000,000 omitted)*	*Prevention, Apprehension and Correction*	*Cost (000,000 omitted)*
Crimes against persons, total	$ 815	Enforcement and justice, total	$4,212
Homicide	750	Police	2,792
Assault and other	65	Corrections	1,034
Crimes against property, total	$3,932	Courts	261
Commercial theft, unreported	1,400	Prosecution and defense	125
Fraud	1,350	Private protection, total	$1,910
Robbery, burglary, larceny, auto theft	600	Prevention services	1,350
Embezzlement	200	Insurance	300
Forgery and other	82	Prevention equipment	200
Arson and vandalism	300	Counsel, bail, witness expense	60
Illegal goods and services, total	$8,075		
Gambling	7,000		
Narcotics	350		
Loan-sharking	350		
Prostitution	225		
Alcohol	150		
Other, total	$2,036		
Driving while intoxicated	1,816		
Abortion	120		
Tax fraud	100		

Source: U.S. Department of Commerce, Bureau of the Census, *Statistical Abstract of the United States, 1972*, p. 151.

should in turn raise GNP above what it would be in the presence of widespread criminal activities. Crime prevention activities can be considered an economic good or service, since GNP is higher with them than it would be without them. Thus we can think of crime prevention activities as being produced; resources—labor and capital—go into their production. The costs of producing these services are measured by applying the alternative-cost principle: the resources used in producing crime prevention are equal to the value these resources would have had in their best alternative uses. The right-hand column of Table 4–1 shows the amounts paid for resources used in crime prevention in 1965. These amounts must be about equal to the economic costs of crime prevention activities, since resources used in the whole range of prevention activities must be paid for approximately in terms of what they are worth in their best alternative use.

INDIVIDUALLY AND COLLECTIVELY CONSUMED GOODS

Would a 5 percent increase in the police force of your city be worth anything to you personally? Would an increase or a decrease in the number of patrol cars on the city's streets affect you directly? Would it benefit you if there were an increase or decrease in the number of courts and judges in the system of justice? Your answers to these questions will be either "No" or "I don't know."

Such questions lead logically to a useful threefold classification of goods and services. The first includes those that are *individually consumed*. The second includes those that are *collectively consumed*. The third is made up of *semicollectively consumed* goods and services.

Individually Consumed Goods

The concept of individually consumed goods and services is straightforward. It includes those that directly benefit the person who consumes them. Much of what we consume is of this nature—hamburgers, suntan lotion, pencils, and the like. The person doing the consuming is able to identify the benefit he receives. For example, eating a hamburger gives pleasure to the eater and reduces his hunger pangs.

Collectively Consumed Goods

Collectively consumed goods and services lie at the opposite pole from those that are individually consumed; in this case, the individual is not able to isolate or identify a specific personal benefit. Consider national defense services. What part of the total defense services provided by the economy can you identify as being consumed by you, and what is your estimate of the resulting increase in your well-being? Services like this contribute to the welfare of the group of which we belong, but it is not possible to pick out the part of the benefit that accrues specifically to any one person.

Many kinds of services produced and consumed by a society are collectively consumed. They include national defense, crime prevention, space exploration, some aspects of public health, and most antipollution measures.

Semicollectively Consumed Goods

Semicollectively consumed goods and services yield identifiable benefits to the one who consumes them, but their consumption by one person yields spillover benefits to other persons. My neighbor's consumption of the various items that lead to beautiful landscaping on his property benefits me as well as him. When other people in a democratic society consume the services of primary education— learn to read, write, and do arithmetic—I benefit from it, too, because a literate population improves the functioning of the democratic processes. When other people purchase sufficient medical care to avoid epidemics, I benefit from the purchase of their health care.

A great many items which people consume and which yield direct benefits to them also yield benefits to others as their consumption occurs. These benefits to persons other than the direct consumers were identified in the last chapter as *social spillover benefits*. We also noted that the consumption of some semicollectively consumed goods may yield *spillover costs* to persons other than the direct consumers. Cigarette smoking in a classroom in which there are nonsmokers may be a case in point. So may onion or garlic eating.

The "Free Rider" Problem

A society may have difficulty in getting collectively consumed goods produced because of a tendency for some of the benefactors of the goods to be *"free riders."* The nature of the free rider problem can be illustrated by an example from the Old West. On the plains of Oklahoma, Texas, Kansas, and other frontier cattle-raising states, cattle rustling posed a serious problem. In order to deal effectively with the problem in one area (say, the Dodge City environs), it was advantageous for the cattle raisers of the area to band together. They organized a vigilante group of sufficient size to make rustling in the area an exceedingly dangerous business—as a few who were caught and hanged would have testified, if they had been able. All the cattlemen of the area contributed to the cost of organizing and maintaining the vigilante group.

As the problem was brought under control, however, it became difficult to meet the costs of holding the vigilante group together. Any one cattleman was inclined to think that if the others maintained the group they could not keep him from benefiting from its activities. If rustlers were afraid to operate in the area *everyone* benefited, whether he helped pay the costs or not. Each cattleman therefore had an incentive to withdraw support from the group and to become a "free rider," since even if he did not pay a part of the costs of the protection it provided he could not be excluded from its benefits.

Government Production of Collectively Consumed Items

Historically, groups of people have found that in banding together they can do things collectively that they are not able to do as individuals. One of the first things discovered was that the group provides better protection from outsiders than individuals can provide on their own. They also found that group action is well suited to protecting the members of the group from predators in their midst.

Group action on a voluntary basis is technically possible, of course. The vigilante group of the Old West provides an excellent example. But voluntary associations to provide collectively consumed goods have a tendency to fall apart because of the incentives that induce some people to become free riders and because free riders cannot be excluded from the benefits of the good. Thus the voluntary association is a tenuous mechanism for this purpose.

Supplanting the voluntary association with the coercive association that we call *government* can effectively remedy the free rider problem. A coercive governmental unit (and the power of coercion is an essential feature of government) simply requires that all who receive the benefits of a collectively consumed good or the service it provides should pay appropriate taxes for it. Thus the provision of national defense, crime prevention, pollution prevention, and other collectively consumed goods and services become a government function. These items are often referred to as *public goods*.

Most modern governments do not confine their production of goods and services to collectively consumed or public goods. Name any good or service, and there will probably be a government somewhere that produces it. A major difference between a private enterprise economic system and a socialistic economic system is that the government of the latter is responsible for the production of individually consumed as well as collectively consumed and semicollectively consumed items. The government of the former will leave the bulk of individually consumed goods to private businesses, although it may play a relatively important role in the provision of such semicollectively consumed goods as education.

THE ECONOMICS OF CRIME PREVENTION ACTIVITIES

The "Correct" Level

The level of expenditures on crime prevention activities by any governmental unit is open to question. Is the $4.2 billion level indicated in the right-hand side of Table 4–1 more or less "correct" for the United States as a whole? The same question can be appropriately asked about any category of government activity and expenditure. To find the answer to any of these questions, *cost-benefit analysis* is used. This analysis estimates the benefits of the activity, determines its costs, and finds the level at which the costs of an increase in the activity begin to exceed the benefits of that increase.

The framework for the problem is set up in Table 4–2. Suppose the annual benefits and costs of crime prevention at various levels have been investigated thoroughly and the results have been recorded in columns 1, 2, and 4. A "unit" of crime prevention is a nebulous concept, a composite of police manpower, patrol cars, courthouses, judges' services, prison costs, and the like. The definition of physical units is avoided by using arbitrary $60,000 units of crime prevention, and it is assumed that each $60,000 chunk is spent in the best possible way.

The money expense of crime prevention to the community is met by levying taxes. The *economic cost* is the value of the goods and services that resources used in crime prevention activities could have produced if they had not been drawn into crime prevention.

TABLE 4–2
Estimated Benefits and Costs of Crime Prevention, Typical U.S. Community

(1) Units of Crime Prevention	(2) Total Benefits	(3) Marginal Benefits	(4) Total Costs	(5) Marginal Costs	(6) Total Net Benefits
1	$ 200,000	$200,000	$ 60,000	$60,000	$140,000
2	380,000	180,000	120,000	60,000	260,000
3	540,000	160,000	180,000	60,000	360,000
4	680,000	140,000	240,000	60,000	440,000
5	800,000	120,000	300,000	60,000	500,000
6	900,000	100,000	360,000	60,000	540,000
7	980,000	80,000	420,000	60,000	560,000
8	1,040,000	60,000	480,000	60,000	560,000
9	1,080,000	40,000	540,000	60,000	540,000
10	1,100,000	20,000	600,000	60,000	500,000

The *benefits* of crime prevention are the community's best estimates of how much better off the suppression of crime will make them —the value of the extra days they can work as a result of *not* being raped, maimed, or murdered, plus the value of property *not* destroyed or stolen, plus the value of the greater personal security they feel, and so on. Obviously, the benefits will be much more difficult to estimate than the costs. In fact, the most difficult and vexing part of the problem is the estimation of the benefits that ensue from various kinds of crime prevention activities.

If the benefits and costs are known, as we assume in Table 4–2 that they are, determination of the correct level of crime prevention is relatively simple. Consider first whether there should be no crime prevention at all or whether one unit would be worthwhile. One unit of prevention yields benefits to the community of $200,000, and it would cost them only $60,000 to obtain it. Obviously, this is better than no prevention; the net benefits (total benefits minus total costs) are $140,000.

Now consider two units of prevention versus one unit. The total benefits yielded are $380,000. But note that the *increase* in total benefits yielded in moving from one to two units is $180,000, somewhat less than the increase in total benefits resulting from a movement from zero to one unit. The increase in total benefits resulting from a one-unit increase in the amount of crime prevention is called the *marginal benefit* of crime prevention. As the number of units of prevention is increased, the marginal benefits would be expected to decline, because each one-unit increase would be used to suppress the most serious crimes outstanding. The more units used, the less serious the crimes to which they are applied, and, therefore, the less the increase in the benefits from each one-unit increase in prevention.

It pays the community to move from the one-unit level to the two-unit level of prevention because the marginal benefits yielded by the second unit exceed the marginal costs of the increase. *Marginal costs* of crime prevention are defined in much the same way as marginal benefits—they are the increase in total costs resulting from a one-unit increase in prevention. Marginal costs of prevention are constant in the example because we are measuring units of prevention in terms of $60,000. Therefore, the total net benefits will be increased by $120,000 ($180,000 − $60,000) if the community increases the prevention level from one to two units. (Make sure you understand this before you go any further.)

Using the same kind of logic, it can be determined that it is worthwhile for the community to use a third, fourth, fifth, sixth, and seventh unit of crime prevention. For each of these increases, the marginal benefits are greater than the marginal costs—that is, each adds more to total benefits than it adds to total costs. Therefore, each brings about an increase in total net benefits. Total net benefits reach a maximum of $560,000 at the seven-unit level. If the level of prevention is raised to eight units, no harm is done. Marginal benefits equal marginal costs, and there is no change in total net benefits. But if the level is raised to nine units, total net benefits will fall to $540,000.

It is wise to review the logic underlying determination of the correct amount of government activity in crime prevention—or in anything else. It is very simple, very important, and frequently overlooked. If a small increase in the level of activity yields additional benefits worth more than the additional costs, it should be expanded. On the other hand, if its marginal benefits are less than its marginal costs, it should be contracted. It follows that the correct level is that at which marginal benefits are equal to marginal costs. (Study Table 4–2 until you understand this thoroughly.)

The foregoing economic analysis suggests something about dealing with increasing crime rates. If, when crime prevention activities are stepped up, the cost of an increase in prevention is less than the benefits it realizes, we ought to be engaged in more crime prevention activities. We are irrational if we do not. However, if a unit of prevention is not worth to us what it costs, then it would be irrational to attempt to suppress crime at present levels of crime prevention activities. Complete suppression of crime is never logical from the point of view of economics. There will be some level of crime prevention at which the benefits of an additional unit of prevention are simply not worth what they cost. (What about ten units of prevention in Table 4–2?)

The economic analysis developed above, as important as it is, fails to touch on a very large part of the problems of crime. It does not consider, for example, such questions as: What gives rise to crime in the first place? What causes children to become delinquent and to grow up as criminals? What causes adults to turn to criminal

activities? Can criminals be rehabilitated, or should they simply be
punished? These and many other questions are psychological, social, and even political in nature. Given the social milieu in which
crime takes place, however, economic analysis is valuable in determining the level at which prevention activities should be
pursued.

Allocation of the Crime Prevention Budget

Economic analysis also has something to contribute in determining the efficiency of crime prevention activities. There are several facets to a well-balanced governmental crime prevention
program. Ideally, it should deter people from engaging in criminal
activities. Failing in this—as it surely will—it must first detect and
apprehend those engaging in criminal activities. This is primarily
a police function. To determine the guilt or innocence of those
charged with criminal acts, the legal system utilizes courts, attorneys,
judges, and juries. Those convicted are fined and/or put in prison.
Reference to the prison system as a corrections system indicates
hope that those incarcerated will somehow be rehabilitated and
deterred from engaging in further criminal activities. In practice,
the sentences of those convicted of crimes usually take on at least
some aspects of punishment.

How much of a governmental unit's crime prevention budget
should be allocated to police departments? How much for courts,
judges, and prosecutors? How much for corrections, rehabilitation,
and punishment? Detection and apprehension of persons thought to
be committing criminal acts is of little value unless there are adequate court facilities for trying them. Trying persons apprehended
and sentencing those convicted presupposes a system of corrections.
No one facet of crime prevention can contribute efficiently unless
the others are there to back it up.

The correct or most efficient mix of the different facets of crime
prevention is determined logically by what economists call the
equimarginal principle. The crime budget should be allocated
among police, courts, and corrections so that the last dollar spent
on any one facet yields the same addition to the benefits of crime
prevention as the last dollar spent on the others. Another way of
saying this is that the budget should be allocated so that the mar-

ginal benefits from a dollar's worth of police effort will equal the
marginal benefits of a dollar's worth of judicial effort and a dollar's
worth of corrective effort in the overall suppression of crime.

As an example, suppose that the crime prevention system is over-
loaded in the area of detection and apprehension. The courts cannot
handle all those who are being arrested, so many of them must be set
free without trial. The mere fact of arrest will have some crime-
deterring effects, but they will be much less than would be the case
if there were adequate court facilities.

The contribution to crime prevention of a dollar's worth of police
activity at this point is low. On the other hand, an expansion of
court facilities would increase the likelihood of trial and conviction
of those apprehended. We would expect the crime-deterring effect
of a dollar's worth of such an expansion to be greater than that of a
dollar spent on detection, apprehension, and subsequent freeing
of those apprehended. Suppose that taking a dollar away from police
work brings about enough of a crime increase to cause a 75-cent
loss to the community. Now suppose that if court activity were increased by one dollar's worth, this increased activity will deter
criminal activity enough to make the community better off by $3.
Under these circumstances, the community will experience a net
gain of $2.25 by a transfer of a dollar from police activities to court
activities. Such net gains are possible for any $1 transfer among
police activities, court activities, and corrections activities when the
marginal benefits of a dollar spent on one are less than the marginal
benefits of a dollar spent on either of the others. No further gains are
possible when the crime prevention budget is so allocated that the
marginal benefits of a dollar spent on any one activity equal the
marginal benefits of a dollar spent on any of the other activities.

THE ECONOMICS OF LEGALIZING ILLEGAL ACTIVITIES

Economic analysis also provides information that is useful in the
determination of whether or not certain activities should be considered illegal. There has been much controversy historically over
legalization of the purchase, sale, and consumption of alcohol. More
recently, drugs have come into the picture—especially marijuana.
So has abortion. Although prostitution is illegal in most parts of the

United States, legalization of the practice comes up for discussion periodically. Various forms of gambling also figure in arguments as to what should and what should not be illegal.

The purchase and sale of abortions provides an excellent example of the contributions that economic analysis can make in a controversy over whether or not an activity should be legal. Most of the states of the United States have had laws making abortions illegal, many of which were struck down by a recent Supreme Court decision. The underlying basis of these laws is morality. Antiabortionists contend that abortion destroys a human life. Proabortionists argue that a woman should be free to make the choice of whether she wants to have a baby, and the passing of an unborn fetus is not equivalent to destroying a human life. The central disagreement is over the point at which a fertilized egg becomes a human being. It must be recognized at the outset that economics can tell us nothing about the moral issues involved. It can, however, provide important information regarding the conditions of purchase and sale when the activity is illegal, as compared with when it is legal.

In Figure 4–1, suppose that D_1D_1 and S_1S_1 represent the demand curve and the supply curve for abortions when this type of medical service is illegal. The fact that abortions are illegal does not drive all potential customers out of the market, but it does suppress the number who would buy abortions at each possible price. Neither does it completely eliminate the supply, but it does affect the segment of the medical profession from which the supply comes. Part of it is rendered by poorly trained personnel of the midwife or unscrupulous druggist variety. Part of it comes from medical doctors who are in difficulty with their professional brothers for one reason or another and who are more or less barred from legally practicing medicine. Almost all of the illegal abortions must be performed with inferior medical facilities—for example, the home "office" of the illegal practitioner—under circumstances that are likely to be unsanitary.

Prices are likely to be very high as compared with other comparable medical services for two reasons: (1) because of the limited quantities of facilities and abortionists available, and (2) in order to compensate the abortionist for the risk of being caught and prosecuted. An interesting side effect is that abortions will be much more readily available to the rich, for whom the high price is less

FIGURE 4–1
Economic Effects of Legalizing Abortions

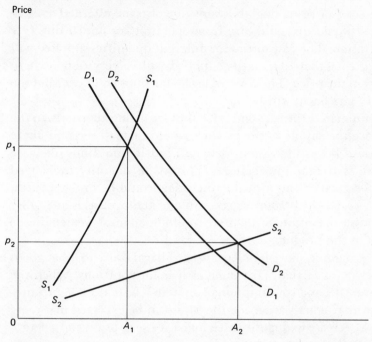

When abortions are illegal, the demand and supply curves are D_1D_1 and
S_1S_1, respectively. Legalization will increase demand to some extent, shifting the demand curve to some position such as D_2D_2. Supply is likely to be
greatly increased, as shown by the shift of the curve from S_1S_1 to S_2S_2. The
quantity exchanged rises from A_1 to A_2, and the price falls from p_1 to p_2.

important, than for the poor, who are priced out of the market. The
price of an illegal abortion in Figure 4–1 is p_1, and the quantity performed is A_1.

Now suppose that abortions become legal. There will be some
increase in demand, say to D_2D_2, since the taint of illegality is removed. There will, of course, still be moral constraints that prevent
some women from aborting unwanted babies. The effects on supply
are likely to be more dramatic. Abortions can now be performed in
hospitals under controlled sanitary conditions, and in medical terms
they are no big deal. They will be performed by doctors whose com-
petency for this operation is as great as for any other. The risk of

being caught and prosecuted has been removed and no longer enters into the cost picture.

The costs of supplying abortions now are the alternative earnings that physicians could earn from operations of similar difficulty and duration. The cost spread for different quantities supplied will not be great—that is, quantity supplied will be very responsive to changes in the price. The price of legal abortions will be p_2, and the quantity purchased will be A_2.

To summarize the economic effects of legalizing abortions, in the first place the supply of the product would increase. Second, there would also be an increase in demand, but it would not likely be as great as the supply increase. Third, the quantity exchanged would be greater, and probably the price would be lower. Fourth, the service would become as accessible to the poor as is any other comparable operation. Fifth, there would be an improvement in the quality of the product.

The economic analysis of legal versus illegal traffic in other goods and services is virtually the same as it is for abortions. When the purchase, sale, and consumption of an item—be it alcohol, prostitution, or marijuana—are made illegal, it can be expected that there will be a decrease in quantity exchanged, a rise in price, and a deterioration in the quality of the product.

SUMMARY

Criminal activities are defined as activities that are illegal. They may or may not be immoral. They are usually classified as (1) crimes against persons, (2) crimes against property, (3) traffic in illegal goods and services, and (4) other.

Crime constitutes a serious problem in the United States; crime rates generally have been increasing over the years. Some of the underlying causes of crime are (1) unrestrained passions or emotions, (2) poverty coupled with high levels of economic and social aspirations, and (3) low standards of social values.

Good information on the costs of crime are not available because many criminal activities go unreported and because it is difficult to place dollar values on the results of some kinds of these activities. Some reported "costs" of crime are not really economic costs to the society as a whole but are transfers of income from the victim of the crime to its perpetrator.

In an economic analysis of crime it is useful to classify goods and services into three categories: (1) individually consumed, (2) collectively consumed, and (3) semicollectively consumed items. Governments, with their coercive powers, are in a unique position to produce such collectively consumed items as crime prevention goods and services. Consequently, collectively consumed goods of this type are usually provided by governments.

Cost-benefit analysis can be used to advantage in determining the level of crime prevention activities in a society. The costs of crime prevention can be easily determined, but the benefits —many of which are intangible—are hard to estimate. Conceptually, they are the difference between what GNP would be *with* crime prevention and what *it* would be without such activities. On the basis of the best estimates that can be made, the society should seek that level of crime prevention at which the total net benefits are greatest. This will be the level at which the marginal benefits of crime prevention are equal to its marginal costs.

Once the level of the government's crime prevention budget is determined, it should be efficiently allocated among the different facets of crime prevention activities. These include detection and apprehension of violators, determination of their guilt or innocence, and corrections. The equimarginal principle is appropriate to use for this purpose. The budget should be allocated so that the marginal benefits from any one of the foregoing facets are equal to the marginal benefits from each of the others.

From time to time certain kinds of activities—usually purchase and sale of items—that have been illegal are made legal. The economic result usually is that greater quantities of the legalized item will be exchanged at a lower price, the item becomes generally more available to the poor, and there will be an improvement in the quality of the product.

Economic analysis alone will not solve crime problems, but it can be very useful in making logical attacks on them.

SUPPLEMENTARY READING

Federal Bureau of Investigation. *Uniform Crime Reports for the United States*. Washington, D.C.: Government Printing Office.
    Sums up all reported crimes in the United States on an annual basis, providing the most complete statistical data available on kinds

of crime and who commits them. It also provides trend data for key types of crime statistics. There is very little analysis of the data.

North, Douglass C., and Miller, Roger L. *The Economics of Public Issues,* chap. 22, "The Economics of Crime Prevention." New York: Harper & Row, 1971.

Discusses the "correct" allocation of a governmental unit's crime prevention budget among the various facets of a balanced crime prevention program.

President's Commission on Law Enforcement and Administration of Justice. *Crime and Its Impact—An Assessment.* Washington, D.C.: Government Printing Office, 1967.

This Task Force Report pulls together and analyzes existing data on the extent of and trends in criminal activities. Of particular interest for our purposes is Chapter 3, "The Economic Impact of Crime." While the report does much with the data available, the need for more complete data reporting and for additional systematic analysis of the economic impact of crime becomes abundantly clear.

Rogers, A. J., III. *The Economics of Crime.* Hinsdale, Ill.: Dryden Press, 1973.

A good elementary exposition of the economic motivations for criminal activities and the economic consequences of those activities. Contains very little on the economics of crime prevention.

Chapter 5

POLLUTION PROBLEMS

CHECKLIST OF ECONOMIC CONCEPTS

Alternative-Cost Principle
Production Possibilities Curve
Cost-Benefit Analysis
Marginal Cost
Marginal Benefit
Economic (or True) Cost
Externalities
Social Cost
Private Cost
Economic Efficiency

5

POLLUTION PROBLEMS
Must We Foul Our Own Nests?

THE HIGH-PITCHED WHISTLE of departing jets was deafening as John Q. Smith stepped outside the terminal building and walked toward the parking lot. He located his three-year-old car, got it started, paid the parking fee, and wheeled out onto the congested freeway, adding his own small carbon monoxide and hydrocarbon contributions to the pall that hung over the city. On his left the Contaminated Steel Company was belching noxious streams of dense smoke into the heavy air, ably assisted by the nearby power and light plant. Where the freeway joined the river's edge, a pulp and paper mill could be seen spewing its wastes into the river. He held his breath as long as he could along the two-mile stretch of road adjoining the stockyards. Then with a sigh of relief he swerved off the freeway and turned down the country road that would take him home. Once out of sight of human habitat, he stopped the car and relieved himself at the side of the road, noting as he did so the accumulating litter of beer cans, paper, and cellophane bags on the shoulder of the road and in the ditch.

John Q's house was located on a lake. Since a group of industrial plants had been built along the lakeshore several miles away, it was not as pleasant to swim and water-ski in the lake as it had been previously. The fishing didn't seem to be as good, either. Recently he had been having problems with a backed-up sewer, and he wondered as he turned in the driveway if the plumber had been there to clean out the sewer line that reached from the house to the lake. John Q. had grown up in the great outdoors (this is why he had built the house on the lake), and he was much concerned about its deterioration.

WHAT IS POLLUTION?

Most of us, like John Q. Smith, are concerned about environmental problems, but we are not quite sure what we can do about them. As individuals, we seem to believe that we can do little. In fact, we are likely to add to the problems by thinking that our own bit of pollution is just a drop in the bucket.

In recent years collective actions to alleviate pollution through governmental units have been initiated. The problem is how to determine what constitutes wise governmental antipollution policies. Should polluting activities be banned altogether, or should some be permitted on a limited scale? What kinds of pollution controls are most effective? Which are most equitable? To get at these and related questions, we must examine the economic nature of pollution and its control.

The Environment and Its Services

We take the environment in which we live so much for granted that we seldom think explicitly about what it is. An explicit definition of the environment is necessary, however, to provide the base on which to build an analysis of pollution problems. The environment consists of air, water, and land, which furnish a variety of important services.

First, the environment provides a *habitat* or surroundings in which both plant and animal life can survive. Temperature ranges on the planet are neither too hot nor too cold for survival. The air, the water, and the land contain the elements needed to sustain living matter as we know it.

Second, the environment contains *resources* that are usable in the production of goods and services. These include minerals such as petroleum, coal, and a wide assortment of ores that can be processed into metals and metal alloys. They include soil properties and plant life supported by the soil. Resources include the plant and animal life yielded by water as well as the inherent properties of water used directly in production processes. They also include oxygen and nitrogen, along with other elements and properties found in the atmosphere.

Third, the environment furnishes many *amenities* that make life more enjoyable. It opens up possibilities of a walk along a river, through an alfalfa field, or in a rose garden. It provides an area in which you can fly kites or have picnics, a place to take your girlfriend or your boyfriend—or even your husband or wife. You can sit in it and enjoy the sunset. Or, if you so desire, you can paint it or photograph it.

Production, Consumption, and Wastes

The services of the environment are used by both production units and household units as they engage in activities of various kinds. Production units lay heavy claims on the environment's resources, but they may also make use of its habitat and amenity characteristics.

As production units engage in the process of transforming raw and semifinished materials into goods and services that will satisfy human wants, there are at least three ways in which the environment can be affected. First, some of the environment's stocks of exhaustible resources may be diminished. These include coal, petroleum, and many mineral deposits. Second, it is called upon for replaceable resources like timber, grassland, oxygen, and nitrogen. Third, it is used as a place to dispose of the wastes of the production and consumption processes—as a gigantic garbage disposal.

The pollution problem arises primarily from the use of the environment by producers and consumers as a dumping ground for wastes. We litter the countryside with cans, paper, and the other residues of consumption and production. We dump the emissions from our automobiles and factories into the atmosphere. We empty sewage and residue from production directly and indirectly into streams, rivers, and lakes.

Recycling of Wastes and the Concept of Pollution

As wastes from production and consumption are dumped into the environment, nature sets recycling processes in motion. Animal life

uses oxygen, giving off carbon dioxide wastes. But plants use carbon
dioxide, giving off oxygen wastes. Dead plants and animal life are
attacked by chemical elements that decompose them, restoring to the
soil elements that the living organisms had withdrawn from it. Living organisms frequently contribute to the decomposition process.
Iron and steel objects rust and disintegrate over time. So does wood
and other matter. Wastes that can be decomposed in air, water, and
soil are said to be *biodegradable*. But there are some wastes that are
not biodegradable. Aluminum containers are a case in point.

Recycling—the transformation of wastes into raw materials that
are again usable—requires variable lengths of time, depending on
what it is that is being recycled. It takes many years for a steel pipe
to rust away. Wood wastes vary a great deal in the time it takes for
their complete disintegration. But many plant and animal products
require only a very short time to decompose.

Pollution consists of loading the environment with wastes that
are either not completely recycled, are not recycled fast enough,
or are not recycled at all. It involves a diminution of the capacity
of the environment to yield environmental services. Pollution occurs when recycling processes fail to prevent wastes from accumulating in the environment.

Common Forms of Pollution

Pollution is as old as mankind itself. Wherever people have con-
gregated, their wastes have tended to pile up more rapidly than the
forces of nature can digest them. As long as the world was sparsely
populated and no permanent cities existed, no great problems were
created. When the extent of pollution in one locale imposed costs
on the people living there that outweighed the costs associated with
moving, they simply moved away from it. Then, given time, natural
recycling processes could in many cases take over and restore the
excess wastes to usable form.

When towns and cities came into existence, pollution raised more
serious problems. How could bodily wastes from humans and an-
imals, as well as refuse from the daily round of living, be disposed
of? Until fairly recent times it was not disposed of in many instances
—levels of sanitation were unbelievably low, and levels of stench
were unbelievably high. As the density of the world's population

has increased and as it has become more difficult to move away from pollution problems, man has turned his attention more and more toward the development of control measures. In order to control pollution, it must be identified as closely as possible.

Air Pollution. In the processes of production and consumption, five major kinds of wastes are dumped into the atmosphere. Most are a result of combustion and have caused local problems for a long time. Since there are millions of cubic miles of atmosphere to absorb these wastes, however, air pollution has not caused great concern until the past few decades. These wastes are carbon monoxide, sulfur oxides, nitrogen oxides, hydrocarbons, and particulates.

Carbon monoxide, an odorless, colorless gas, makes the atmosphere a less hospitable habitat for animal life. In concentrated amounts, it causes dizziness, headaches, and nausea in humans. Exposure to a sufficiently high concentration—about 100 parts per one million parts of atmosphere—for a few hours can be fatal. About 64 percent of the carbon monoxide emissions into the atmosphere in the United States comes from automobiles, and another 12 percent comes from industrial sources of one kind or another.[1] The greatest concentrations of carbon monoxide occur in large cities. On New York City streets concentration levels as high as 13 parts per one million parts of atmosphere have been recorded.

Sulfur oxides constitute a second major source of atmospheric pollution. Where they are heavily concentrated, they cause damage to both plant and animal life. Oxides result largely from the combustion of fuel oils and coal. Consequently, high levels of concentration are most likely to occur where these are used for the generation of electricity and for residential heating.

A third atmospheric pollutant is *nitrogen oxides.* These can cause lung damage in human beings and may also retard plant growth. The main sources of the pollutant are automobiles and stationary combustion processes such as those used in generating electric power.

Hydrocarbons constitute a fourth kind of waste emitted into the air. At their present concentration levels no direct harmful effects

---

[1] U.S. Department of Health, Education, and Welfare, National Air Pollution Control Administration, *Nationwide Inventory of Air Pollutant Emissions, 1968* (August 1971).

have been attributed to them. However, they combine with nitrogen oxides and ultraviolet rays of the sun to form photochemical smog. The smog may produce breathing difficulties and eye irritation for human beings. In addition, it speeds up the oxidation processes to which paints and metals are subject, resulting in substantial damages to industrial plants and equipment. Over 50 percent of hydrocarbon emissions in the United States comes from automobiles, and the rest from other combustion processes.

A fifth air pollutant consists of a heterogeneous mixture of suspended solids and liquids called *particulates*. These are largely dust and ash, along with lead from automobile exhausts. The major source of particulates, however, is fuel combustion in stationary sources and in industrial processes. Open fires used to burn trash and garbage also make their contributions. Particulates serve to lower visibilities. Some, such as lead from automobile exhausts, may be directly harmful to human beings.

Water Pollution. Water pollution is ordinarily measured in terms of the capacity of water to support aquatic life. This capacity depends upon (1) the level of dissolved oxygen in the water and (2) the presence of matters or materials injurious to plant and animal life.

The level of dissolved oxygen is built up through aeration of water and through the photosynthetic processes of plant life living in the water. It is destroyed by its use to decompose organic matter that occurs in or is dumped into the water. The oxygen needed for decomposition purposes is referred to as *biochemical oxygen demand,* or BOD. The level of dissolved oxygen available for supporting aquatic life, then, depends upon the balance between aeration and photosynthesis on the one hand and BOD on the other.

The level of dissolved oxygen is affected by several factors. First, it tends to be higher the greater amount of water exposed to the atmosphere. In nature, fast-running streams, rapids, and waterfalls contribute to aeration. Artificial aeration is frequently accomplished by shooting streams of water through the air. Second, it also tends to be higher the greater the amount of photosynthesis that occurs in the water. In some instances the amount of photosynthesis that occurs in aquatic plant life may be reduced by air pollution. In this way, air pollution may be a source of water pollution. Third, it tends to be higher the lower the temperature of the water—use of the water for cooling by firms such as steel mills, oil refineries, and electricity-generating plants raises the temperature of the water and lowers its capacity to hold dissolved oxygen. Fourth, organic wastes that create BOD come from both domestic and industrial sources, so the level of dissolved oxygen varies inversely with the amounts that are dumped. The decomposition of such wastes can be greatly facilitated and BOD can be correspondingly reduced by chemical treatment of such wastes before they are discharged into streams, rivers, lakes, or oceans.

The capacity of water to support aquatic life is reduced when various kinds of materials and matters are dumped into it. Among these are toxins which do not settle out of the water and are not easily broken down by biological means. Mercury is a toxin that has created problems of contaminated tuna and salmon. So are phenols, herbicides, and pesticides. There have been heated discussions in recent years over the propriety of using them in large quantities. Questions have been raised also as to whether the oceans should be used for the dumping of nuclear wastes and for undersea nuclear explosions.

Land Pollution. Land pollution results from the dumping of a wide variety of wastes on the terrain. Highways are littered with refuse thrown from passing automobiles. Junkyards grow as we scrap over seven million automobiles per year, to say nothing of the prodigious amounts of other machinery and appliances that are retired from use. Mining areas are covered with slag and rock piles. Strip mining often leaves huge, unsightly blemishes on the countryside. Garbage dumps and landfills grow as towns and cities dispose of the solid wastes they collect and accumulate. All of these reduce the capacity of the terrain to render environmental services.

ECONOMICS OF POLLUTION

No one likes pollution. Almost everyone would like to see something done about it. Toward the end we shall consider in this section the fundamental economics of the pollution problem. Accordingly, we shall examine the reasons why pollution occurs, analyze the effects of pollution on resource allocation, look at the costs of pollution control, and identify its benefits. Finally, we shall establish criteria for determining the appropriate level of control.

Why Polluters Pollute

Why is it that pollution occurs? What is there about environmental services that enables consumers and producers to use the environment as a free dumping ground? Ordinarily, pollution results from one or both of two basic factors: (1) the fact that no one has property rights or enforces them in the environment being polluted, and (2) the collectively consumed characteristics of the environment being polluted.

If no one owns a portion of the environment or if an owner cannot police it or have it policed, then it becomes possible for people to use a river, a lake, the air, or an area of land as a waste basket without being charged for doing so. Because no one owns the air above city streets and highways, automobile owners can dump combustion gases into it without paying for the privilege of doing so. Similarly, a paper mill can dump its wastes into the river without charge because no one owns the river. But even ownership of the environment may not be enough to keep pollution from occurring. How many times have you seen litter accumulate on a vacant lot, or junk dumped in a ditch in a pasture away from town, because the owner was not there to prevent the dumping?

In addition, environmental services are usually collectively consumed or used. It is hard to single out and determine the value of the air that one person—or his automobile—uses. Similarly, it is often difficult to attach a value to the water deterioration caused by one industrial plant among thousands that dump their wastes into a river. Would any one person be willing to pay someone *not* to take some action that would destroy a beautiful view across the countryside? When values cannot be placed on the amounts of environmental services used by any one person, it is difficult to induce people not to pollute by charging them for the right to do so.

Pollution and Resource Use

In the process of using environmental services, a polluter may be induced to overuse environmental services at the expense of other users; pollution frequently involves inefficient use or misallocation of environmental services among those who use them. Suppose, for example, that two business firms are located along a riverbank. The upstream firm produces paper, using the river as a place to discharge its wastes. Just downstream is a power plant that requires large amounts of clean water for cooling purposes. If the paper mill were not there, the water from the river would be clean enough for the power plant to use. But since it is there—just upstream—the power plant must clean the water before using it.

Since the use of the river by one party as a dumping place for wastes may reduce the value of the river's services to some other party, economic costs may be incurred by the dumping. According to the alternative-cost principle, the economic cost of the dumping is equal to the reduction in the value of the river's services to others. If recycling of the dumped wastes occurs fast enough, or if the environment is large enough relative to the wastes dumped into it so that no one is injured by the dumping, no economic costs or pollution problems occur.

The use of the river for waste disposal by the paper mill decreases the value of the river's services for power production in the example, so economic costs are involved in that dumping. In effect, the paper mill shifts some of its costs of production to the power plant. It is the power plant that must pay for cleaning the water, but it is the paper mill that makes it dirty.

The pollution problem affects the supply curves of the power plant. Suppose in Figure 5–1 that the power plant's supply curve of electricity would be S_eS_e if the river *were not polluted* by the paper mill. The curve shows the alternative prices per kilowatt hour necessary to induce the power plant to produce the various quantities of electricity indicated on the horizontal axis. Ignore the D_eD_e line for the present, and consider the effects of pollution by the paper mill. Suppose that the power plant must clean the water before using it. Since the power plant must cover its costs, the price that it must receive in order to induce it to produce any specific quantity of electricity will be higher by an amount equal to the costs per kilowatt hour of cleaning the water. The supply curve is thus shifted upward to some position such as $S_{e_1}S_{e_1}$. If the output of the power plant were e_1 kilowatt hours, the price necessary to bring forth that output in the absence of pollution is e_1c_1. With pollution occurring, the necessary price is e_1f_1, with c_1f_1 being the cost per kilowatt hour of cleaning the water. Similarly, for an output level of e, the required price in the absence of pollution is ec, with pollution it is ef, and the cost per kilowatt hour of cleaning is cf. So the supply of

FIGURE 5–1
Effects of Water Pollution on a Water User

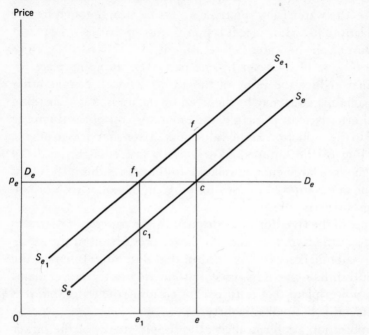

Kilowatt Hours per Day

The demand curve for the output of a power plant is D_eD_e. Its supply curve, when it can obtain clean water for its use, is S_eS_e. Consequently, it will produce and sell e kilowatt hours per day. However, if a paper mill located upstream pollutes the water, costs of cleaning the water before using it move the supply curve upward (or to the left). The power plant accordingly reduces its output to e_1. The power plant—or its customers—thus pays the costs of cleaning the paper mill's wastes from the water.

electricity is decreased by the pollution of the paper mill from what it would be in the absence of pollution.

The supply curve of the paper mill is increased by its access to the river for waste disposal. In Figure 5–2 let S_rS_r be the paper mill's supply curve, assuming that the river is not available as a "free" dumping space. The supply curve shows the alternative prices that must be received by the paper mill to induce it to produce and sell various quantities of paper. To induce the mill to produce and sell r reams, the price per ream must be rg. To induce it to place r_1 reams on the market, the price must be r_1g_1. Suppose now that the river

FIGURE 5–2
Effects of Water Pollution on the Polluter

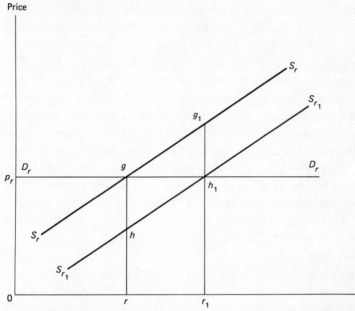

The demand curve for the output of a paper mill is D_rD_r. When it must clean its own wastes, its supply curve is S_rS_r, and its output level will be r reams of paper per day. If it can dump its wastes into the river, cleaning costs are saved, and its supply curve shifts downward (to the right). Its output will increase to r_1. It is able to shift a part of its costs to downstream users of the water, such as a power plant.

is made available to the paper mill as a "free" dumping ground for wastes. The costs of producing a ream of paper are now reduced, and for an output level of r reams per day the price need not be higher than rh—if the cost saving per ream is hg. Similarly, for r_1 reams and a cost saving of h_1g_1, the necessary price is r_1h_1. The supply of paper is thus increased by the accessibility of the river as a "free" place to dispose of its wastes.

The shifting of a part of the paper mill's production costs to the power plant induces the power plant to underproduce. Suppose in Figure 5–1 that the price of electricity is p_e per kilowatt hour and that the power plant can sell as much or as little as it desires to sell at that price. The horizontal line D_eD_e is the demand curve facing the firm for its power output.[2] If it were not necessary for the power plant to clean the water, its supply curve would be $S_e S_e$ and its output would be e kilowatt hours per day. However, since the operation of the paper mill makes it necessary to clean the water before using it, the supply curve becomes $S_{e_1} S_{e_1}$. These higher levels of costs induce the firm to cut back its production when the price is p_e to e_1 kilowatt hours per day. The evidence of underproduction is that at this level of production, electricity is worth more per kilowatt hour to consumers than the economic cost of producing it. The *economic costs* per kilowatt hour at this output level are $e_1 c_1$. This is what the resources used in producing a kilowatt hour are worth in alternative uses—what the power plant must pay for them to retain them. The rest of the cost— $c_1 f_1$—is the cost per kilowatt hour of cleaning the water or of undoing what the paper mill has done.

Similar reasoning leads to the conclusions that the paper mill overproduces. In Figure 5–2 if the price per ream of paper is p_r and the paper mill can sell as much or as little as it desires at that price, $D_r D_r$ is the demand curve facing the firm. If the paper mill were to bear the costs of its dumping of wastes by leaving clean water for the power plant, its supply curve would be $S_r S_r$, and its equilibrium output level would be r. However, since it is able to use the river for waste disposal, its supply curve is $S_{r_1} S_{r_1}$, and it produces r_1 reams of paper per day. The evidence of overproduction is that *economic costs* per ream of paper exceed what consumers pay to get it. The economic costs per ream are $r_1 g_1$. Of this amount, $r_1 h_1$ is the cost to the paper mill of resources used in the production of a ream of paper at output level r_1, and $h_1 g_1$ is the cost imposed on the power plant per ream of paper produced. This latter amount is not taken into account by either the paper mill or its customers, so the economic or true cost of a ream of paper exceeds what it is worth to consumers.

The Costs of Controlling Pollution

Our reactions to pollution often take the form of, "Let's make it illegal." We maintain that we are entitled to clean air, clean water, and clean land. But how clean is clean? Cleanliness, like goodness,

---

[2] Actually, since the power plant is likely to have some degree of monopoly in the sale of electricity, the demand curve facing it may not be horizontal. Assuming that it is horizontal makes no essential difference in the sense of the analysis, and it does make the analysis simpler.

is a relative rather than an absolute quality. To determine the amount of pollution, if any, that should be allowed, the costs of keeping the environment clean must first be considered.

Pollution control is not costless. An industrial plant that scrubs or cleans its combustion gases before discharging them into the air must use resources in the process. Labor and capital go into the making and operation of antipollution devices, and resources so used are not available to produce other goods and services. The value of the goods and services that must be given up is the cost of the plant's pollution control activities. The cost of pollution control is a straightforward application of the alternative-cost principle.

The costs of pollution control to society are illustrated graphically

FIGURE 5–3
The Costs of Pollution Control

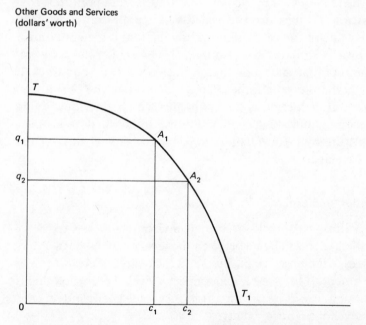

The combinations of other goods and services and pollution control that the resources of the economy can support are shown by the production possibilities curve TT_1. By giving up q_1T of other goods and services, the economy can have c_1 units of pollution control, as shown at point A_1. If c_1c_2 more units of pollution control are to be obtained, the cost will be q_2q_1 additional units of other goods and services.

by the production possibilities curve of Figure 5–3. Dollars' worth of all goods and services other than pollution control are measured on the vertical axis, and dollars' worth of pollution control are measured on the horizontal axis. At point A_1 the labor and capital of the economy are producing q_1 dollars' worth of goods and services and c_1 dollars' worth of antipollution activities. If still more pollution control—a cleaner environment—is desired, some value of goods and services must be sacrificed. By giving up $q_2 q_1$ dollars' worth of goods and services, pollution control can be increased by $c_1 c_2$ dollars' worth. Thus, $q_2 q_1$ dollars' worth of goods and services is the economic cost of an additional $c_1 c_2$ dollars' worth of control or of a cleaner environment.

The Benefits of Controlling Pollution

The benefits of pollution control consist of the increase in well-being of the members of the society that results from pollution control activities. To measure the benefits of a pollution control activity, the value of the increase in well-being that it generates must be determined. Suppose, for example, that smog permeates a particular metropolitan area but that pollution control activities can reduce or perhaps even eliminate it. To determine the benefits of, say, a 50 percent reduction in smog, we can ask each individual living in the area how much such a reduction would be worth to him. By totaling all the replies we would arrive at the dollar value of the expected benefits.

The Appropriate Level of Pollution Control

Since pollution control—a cleaner environment—has costs, society must make some choice between the level of goods and services its resources will be used to produce and the degree of cleanliness of its environment. If the society experiences a level of pollution that is distasteful to it, it will be willing to sacrifice some goods and services for some level of pollution control.

The appropriate level of pollution control is determined by weighing the benefits of control against the costs. If the benefits of additional control—what cleaner air is worth to the citizens of the society—exceed the costs of the additional control, then pollution control should be increased. However, if the benefits of additional control are less than what it costs in terms of sacrificed goods and services, the additional control is unwarranted.

As an illustration, consider a community of 10,000 persons pervaded by a nauseating stench from an incinerator used to dispose of the community's garbage. Suppose that the odor can be completely eliminated by an expenditure of $100,000 per year for an alternate method of garbage disposal (carrying it away and burying it in a landfill outside the town) and that it can be partially controlled by using various combinations of burning and burying.

Suppose that the costs of different levels of partial control are those of columns 1, 2, and 3 of Table 5–1. By spending $10,000 on carrying and burying, the community can eliminate 10 percent of the stench; each additional $10,000 expenditure eliminates another 10 percent of the original total stench, until with a $100,000 expenditure the pollution is entirely eliminated.

Column 3 of Table 5–1 lists the *marginal costs* of pollution control. The concept is essentially the same as the marginal costs of crime prevention—it shows the change in total costs per unit change in the amount of pollution control. Since each increment in pollution control (an increment is defined as 10 percent of the control needed to eliminate the odor) adds $10,000 to the total cost of pollution control, the marginal cost of pollution control at each control level is $10,000.

The benefits of pollution control to the community are shown in columns 4, 5, and 6. Before any control is undertaken, each person in the community is asked what a 10 percent reduction in the stench is worth to him. Suppose each person indicates that he would be willing to pay $10 for it. We conclude that $100,000 measures the total benefits yielded by the first 10 percent reduction. Since the benefits exceed the costs by $90,000, the first 10 percent reduction is clearly warranted.

The question now arises as to whether a second 10 percent reduction in the stench is worthwhile. Since the pollution is not as intense as it was with no control, a second 10 percent reduction is of less value than was the first one. Suppose each person values the move from 10 percent control to 20 percent control at $8, so that the community valuation of the extra control—or the marginal benefits of it—is $80,000. Since the marginal costs of the additional

TABLE 5-1
Annual Costs and Benefits of Pollution Control

(1) Pollution Control or Eliminated Stench	(2) Total Cost of Control	(3) Marginal Cost of Control	(4) Per Person Marginal Benefits of Control	(5) Community Marginal Benefits of Control	(6) Total Benefits of Control	(7) Net Benefits of Control
1st 10%	$ 10,000	$10,000	$10 ea.	$100,000	$100,000	$ 90,000
2nd 10%	20,000	10,000	8 ea.	80,000	180,000	160,000
3rd 10%	30,000	10,000	6 ea.	60,000	240,000	210,000
4th 10%	40,000	10,000	4 ea.	40,000	280,000	240,000
5th 10%	50,000	10,000	2 ea.	20,000	300,000	250,000
6th 10%	60,000	10,000	1.60 ea.	16,000	316,000	256,000
7th 10%	70,000	10,000	1.20 ea.	12,000	328,000	258,000
8th 10%	80,000	10,000	.80 ea.	8,000	336,000	256,000
9th 10%	90,000	10,000	.40 ea.	4,000	340,000	250,000
10th 10%	100,000	10,000	.10 ea.	1,000	341,000	241,000

control are only $10,000, putting it into effect adds $70,000 to the total net benefits of control and is, therefore, a good investment for the community.

Column 5 shows the community's *marginal benefit* at different levels of control. Marginal benefits of pollution control, like the marginal benefits of crime prevention, are defined as the *change* in total benefits per unit *change* in whatever it is that yields the benefits. Note that the *total benefits* at any given level of control are obtained by adding up the marginal benefits as the level of control is increased unit by unit up to that level.

Marginal benefits, as shown in Table 5–1, decline as the level of pollution control is increased (the level of the stench is decreased). This is what we would expect to happen in the case at hand. The greater the amount of control, or the lower the level of the stench, the less urgent additional control becomes. This will be the usual situation in controlling pollution.

The level of pollution control yielding the maximum net benefits to the people of the community is that at which the marginal benefits just cease to exceed the marginal costs. The marginal benefits of the first two 10 percent increments in the total amount of control needed to eliminate the stench exceed the marginal costs of making them. Thus, net benefits are increased by increasing control at least to the 20 percent level. The third, fourth, fifth, sixth, and seventh 10 percent increments also yield marginal benefits exceeding their marginal costs, and they increase the net benefits of control to the community. Now consider the eighth 10 percent increment. Marginal benefits are $8,000, and marginal costs are $10,000. Extending pollution control from the 70 percent level to the 80 percent level *reduces* the net benefits by $2,000. The eighth 10 percent increment is not worth to the community what it costs.

The principle is perfectly general. Net benefits will always be increased by increasing control if the marginal benefits of the increase are greater than the marginal costs of making it. Net benefits will decrease from an increase in the control level if the marginal benefits of that increase are less than its marginal costs. The appropriate level of control is the one that approaches as closely as possible the one at which the marginal benefits equal the marginal costs but does not go far enough for marginal costs to exceed marginal benefits.

WHAT CAN BE DONE ABOUT POLLUTION?

Human beings often react to problems with their emotions rather than with the capacity for logic with which they are endowed. Policies recommended to control pollution reflect this human characteristic. Typical recommendations call for direct control of pollution by the state. But this is only one of the possible avenues of reducing pollution problems. Others include indirect control by the state through a system of incentives encouraging potential polluters not to pollute or to limit their pollution, and an examination of the institutions of private property rights and markets to see if they can be modified to provide the desired limitations on polluting activities.

Direct Controls

An appealingly simple way to control pollution is to have the government ban polluting activities or agents. If phosphates contaminate water, then ban the use of phosphates in detergents. If DDT pollutes water and land, ban the use of DDT. If the burning of fuel oil and coal increases the sulphur oxide content of the atmosphere, prohibit their use. Require industrial plants to clean the pollutants from whatever it is they discharge into the atmosphere or water. The method is straightforward and, on the face of it, seems eminently fair.

The case of the city with the terrible stench shows that complete prohibition of pollutants is not likely to be worth its costs. Pollution control uses resources that could have produced goods and services, and the value of the goods and services foregone is the cost to society of controlling the pollution. If the damage done by an additional unit of pollution is less than the costs of preventing it from occurring, community welfare is greater if it is allowed to occur. Consequently, direct controls usually should aim at a less idealistic goal than a pollution-free environment. They may take the form of controlling the level of pollution by such devices as setting emissions standards or limits for industrial plants, automobiles, and the like.

One problem raised by the use of direct controls to limit the amount of pollution is that it presupposes the regulatory body can determine what the economically desirable levels of pollution are. This is not an insurmountable problem. Tolerance limits on the amount of pollution to be allowed can be reasonably well established. Within those limits, overall costs can be weighed continually against benefits to establish an approximation of the desirable levels of pollution.

A second problem is the difficulty facing a regulatory body in achieving an efficient allocation of the permissible pollution among different polluters. For example, it may be more costly for a steel mill to eliminate a unit of sulphur oxide from its emissions than it is for a power plant. In the interests of economic efficiency, it is best to eliminate pollution where it is least costly to do so. Thus the power plant should be required to reduce its sulphur oxide emission before the steel mill is required to do so. This is a difficult kind of decision for a regulatory body to make, since it is responsible to a political body for which economic efficiency is not a primary goal. In addition, it is unrealistic to suppose that the regulatory body has a working knowledge of the nature of costs for every polluter.

A third problem is that of enforcing the standards of emissions once it has been determined what those standards should be. Direct controls do not give polluters an economic incentive not to pollute. In fact, it will pay them to seek ways and means to evade the pollution standards set for them. But we should not overstate the enforcement problem. Almost any prohibition of activities that individuals and business firms want to engage in creates enforcement problems.

Indirect Controls

The state may control many types of pollution by placing taxes on polluting activity. Where the amounts of polluting discharges can be measured for individual polluters, a tax can be placed directly on each unit of discharge. This will induce the polluter to reduce the amount of pollution that is discharged. In some cases where such measurement is not possible, polluters may be taxed indirectly —automobiles not equipped with pollution control devices can be subjected to a tax on a mileage basis. This will induce their owners either to install pollution control devices or to drive less.

Figure 5–4 illustrates the use of a tax to control the amounts of pollutants discharged into the environment. Consider an industrial

FIGURE 5–4
Control of Pollution by Means of a Tax on Polluted Discharges

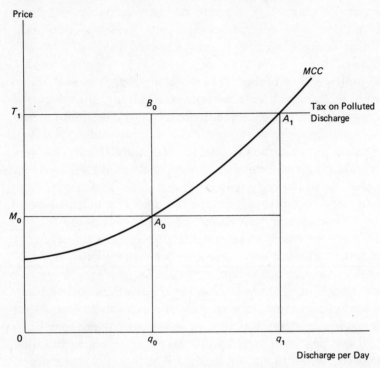

If the level of a tax on polluted discharges exceeds the marginal costs of cleaning the discharge, a firm will elect to clean the discharge. This will be the case for all discharge levels up to q_1. If the level of the tax is less than the marginal cleaning costs, the firm will elect to pay the tax rather than clean the discharge. This will occur for all of the discharge in excess of q_1.

concern that discharges its polluting wastes into a river. Processes for cleaning the wastes so that the pollution they cause is eliminated or diminished are available. *Marginal cleaning costs,* defined as the change in total cleaning costs per one unit change in the firm's discharge of wastes, are shown by MCC. For example, if the level of discharge is q_0, then q_0A_0 is the addition to the firm's total cost of cleaning brought about when the amount of discharge is increased from one unit less than q_0 to the q_0 level. Similarly, the addition to total cleaning costs when the firm moves from one unit of less than q_0 units per day, it pays the firm not to pollute. It is less costly to upward to the right, indicating that the larger the firm's rate of waste discharge the greater is the cost to it of cleaning an additional unit. This may or may not be the case—we assume here for illustrative purposes that it is. The level of the tax on polluted discharge is T_1 per unit, regardless of the level of the discharge.

A tax per unit of polluted discharge will induce the firm to reduce its polluting activity if the amount of the tax exceeds the marginal costs of cleaning the discharge. If the discharge is less than q_1, say q_0 units per day, it pays the firm not to pollute. It is less costly to clean the discharge than it is to pay the tax. For the q_0 unit of discharge, $q_0 B_0$ would be added to the firm's total costs if it elects to pay the tax and not to clean up the discharge. Only $q_0 A_0$ would be added to its total costs if it elects to clean the discharge and pay no tax. This will be the case for any discharge level up to q_1 units per day. On the other hand, for a discharge level exceeding q_1 per day, the firm will clean q_1 units and pay the tax on the remainder of the discharge. It is cheaper to clean than to pay the tax on each unit up to that level. For units of discharge exceeding q_1, it is cheaper to pay the tax than to clean them.

The tax can be set at any desired level, depending upon the amount of pollution the government decides to allow. Raising the tax will decrease the amount of pollution, and lowering the tax will increase it. Ideally, the tax should be set at a level at which the marginal benefits to society of cleaning a unit of discharge equal the marginal cleaning costs. If the level of polluted discharge permitted is such that the marginal benefits of cleaning the discharge exceed the marginal costs of cleaning it, the tax is too low and should be increased. If the level of polluted discharge permitted is such that marginal benefits of cleaning are less than the marginal costs of cleaning, the tax is too high and should be decreased.

The use of taxes to control pollution has its advantages. A major one is that it provides an incentive to the polluter to seek improved ways and means of cleaning up his discharge. Another advantage is that it prevents the polluter from shifting some of his production costs (pollution costs) to others; it reduces his incentives to overproduce.

There are also disadvantages. First, it would be difficult to determine the benefits—total and marginal—to society of cleaning the discharge. Second, enforcement of the tax will not be easy. Policing will be necessary to determine that the discharge is indeed properly cleaned. Third, taxes are levied by political rather than economic bodies, and politics may well get in the way of the enactment of appropriate tax levels.

Private Property Rights

Since the absence of well-defined property rights provides a primary incentive to polluters to dump their wastes in certain segments of the environment, the assignment of property rights either to firms that pollute or to those that benefit from a clean environment may provide a means of control in some cases. Consider, for example, the upstream paper mill–downstream power plant case described above. Since neither firm owns the river, the paper mill is able to use it for waste disposal, and the costs of the waste disposal fall on the power plant.

Suppose that rights to the river are sold at auction by the government. These rights will be purchased by the firm to which they are most valuable. If the annual value to the paper mill of using the river for waste discharges (i.e., the costs of alternative means of disposing of the wastes) exceed the annual cost to the power plant of cleaning the water, the paper mill will buy the rights. The river will be put to its most valuable use—that of being a sink for waste disposal. However, if the value of clean water to the power plant (the costs of cleaning it for power plant use) exceeds the value to the paper mill of using the river to discharge wastes, the power plant will purchase the rights and the river will be put to its most productive (valuable) use—that of furnishing clean cooling water for the generation of electricity.

Regardless of which firm buys the rights, changes in the relative values of the two uses will provide incentives for the river to be put to the use in which it is most valuable. If the paper mill holds the rights to the river but the annual value of clean water to the power plant exceeds the annual value of the river as a waste disposal, the power plant will be willing to pay the paper mill enough to induce it not to pollute—to use alternative means of disposing of its wastes. On the other hand, if the power plant owns the rights and the annual value of the river to the paper mill as a waste disposal exceeds the annual cost to the power plant of cleaning the water, the power plant will sell the paper mill pollution privileges.

SUMMARY

The environment provides environmental services that are used by both household units and producing units of the economy. In the processes of consumption and production wastes are generated. If the ecological system cannot recycle these wastes as fast as they are generated, wastes accumulate. This constitutes pollution.

Economic analysis of pollution provides a perspective on its causes and its effects, along with the costs and benefits of controlling it. Incentives to pollute stem from (1) an absence of property rights in the environment and (2) the collectively consumed nature of whatever is being polluted. Polluters, by polluting, transfer a part of their costs to others. Cost-benefit analysis is useful in determining how much pollution should be allowed. It indicates that it is seldom in the common interest to forbid pollution altogether.

There are three main avenues that governmental pollution control policies can take. First, certain polluting activities may be controlled directly through prohibitions or limitations on polluting activities. Second, they may be controlled indirectly by providing polluters with incentives not to pollute—say through taxation of polluting activities. Third, much pollution can be controlled by selling or assigning individuals property rights to whatever is being polluted, then allowing them to sell pollution rights to would-be polluters.

SUPPLEMENTARY READING

Crocker, Thomas D., and Rogers, A. J., III. *Environmental Economics.* Hinsdale, Ill.: Dryden Press, 1971.

Provides a good elementary treatise of the nature of pollution, the economics of pollution, and alternatives available for controlling it. Writing style holds the reader's interest.

Dolan Edwin G. *Tanstaafl,* chaps. 1, 3, 4, and 6. New York: Holt, Rinehart & Winston, 1971.

A short, interesting book on the broad range of ecological problems —pollution, population, and depletion of natural resources. Elementary economics is used to evaluate the problems and suggest policy alternatives.

Freeman, A. Myrick, III. *The Economics of Pollution Control and Environmental Quality.* New York: General Learning Press, 1971.

This monograph is intended to show how economic analysis can contribute to an understanding of pollution and its control. It is compact and thorough. Although some of the analysis may be beyond the grasp of elementary students, most of it will be readily understandable.

North, Douglas C., and Miller, Roger Leroy. *The Economics of Public Issues,* chaps. 13, 14, 19, 20, and 28. New York: Harper & Row, 1972.

Short chapters on several different pollution problems—air pollution, oil spills, hydroelectric projects, and the like. Cost-benefit analysis is introduced, and considerable use is made of the concept of spillovers and the alternative-cost principle.

Ruff, Larry E. "The Economic Common Sense of Pollution." *The Public Interest,* (Spring, 1970), pp. 69–85.

Provides an elementary economic analysis of pollution. The marginal concept is introduced, along with concepts of social costs, resource allocation, and economic efficiency. The author builds his economic analysis around the problems that must be met and solved by a pollution control board.

Chapter 6

HEALTH ISSUES

CHECKLIST OF ECONOMIC CONCEPTS

Elasticity of Demand
Changes in Demand
Per Capita Income
Tastes and Preferences
Relative Prices
Substitution Effects
Less than Full-Cost Pricing
Elasticity of Supply
Changes in Supply
Principle of Diminishing Returns
Investment
Technological Advancements

6

HEALTH ISSUES
Is It Worth What It Costs?

Even though we are a nation that places a high value on health, we have done very little to insure that quality health care is available to all of us at a price we can afford. We have allowed rural and inner-city areas to be slowly abandoned by doctors. We have allowed hundreds of insurance companies to create thousands of complicated policies that trap Americans in gaps, limitations, and exclusions in coverage, and that offer disastrously low benefits which spell financial disaster for a family when serious illness or injury strikes. We have allowed doctor and hospital charges to skyrocket out of control through wasteful and inefficient practices to the point where more and more Americans are finding it difficult to pay for health care and health insurance. We have also allowed physicians and hospitals to practice with little or no review of the quality of their work, and with few requirements to keep their knowledge up to date or to limit themselves to the areas where they are qualified. In our concern not to infringe on doctors' and hospitals' rights as entrepreneurs, we have allowed them to offer care in ways, at times, in places, and at prices designed more for their convenience and profit than for the good of the American people.

When I say "we have allowed," I mean that the American people have not done anything about it through their government, that the medical societies and hospital associations have done far too little about it, and that the insurance companies have done little or nothing about it.

I believe the time has come in our nation for the people to take action to solve these problems.[1]

GROWTH AND NATURE OF HEALTH SERVICES

National health expenditures in the United States grew spectacularly in the 1940s, 1950s, and 1960s, at least doubling every decade. The same upward trend looks likely for the 1970s. These expenditures include such health services and supplies as hospital services, physicians' and dentists' services, and drugs and drug supplies, as well as expenditures on research and on construction of medical facilities. In the 32-year span from 1940 to 1972, health expenditures rose from $3.9 billion to $83.4 billion, from $29 per capita to $394 per capita, and from 4.1 percent of the nation's income to 7.6 percent. Figure 6–1 shows these trends and a projection to 1980 which indicates that per capita health expenditures may reach $814 by the beginning of that decade.

Factors Explaining the Rise in Personal Health Costs

A number of factors can explain the rise in personal health costs, that is, money spent for health services for the direct benefit of the individual.[2] These factors are the rise in prices for medical services, population growth, and increases in the use and quality of medical services. Figure 6–2 shows the relative importance of these factors in the rising costs of physicians' services and hospital care between 1966 and 1971.

Price Increases. Between 1966 and 1971, price increases accounted for 91 percent of the increase in the costs of hospital care and 71.1 percent of the increase in the costs of physicians' services. Thus most of the increase in the total costs for hospital and physicians' services is not attributable to a larger quantity or better quality but to higher prices for given quantities and qualities of health services.

---

1 Edward M. Kennedy, *In Critical Condition: The Crisis in America's Health Care* (New York: Simon & Schuster, 1972), pp. 16–17.

2 Personal health expenditures do not include outlays which are spent for the community, such as in construction, research, or disease control.

FIGURE 6–1

National Health Expenditures in Selected Years, 1940 to 1972, and Projected in 1975 and 1980

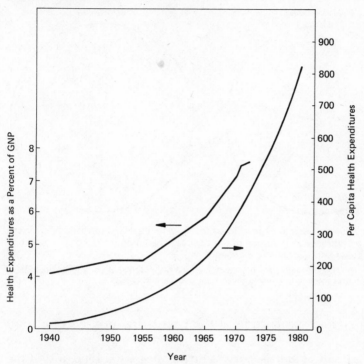

Health expenditures, whether measured as a percent of GNP or per capita, are increasing rapidly.

Source: U.S. Department of Health, Education, and Welfare, Social Security Administration, Office of Research and Statistics, *Medical Care Costs and Prices: Background Book* (January 1972), pp. 79, 90; Barbara S. Cooper and Nancy L. Worthington, "National Health Expenditures, 1929–1972," *Social Security Bulletin*, January 1973, p. 5.

Population Growth. Population growth accounted for 6.4 percent and 10.3 percent of the rise in the cost of hospital care and physicians' services, respectively, between 1966 and 1971. In general, the larger the number of people, the more health care is needed and the more resources are channelled into health care. The current slowdown in population growth can be expected to reduce the growth in the costs of medical care. However, the average age of population will increase with a slower growth rate; as a conse-

158   Economics of Social Issues

FIGURE 6–2
Factors Explaining the Increase in the Costs of Physicians' Services and Hospital Care between Fiscal Years 1966 and 1971

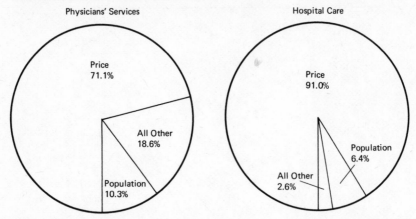

Most of the increase in expenditures for hospital care and physicians' services is due to an increase in the price of the service. The category "all other" refers to per capita rise and quality improvements.

Source: U.S. Department of Health, Education, and Welfare, Social Security Administration, *Medical Care Costs and Prices: Background Book*, (January 1972), p. 81.

quence, a larger proportion of the population may need medical care.

Per Capita Use and Quality. During the period 1966 to 1971 the remaining part of the increase in the costs of hospital care and physicians' services, 2.6 percent and 18.6 percent respectively, was due to the increase in per capita use of these services and quality improvements. Hospital use may be measured by the number of hospital admissions, hospital patient-days, average length of hospital stays, and hospital occupancy rates. Over the years, these measures indicate greater use of hospital services. However, between 1971 and 1972 hospital patient-days, average length of hospital stay, and occupancy rates decreased, indicating a slowdown in hospital use and better hospital services.[3] Hospital costs per patient-day continued the upward trend in 1972 because hospital fixed costs were spread over fewer days of care, and because hospitals were providing better care.

---

[3] Barbara S. Cooper and Nancy L. Worthington, "National Health Expenditures, 1929–1972," *Social Security Bulletin,* January 1973, p. 5.

Is There Anything Special about the Rising Costs of Medical Services? There is nothing special or unusual about the rising cost of medical services. Price increases, population growth, and a greater quantity and better quality of services will explain the rise in costs of most, if not all, goods and services. The reason people are so uptight about the rising costs of medical services lies, in part, in the special characteristics of health services.

Special Characteristics of Health Services

The Role of the Physician. A special characteristic of health services involves the role of the physician, who operates on both sides of the market. He is both a supplier and a demander of health services. It is the physician who provides the consumer directly with services and determines the services he needs from other suppliers —hospitals and suppliers of drugs and medicines. Decisions about medications, getting well at home or in the hospital, number of days spent in the hospital, and special medical services required are all made by the physician. Consumers usually do not even determine where they will receive hospital care. The selection of a hospital depends largely on where the physician happens to hold staff positions and which hospital the physician prefers.

Consumer Ignorance. Consumers are probably less informed about medical services than about anything else they buy. They usually can shop around, look, try, and compare goods and services they wish to buy. *Consumer Reports* publishes the results of testing certain products and provides valuable information that can serve as a guide to rational decision making by the customer. Almost no objective information is available concerning the quality of health services, however. Physicians are reluctant to give evaluations of the work of other physicians. Hospital and physicians' services generally are not subject to quality controls. Human errors, mistakes, and incompetencies in the supply of medical services may go undetected until it is too late for the individual buyer.

It is not a usual practice in the health field to disclose a list of prices for units of services. In many instances, consumers do not inquire about and do not know the prices of medical services until they receive their bills—at which time their choices are narrowed down to paying the bills or going to jail. The prices, quantities, and qualities of medical services are well-kept secrets to most consumers. The suppliers of health services have done little to change this situation.

Spillover Benefits. In Chapter 3, on education, it was noted that benefits which flow to the specific users of goods and services are called direct benefits. As they use the goods and services, there may be indirect or social *spillover benefits* to other individuals.

The best illustration of social spillover benefits in health services involves communicable diseases. The use of medical services to get well from a disease that may spread to others directly benefits the user of the service and indirectly benefits others. Immunization shots benefit not only the person receiving the immunity from a disease, but the benefit extends beyond the individual user to others in society.

However, benefits from many medical services flow only to the individual users of these services. A heart or kidney transplant benefits primarily the individual receiving the transplant. The increased quantity and quality of medical services from the use of new equipment and intensive-care hospital rooms increases the chances of survival to the individual buyers of these services.

A "Right" to Good Health. Most people regard good health as a "right." They believe that a sick person should have access to medical services regardless of his income. This is why people are appalled when they hear on the radio, see on TV, or read in the newspaper that a person in a serious accident or with a serious illness was refused admittance to a hospital because he did not have either money or health insurance to pay for the services needed. The basic idea that health services are essential needs and people have a right to receive them runs consistently through American thought.[4]

Unpredictability of Illness. Individuals and families, through budgeting, may carefully plan what goods and services they will buy, the quantities of each, and how much they will save. Some medical and health services can be planned for in this way, and others cannot be. A family may plan to fulfill medical and health needs that are predictable, such as physical examinations or immunization shots, but it is difficult to plan for illnesses or accidents. For one

---

[4] Herbert E. Klarman, "Requirements for Physicians," *American Economic Review,* May 1951, p. 633.

thing, people do not usually like to consider the prospects of illness. Second, and more critical from the viewpoint of family planning, the incidence of illness is uneven and unpredictable for a family.

Voluntary health insurance provides a way for individuals and families with the desire and ability to pay for it to plan for and cover the major risks of illness or injury. The incidence of illness is predictable, and therefore insurable, for the population or large numbers of people. Private health insurance companies cannot provide full protection against the exceptional or extremely high-cost illness, however. The consumer remains in general unprotected against prolonged and catastrophic illnesses or injuries.

HEALTH-CARE PROBLEMS

The special characteristics of health services provide a good background for an understanding of the nature of health services. They do not, however, give rise to a unique set of problems. The major economic problems in the health-care industry are those of efficiency in the supply of health services and equity in their distribution.

The Public View

The view of the public concerning the problem in health care is reflected in the following quote:

A decade ago, one medical group in Manhattan charged $35 for a basic physical checkup; today it charges $65. In those same years the going rate for an appendectomy in New York rose from $485 to $1,175 and the cost of an average hospital stay, for the nation as a whole, rose from $265 to $785.[5]

Most people view the rising costs of health care as the problem. Are they in fact the problem, or, perhaps, the symptom?

The Economist's View

Economists in general do not look upon the rising costs of any good or service as necessarily a problem. Changes in prices and

---

[5] Richard A. Lyons, "Dilemma In Health Care: Rising Cost and Demand," *New York Times*, September 13, 1971, p. 1.

quantities of individual goods and services bought and sold may reflect changes in demand and supply in the market. The total amount of money spent for individual goods and services increases when demand and supply for these goods or services rise. There is no problem here. This is what is expected in a market economy.

However, the rising costs of health care may indicate or be a symptom of factors economists are concerned about, such as the restrictions on entry into the health-care industry, the response of supply to demand changes, and the impact of government subsidies on the demand for health services. A central economic problem as seen by economists involves the efficient use of scarce resources in the health-care industry. The analysis of demand for and supply of health services that follows provides a framework for an evaluation of the health-care industry in terms of economic efficiency.

ANALYSIS OF DEMAND FOR HEALTH SERVICES

Elasticity of Demand

Consumers of certain health services, such as hospital and physicians' services, are not very responsive to price changes. An increase in price will not reduce the quantity demanded very much, and a decrease in price will not increase it much. In other words, the elasticity of demand for health-care services is low, or inelastic.[6]

This situation is illustrated in Figure 6–3. An increase in price from p_1 to p_2 decreases quantity demanded from q_1 to q_2. When demand is inelastic, the percentage decrease in quantity demanded is less than the percentage increase in price. Suppose p_1 and p_2 are $4 and $5, respectively, for a visit to a doctor's office and that q_1 and q_2 are 10 visits and 9 visits, respectively, per month. An increase in price of 25 percent $(5 - 4/4)$ causes the number of visits to the doctor's office to be reduced from ten visits to nine visits per month—a percentage decrease in quantity demanded of approximately 11 percent $(10 - 9/9)$.[7] The elasticity coefficient is $11/25$,

---

6 Herbert E. Klarman, *The Economics of Health* (New York: Columbia University Press, 1965), pp. 24–25.

7 In calculating the percent change in price and percent change in quantity demanded, the lower of the two prices and the lower of the two quantities should be used. Also, it should be noted that elasticity more precisely refers to the response of quantity demanded to a small change in price and that the slope of a demand curve is not a reliable indicator of the degree of responsiveness of quantity demanded to price changes.

FIGURE 6–3
An Inelastic Portion of Demand

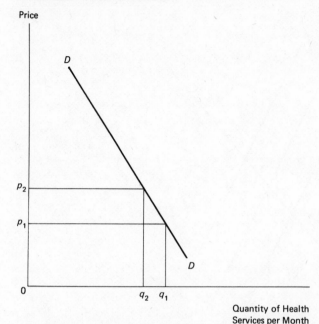

The inelastic portion of a demand curve is that over which a given percentage change in price results in a smaller percentage change in quantity demanded. For demand to be inelastic between prices p_2 and p_1, the percentage change from q_2 to q_1 must be smaller than the percentage change from p_2 to p_1.

or .44, in this illustration. The price elasticity of demand is said to be inelastic when the elasticity coefficient is less than 1.

Factors Changing the Demand for Health Services

Changes in Per Capita Income. Rising per capita incomes in the United States have caused the demand curve for health services to shift to the right. This is illustrated in Figure 6–4. Increases in income cause the increases in demand from D to D_1 to D_2. The increases in price from p to p_1 to p_2 and the increases in quantity demanded from q to q_1 to q_2 are due to the rise in demand for health services.

FIGURE 6–4
An Increase in Demand Due to Income Growth

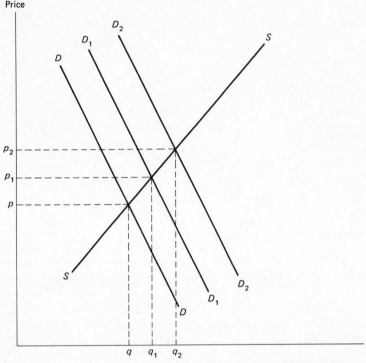

Quantity of Health
Services per Month

The demand curve is shifting outward because of increasing income and changing tastes and preferences. As a result, both the price and quantity demanded of health services are increasing.

Changes in Tastes and Preferences. Changes in consumer tastes and preferences also change demand. An increase in tastes and preferences for medical services increases demand for these services. This means that consumers are willing to buy larger quantities of medical services at every possible price. It cannot be said for certain, but an increase in tastes and preferences for medical care appears to have played at least a small part in stimulating the demand for health services.

Changes in Relative Price. Changes in prices of goods and services which may be substituted for medical services change the demand for medical services. For example, suppose the price of recreational services declines relative to the price of medical physical examinations. The effect of this will be to encourage consumers to substitute the less costly service for medical services, if this is feasible. The result is a decline in the demand for medical services. Since there are a limited number of substitutes for medical services, however, the demand for medical services is probably not appreciably affected by changes in relative prices.

Less than Full-Cost Pricing. Consumers do not directly pay the full costs of health services. Direct consumer payments represent about 37 cents out of each dollar spent for personal health; the remaining part of each dollar is paid by third parties—health insurance, private gifts, and government. The rise in the relative importance of third-party payments is shown in Figure 6–5. The

FIGURE 6–5
Percent Distributions of Personal Health Care Expenditures by Direct and Third-Party Payments in Selected Years, 1950–71

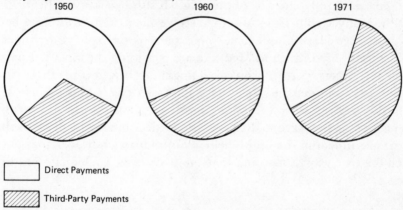

Direct Payments

Third-Party Payments

Third-party payments increased from 31.7 percent of health-care expenditures in 1950, to 44.7 percent in 1960, to 62.8 percent in 1971.

Source: U.S. Department of Health, Education, and Welfare, Social Security Administration, *Medical Care Costs and Prices: Background Book* (January 1972), p. 83.

impact of these third-party payments is to increase the demand for medical services. Consumers view medical care as a "good buy," since a dollar's worth of services may be bought for less than a dollar out of their own pockets. Of course, they have to pay the remainder of the full cost in the form of higher taxes and health insurance premium payments. A higher rate of consumption of goods and services will likely ensue when they are priced at less than full cost to the user.

Medicare and Medicaid. An important reason for the increase in demand for medical care and the rise in medical-care costs has been the development since 1966 of two large government health programs—Medicare and Medicaid. The Medicare program covers the major costs of hospital and physicians' services provided to the aged under social security, and Medicaid pays for the costs of hospital and physicians' services provided to people who are poor. The combined cost of Medicare and Medicaid in fiscal year 1971 was $14.4 billion. Medicare and Medicaid expenditures account for an important portion of the growth in medical care costs in recent years. Between fiscal years 1970 and 1971, for an example, about one fifth of the growth in personal health costs of $6.4 billion was attributable to the growth in Medicare and Medicaid expenditures.

The growth in the cost of medical care due to Medicare and Medicaid is only one side of the coin. Health benefits are the other side. Many aged persons now can receive adequate medical care because of Medicare, and many poor persons can receive it under Medicaid. Medicare and Medicaid are providing the means of payment for many persons who could not afford health care otherwise. By increasing demand, they have increased prices and the use of health services. In addition, the tradition among doctors of providing free medical care to the poor may be discouraged by the growth of government in the health field. This tradition, however, may not be the best way of assuring that the poor receive adequate health care.

ANALYSIS OF SUPPLY OF HEALTH SERVICES

Supply Characteristics: Physicians

Source of Supply. The main source of supply of physicians in the United States is, of course, the U.S. medical schools. These schools are graduating more than 8,000 doctors annually. In 1971, they graduated 63 percent more doctors than in 1950.[8] Another supply source of physicians is from abroad. Physicians trained abroad have

---

[8] Charles T. Stewart, Jr., and Corazon M. Siddayao, *Increasing the Supply of Medical Personnel* (Washington, D.C.: American Enterprise Institute, 1973), p. 16.

come into this country to practice medicine at a rapidly rising rate —exceeding 3,000 in 1971. Physicians trained abroad constitute 18.4 percent of all physicians practicing in the United States.[9]

Elasticity of Supply. The supply of physicians is inelastic in the short run. Thus an increase in demand for physicians in the short run will have an impact primarily on prices. However, in the long run the supply curve of physicians is more elastic, and a rise in demand is expected to increase the number of physicians. After remaining approximately the same in the 1950s, the ratio of physicians to the population increased in the 1960s and early 1970s (see Table 6–1).

TABLE 6–1
Health Personnel and Facilities per 100,000 population, Selected Years, 1950–70

Year	Physicians*	Nurses	Hospital Personnel	Short-Term Hospital Beds
1950	149	249	697	333
1955	150	259	788	344
1960	148	282	888	355
1965	153	319	1,009	383
1969	163	338	1,205	410
1970	171	345	1,245	411

° Doctors of medicine and osteopathy.
Source: Charles T. Stewart, Jr., and Corazon M. Siddayao, *Increasing the Supply of Medical Personnel* (Washington, D.C.: American Enterprise Institute, 1973), p. 19.

Estimated Supply and Requirements. Figure 6–6 shows estimated supply of physicians and requirements for physicians during the period 1970–80. On the assumption that 100 physicians are required for every 100,000 people, the U.S. Public Health Service estimated that there was a shortage of 50,000 physicians in 1969. Beginning with this shortage, and on the same assumption about the required ratio of physicians to the population, it is estimated that supply will catch up and there will be a surplus of 3,000 physicians by 1980.

Physicians' Income. The median income of physicians almost doubled between 1959 and 1969, increasing from $22,000 to $40,550. This growth in income and the relatively high income of physicians attract foreign-trained physicians to this country to prac-

---

[9] Ibid., p. 65.

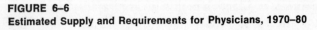

FIGURE 6–6
Estimated Supply and Requirements for Physicians, 1970–80

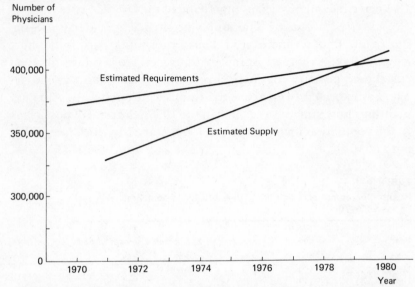

There will continue to be a shortage of physicians through the 1970s. However, by 1980 it is estimated that the shortage will disappear, and a surplus of physicians may occur.

Source: Charles T. Stewart, Jr., and Corazon M. Siddayao, *Increasing the Supply of Medical Personnel* (Washington, D.C.: American Enterprise Institute 1973), p. 25.

tice medicine and encourage more qualified persons in this country to select medicine as a profession. Supply, then, has responded to the rising demand for physicians, but not fast enough to prevent rapidly rising prices for physicians' services. There are two reasons for this. We have mentioned one reason for the slow response of supply, namely the low elasticity of supply in the short run. The second is the restrictions on entry into the field of medicine. The first reason is a technical characteristic associated with the time it takes to train physicians. The second is a market defect attributable to the establishment of barriers to keep human resources out of the medical field.

Supply Characteristics: Hospitals

The short-run supply curve of hospital services is the quantity of hospital services that will be supplied at different prices, given or holding constant the number of hospitals and hospital equipment, technology, and the prices of hospital inputs. The long-run supply curve differs from the short-run curve in that hospital investment (hospital facilities and equipment) may vary in the long run. Changes in hospital investment, technology, and the prices of inputs cause shifts in the short-run supply curve.

We expect the short-run supply curve of hospital services to be upward sloping, indicating that greater quantities supplied are associated with higher prices to patients.[10] These higher quantities result in higher costs per unit because of the principle of diminishing returns. Given the fixed sizes and facilities of the hospitals, the application of more and more variable resources (nurses, medical personnel, supplies, etc.) will eventually result in smaller and smaller increases in output. These smaller increases in output associated with given increases in variable resources or inputs mean higher costs per unit. Higher costs of hospital services may be eventually encountered, also, if hospital size increases. A wider range of services and, thus, more costly services are often associated with large hospitals. In addition, there may be diseconomies connected with larger outputs, due to increasing complexities of management.[11]

Factors Affecting the Supply of Hospital Services

Investment. An increase in hospital investment, that is, the construction of new hospitals, the expansion of existing hospitals, and the purchase of new equipment, increases the capacity of the hospital industry to provide hospital services. Hospital investment is a way to increase the supply of hospital services to meet the growing demand for these services.

Technology. Technological advancements increase the quantity and quality of hospital services. As a result of new technology, a greater quantity of the same services may be provided at lower prices, or new and better services may be provided. New medical technology (procedures and techniques such as open-heart surgery,

---

[10] Some statistical studies indicate that the supply curve for hospital services may be perfectly elastic, indicating that additional quantities may be supplied at the same price. See Klarman, *The Economics of Health*, p. 105.

[11] Ibid., p. 107.

cobalt therapy, and intensive care) usually result in both improved hospital care and higher hospital costs to patients. Between 1966 and 1970, hospital costs per patient day increased 13.9 percent annually, and 44 percent of the increase was due to the improvement in hospital services.[12]

Wages and Other Costs. Hospitals are buying greater quantities of labor and medical supplies and are having to pay higher prices for these inputs. Wages paid to hospital employees and prices paid for drugs and medical supplies increased at an average annual rate per patient-day of 7.8 percent between 1966 and 1970.[13] This growth in the cost of hospital inputs accounts for 56 percent of the growth in the hospital cost per patient-day. Unless higher wages and prices paid by hospitals are offset by increases in productivity, these increases represent the added cost incurred in producing the same amount of hospital services. With reference to supply, this means that the supply curve of hospital services shifts to the left, illustrating that the same quantity may be supplied, only at higher prices.

EVALUATION OF THE U.S. HEALTH-CARE SYSTEM

The U.S. health-care system is under severe criticism. Herman M. Somers describes the system of health care in this country "as a technically excellent product thrown into a Rube Goldberg delivery contraption which distorts and defeats it, and makes it more expensive than it need be."[14] A committee reported to the Secretary of the Department of Health, Education, and Welfare that "the key fact about the health service as it exists today is the disorganization . . . fragmentation and disjunction that promote extravagance and permit tragedy."[15]

The health-care industry is not performing very well for two reasons: (1) entry into the industry is restricted and (2) the industry is inefficiently organized.

---

12 U.S. Department of Health, Education and Welfare, Social Security Administration, *Medical Care Costs and Prices: Background Book* (January 1972), p. 25.

13 Ibid., p. 25.

14 Herman M. Somers, "Economic Issues in Health Services," in Neil W. Chamberlain (ed.), *Contemporary Economic Issues*, rev. ed. (Homewood, Ill.: Richard D. Irwin, 1973), pp. 145–46.

15 Ibid., p. 145.

Reducing Entry Barriers

Competition in the health-care industry could possibly be restored and certainly encouraged by changing the admission practices of medical schools, by reducing the control of the American Medical Association (AMA) over the medical industry, by breaking up the influence of county medical societies, and by eliminating state licensing and examining procedures.

Admission Practices of Medical Schools. The admission practices of medical schools check the supply of physicians and work to keep supply from catching up with the demand for physicians. Medical schools reject a high rate of *qualified* applicants. It was estimated in 1972 that one half of the qualified applicants to medical schools were turned down.[16] To the extent that the high rejection rate of medical schools is due to limited capacity, a lowering of the rejection rate will require an expansion in medical school facilities.

Monopoly Power of the AMA. The AMA virtually controls the supply of physicians. The source of this control is traced to the dominance of the association over medical education.[17] The AMA has controlled the number of medical schools by the use of its power to certify or fail to certify a medical school as a Class A rated school. The effects of its power to certify the quality of medical schools were never more in evidence than between 1906 and 1944, when the number of medical schools in the United States was reduced from 162 to 69. The AMA's dominance over medical education extends, also, to the internship and residency training programs. Its influence and power in this instance is due to the fact that it can approve or disapprove hospitals for administering internship and residency programs. Hospitals strongly favor having interns and residency personnel because these resources are made available at prices below their productivity.[18]

Influence of County Medical Societies. County medical societies are private clubs which keep a close surveillance on their members. These societies have their own judicial system and may expel physi-

---

16 Stewart and Siddayao, *Increasing the Supply,* p. 18.

17 Reuben A. Kessel, "Price Discrimination in Medicine," in William Breit and Harold M. Hochman (eds.), *Readings in Microeconomics,* 2d ed. (New York: Holt, Rinehart & Winston, 1971), p. 375.

18 Ibid., p. 378.

cians from membership or refuse membership to physicians who do not act in the best interest of the group.[19] For example, physicians who reduce prices in order to expand business may be labeled "unethical" and expelled. Expulsion from the society may be tantamount to denying a physician access to the facilities of a hospital, for hospitals may require and usually prefer their staff to be members of the society.

State Licensing Systems. Physicians cannot practice in any state solely by virtue of having completed their medical education. Supported by the AMA, states require that physicians be examined and licensed before practicing medicine. Licensing and examining procedures can be an effective way of controlling the supply of physicians coming from abroad. Foreign-trained physicians and other medical personnel may be encouraged or discouraged from practicing medicine in this country by changes in the difficulty of the examinations and other costs associated with getting a license.

Summary. The supply of medical services, especially physicians' services, is kept artificially low by restrictions to entry imposed directly or indirectly by the AMA, county medical societies, and the state. Until barriers to entry are broken down, the supply of medical and health services will not be responsive to competitive market forces, and the services will not be supplied at competitive prices.

Increasing Efficiency

Paramedical Personnel. Paramedical personnel are medical personnel who have had less training than a doctor. The use of paramedical personnel to do some of the work that doctors usually perform can save the time of doctors, increase their productivity, reduce costs, and increase the supply of medical services.

Although progress has been made in the use of such auxiliary personnel, the idea of a lesser trained and lower paid doctor's assistant is not generally accepted.[20] Many patients prefer the expertise and the bedside manner of the licensed physician. This attitude could be changed by an education program pointing out the savings to the patient and the more efficient use of the physician's time.

---

19 Ibid., pp. 379–80.
20 Stewart and Siddayao, *Increasing the Supply,* p. 41.

Health services jobs would have to be redefined so that the doctor's assistant could perform the job assigned as competently as the doctor could. One study indicates that the use of paramedical personnel could be doubled, and the increase in productivity (output per physician) would be at least 20 percent.[21]

Group Practice. The usual way of providing doctor's services is through a solo practice. A doctor receives an M.D. degree, obtains a license to practice medicine in a state, rents office space, buys furniture, supplies and equipment, puts up a sign, and goes to work. The chances are that business will be thriving in a short time. In some instances, a young physician may join the practice of an older one.

Solo practices are not usually efficient. Modern medical equipment may not be available and, if available, may not be fully utilized. A solo practice does not favor the maximum use of paramedical personnel and does not permit the pooling of human and capital resources. In contrast, *group practices* may permit better utilization of human and capital resources, as well as productivity gains from specialization and division of labor.

Group practices vary in size, type of legal organization (partnership, corporation, etc.), services provided, method of pricing, and method of financing. The one thing that is usually common to group practices is the sharing of costs and revenues.[22] A type of group practice that has attracted substantial support is a prepaid plan called a Health Maintenance Organization (HMO). Medical services are supplied to people in a certain area at fixed fees contracted for in advance. There is an incentive under the HMO for medical services to be provided at the lowest possible cost, since the net income of the organization varies inversely with the cost of providing medical services.

Hospital-Based Health Centers. An extension of the concept of a group practice is the health center. In the health-center concept patients would be tested, classified, and distributed to the area of the center that is best staffed and equipped to treat and cure them. Diagnostic tests could be handled by paramedical personnel. A computer could be used to classify patients as to the type of medical

---

21 Ibid., p. 43.
22 Ibid., p. 44.

care needed and distribute them to center areas in accordance with their respective health needs.

An important role of a health center is to maintain a check on the quality of health care on its premises and throughout the community it serves.[23] Local health centers, nursing homes, first-aid stations, and clinics would be a part of the organizational structure of the health center. The center could have mobile health teams to provide advice and assistance to local health units and supply health services to areas that are without adequate health-care personnel and facilities.

Health-care centers can be organized and developed around the modern hospital.[24] This is logical, since the hospital is the focal point of health activities today. A hospital-based health center could mean that many hospitals in a given area would be under a single management. Each hospital could provide specialized health services. The physician who now makes key decisions with little regard to hospital cost would be made more aware of the economic consequences of his decisions and would be held accountable for the overuse of medical facilities.

Medical Training Time. It usually takes about eight years to become an M.D.—four years in college and four years in "med" school. A person who specializes, of course, receives training beyond the M.D. degree. It has been suggested that two years could be saved from the time it takes to become a doctor by admitting candidates to medical schools after three years of college and reducing the medical program to a three-year period.[25] Medical schools could thus turn out more doctors without expanding medical facilities. The supply of physicians would increase, the price of physicians' services would thereby be reduced.

Summary. The efficiency of the present health-care system could be greatly improved. This could be accomplished through the use of paramedical personnel, the development of group practices and health centers, and the shortening of the period and cost of medical training. The survival of the system of health care as we know it today may depend upon what improvements can be made in the supply and price of health services.

---

23 Somers, *Economic Issues,* p. 149.
24 Ibid., pp. 149–50.
25 Stewart and Siddayao, *Increasing the Supply,* p. 50.

NATIONAL HEALTH INSURANCE PROPOSALS

In addition to the problem of efficiency, two other problems in the health-care field remain unsolved: the problem of meeting the health needs of the poor and the problems facing those with catastrophic health-care expense. National health insurance schemes have been proposed primarily because of these unsolved problems in the health-care field.

The Nixon Administration's Proposal

The national health insurance plan of the Nixon administration consists of two parts.[26] The first part is a mandatory private health insurance program under which all employers would provide their full-time employees with a health insurance package. This package would include basic health benefits and protection against catastrophic medical expense. The second part is a federally financed health insurance plan to provide health insurance coverage to poor families with children who are not covered by the mandatory employer-employee plan. Persons on public assistance who receive health benefits under Medicaid would continue to receive health care under this program.

The Nixon administration's proposal has met with opposition. In the first place, many poor persons would not be covered under the plan. Those who work full time, who do not work full time but have children, and who are on public assistance would be covered. Individuals and couples who are not employed full time and who are not on public assistance would not be covered, however. Secondly, health benefits and coverage would vary, depending upon whether the patient qualified under the mandatory employer plan or the federally financed plan.

Feldstein's Proposal

An appealing proposal by Martin S. Feldstein of Harvard University is based on the idea that government subsidies should vary

---

[26] Charles L. Schultze and others, *Setting National Priorities: The 1973 Budget* (Washington, D.C.: Brookings Institution, 1973), p. 239.

inversely with a person's income.[27] Under his scheme, everyone
would be covered (except the elderly who are covered under Medicare) with a basic health insurance plan including protection against
catastrophic expenses. The cost of the health insurance to the individual would be graduated so that a person with an income under a
certain amount would not pay anything. Also, everyone would be
protected against catastrophic expense by the establishment of a
maximum out-of-pocket medical expense in a given year.

Kennedy-Griffiths Program

The most thorough and far-reaching national health program is
the one proposed by Senator Edward M. Kennedy and Representative Martha W. Griffiths.[28] The Kennedy-Griffiths program calls for
a reorganization of the health-care system and free health care for
everyone. The program would be financed by federal payroll taxes
and general revenues. The way the program would work is that
each year a medical budget would be determined. This budget
would be allocated to ten regions and further within each region
to about 100 subareas. Then the administrative agency in each
subarea would allocate moneys among the suppliers of health
services based upon a price for which they would agree to take care
of a patient for one year. The quality and cost of medical care would
be closely supervised and monitored. The suppliers of health services would have options but would be encouraged to provide
services through an HMO on a fixed-fee basis.

Summary of Health Insurance Proposals

National health insurance programs have two objectives; to
meeting the health needs of the poor and to assist those who have
catastrophic expenses. The Nixon administration's national health
insurance proposal fails to meet the health needs of poor individuals
and couples, and health benefits vary depending upon qualification
under the mandatory employer plan or the federally financed plan.
Feldstein's proposal fulfills the two major objectives of national
health insurance and varies the cost of the program depending upon

---

27 Ibid., p. 245.
28 Ibid., p. 247.

a person's income. This feature of Feldstein's proposal is appealing because it shifts to the taxpayer only the cost of providing health insurance to those who are poor and who have relatively low income. The Kennedy-Griffiths national health insurance plan is the most comprehensive program. It encourages the use of HMO's and provides for health services on a fixed-fee basis. The main drawback of the Kennedy-Griffiths plan is that it transfers to the federal budget the major cost and responsibility of providing health services to all people—the poor and the rich.

SUMMARY

The recent spectacular rise in the cost of medical care reflects growth in demand, slow response of supply, improvements in the quality of medical services, and the inefficient organization of the health-care system. The growth in demand for health services is primarily due to the rise in per capita income in our society and the development of third-party payments. There are more people with more income who desire greater quantities of health-care services and are willing to pay higher prices for them. Third-party payments, that is, payments for health care made by government and private health insurance companies on the behalf of people, have extended health care to more people and have encouraged the utilization of health services. Government payments for medical services have increased demand by providing the means of payment to people covered under Medicare and Medicaid. Prepaid voluntary health insurance reduces the out-of-pocket costs of medical care to the consumer and, consequently, increases the use of health services.

The impact of more people, higher income, and third-party payments on prices of health services would be minimized if the supply of health services responded quickly to the rise in demand. However, supply has been slow to respond. It takes time to construct new hospitals and to train doctors, nurses, and other medical personnel. In addition, human resources cannot move freely into the health field because of restrictions on entry.

Medical services have improved in quality. New and better medical equipment has been introduced. New medical procedures and treatment are being used. A part of the rising cost of medical care, then, is due to the technically better product being supplied.

Increases in productivity can offset in part or entirely an increase in cost. Although the health-care systems have had some increases in productivity, the system in general is inefficient. A great deal of progress cannot be made toward increasing the efficiency with which health services are supplied without major changes in the organization and structure of the health-care system. A hospital-based health center is one type of organization within which health services may be supplied more efficiently.

The three basic issues in health, namely, supplying health services efficiently, protecting families against catastrophic costs, and providing adequate health care to the poor, remain largely unsettled. A national health insurance scheme is likely to be developed if these issues remain unresolved.

SUPPLEMENTARY READINGS

Committee for Economic Development. *Building a National Health-Care System.* New York, 1973.

A pamphlet stating the policy recommendations of the C.E.D. concerning a program for national health insurance. This reference could be distributed and used as a basis for class discussion.

Ginzberg, Eli. *Men, Money and Medicine.* New York: Columbia University Press, 1969.

Well-written and easy to understand book. Presents the view that physicians create their own demand. Chapter 6 on the physician and market power and Chapter 7 on the physician shortage are interesting contrasting reading.

Klarman, Herbert E. *The Economics of Health.* New York: Columbia University Press, 1965.

An economic analysis of the demand and supply of health care is presented in Chapters 2, 4, and 5. Economic concepts and principles are introduced throughout the analysis of health. A background in economic theory would be helpful in comprehension of the analysis.

Lambert, Richard D., (ed.). *The Annals of the American Academy of Political and Social Science,* Vol. 399 (January 1972).

The entire volume is devoted to health issues. Articles by Irving Levesin, "The Challenge of Health Services for the Poor," and by Anne R. Somers, "The Nation's Health: Issues for the Future," are suggested supplementary readings.

Schultze, Charles L., and others. *Setting National Priorities: The 1973 Budget,* chap. 7. Washington, D.C.: Brookings Institution, 1972.

Chapter 7 provides coverage of major issues in health insurance and national health insurance proposals.

Stewart, Charles R., Jr., and Siddayao, Corazon M. *Increasing the Supply of Medical Personnel.* Washington, D.C.: American Enterprise Institute, 1973.

The main theme is that government subsidies to medical students are unnecessary, since there is a surplus of qualified medical students. This is a good general reference. Chapter 4 is especially recommended to supplement the section above on the health-care system.

Part II

DISTRIBUTION
OF INCOME

Chapter 7
POVERTY PROBLEMS

CHECKLIST OF ECONOMIC CONCEPTS

Income Inequality
Demand for Labor
Supply of Labor
Wage Rate Determination
Determinants of Income Distribution
Ownership Pattern of Resources
Negative Income Tax

7

POVERTY PROBLEMS
Is Poverty Necessary?

The young today are just play-acting in courting poverty. It's all right to wear jeans and eat hamburgers. But it's entirely different from not having any hamburgers to eat and no jeans to wear. A great many of these kids—white kids—seem to have somebody in the background they can always go to. I admire their spirit, because they have a strong sense of social justice. But they themselves have not been deprived. They haven't experienced the terror. They have never seen a baby in the cradle crying of hunger. . . .

I think the reason for the gap between the black militants and the young white radicals is that the black kids are much more conscious of the thin edge of poverty. And how soon you can be reduced to living on relief. What you know and what you feel are very different. Terror is something you feel. When there is no paycheck coming in—the absolute, stark terror.[1]

"Poverty amidst plenty" is a striking feature of the American scene. Our nation is the richest in the world, yet millions of people are poor, and millions more that do not live in poverty are poor relative to others. This is not the American dream; it is the American paradox.

---

[1] Quote from Virginia Durr in Studs Terkel, *Hard Times* (New York: Random House, 1970), p. 462.

Poverty may be a more serious problem in our society than in so-cieties with much less income and wealth. Poverty amidst poverty is easier to understand and even condone. But, in a land of abundance it is difficult to comprehend why some people are inadequately fed, clothed, and sheltered. Poverty is a reality that needs to be studied, understood, appreciated, and then eradicated.

Our study of poverty in the United States will be approached in two ways. First, poverty will be examined in reference to *absolute* income levels. This approach permits the identification of people who live below a designated poverty level of income. Second, it will be studied in terms of *relative* incomes, that is, the share or percent of national income that people receive.

POVERTY IN TERMS OF ABSOLUTE INCOME LEVELS

The poverty problem in the United States is essentially an in-come distribution problem. There is enough income to go around so that no one would have to live in poverty. But enough income does not go to everyone, and some people do live in poverty.

FIGURE 7–1
Poor Persons in 1960 and 1971

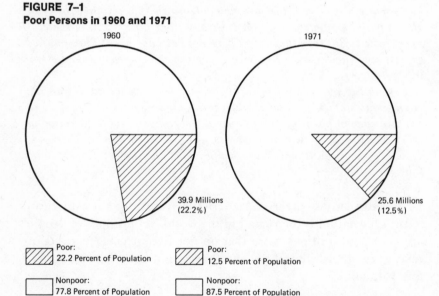

The number of poor persons decreased from 39.9 millions (22.2 percent of the population) in 1960 to 25.6 millions (12.5 percent of the population) in 1971.

Source: U.S. Department of Commerce, Bureau of the Census, *Consumer Income,* Current Population Reports, Series P–60, No. 82 (July 1972).

Median family income in the United States is over $10,000 ($10,290 in 1971). As Figure 7–1 shows, more people and families move out of poverty each year due to growth in family income. This is the good news. The bad news is that over 25 million persons were poor in 1971.

What Is Poverty?

Poverty is not easily defined. Yet, a precise definition has been implied in the statement that many Americans are poor. We shall use the definition of poverty developed by the government.

Poverty is concerned with the relationship between the minimum needs of man and his ability to satisfy these needs. The difficulty with any definition of poverty involves the meaning of "minimum needs" and the amount of money required to satisfy these needs. The approach taken by the government is essentially, first, to determine a minimum food budget and the money cost of that budget. Second, the cost of the food budget is multiplied by three because the cost of food represents about one third of consumer spending, according to studies of consumer spending patterns. For an illustration, $1,379 represents the cost of the minimum food budget for an urban family of four. The cost of food times three equals $4,137, the official poverty level for this type of family in 1971. Poverty levels as defined for different family sizes are listed in Table 7–1.

TABLE 7–1
Poverty Levels in 1971

Family Size	Urban	Rural
2	$2,633	$2,219
3	3,229	2,745
4	4,137	3,527
5	4,880	4,159
6	5,489	4,688

Poverty levels as defined vary by family size and residence of family. For example, a family of four living in an urban area in 1971 had a poverty level of $4,137.

Source: U.S. Department of Commerce, Bureau of the Census, *Consumer Income*, Current Population Reports, Series P–60, No. 82 (July 1972).

Who Are the Poor?

Table 7–2 lists family groups that have a high incidence of poverty. Note that some of these groups overlap with others.

TABLE 7–2
Selected Characteristics of Families below the Poverty Level in 1971

Selected Characteristics	Total Families	Families below Poverty Level	
		Number	Percent
All families	53,296,000	5,303,000	10.0%
White families	47,641,000	3,751,000	7.9
Black families	5,157,000	1,484,000	28.8
Age of family head			
Under 25 years	3,993,000	719,000	18.0
65 years and over	7,478,000	1,062,000	14.2
Size of Family			
2 persons	18,862,000	1,901,000	10.1
4 persons	10,524,000	790,000	7.5
7 or more persons	2,919,000	697,000	23.9
Educational attainment of family head			
Less than 8 years	6,422,000	1,505,000	23.4
High school, 1–3 years	8,275,000	947,000	11.4
High school, 4 years	15,996,000	933,000	5.8
College, 1–3 years	5,557,000	268,000	4.8
College, 4 years	7,104,000	143,000	2.0
Employment status of family head			
Employed	40,776,000	2,247,000	5.5
Unemployed	1,559,000	334,000	21.4
Not in labor force	9,941,000	2,650,000	26.7
Nonfarm families	50,703,000	4,851,000	9.6
Farm families	2,593,000	452,000	17.4

Source: U.S. Department of Commerce, Bureau of the Census, *Consumer Income*, Current Population Reports, Series P–60, No. 82 (July 1972).

Blacks and Other Minority Groups.   Blacks and other minority groups have a very high incidence of poverty. The poverty rate among black families is over three times that of white families. For example, 29 percent of black families were poor in 1971, as compared to 8 percent of white families. The incidence of poverty may be as high or higher among some other minority groups, such as Indians and Chicanos (Mexican-Americans), than among blacks. It was estimated that the unemployment rate among Indians was 40 percent when the national average was 3.8 percent in 1966.[2]

The Young.   The incidence of poverty is very high among young families. Some families headed by young persons, say under 25

2 Gustav Schachter and Edwin L. Dale, Jr., *The Economist Looks at Society* (Lexington, Mass.: Xerox College Publishing, 1973), p. 27.

years old, have difficulties making ends meet because the family head frequently lacks education and work experience. About one out of every five families headed by young persons is poor.

The Aged. Families headed by persons of 65 years of age and over frequently have low levels of family income due to retirement or illness of the family head. Most of the aged poor are couples or widows attempting to live on private or public retirement payments such as social security payments. Some own their homes, but many live in rented rooms and apartments. Among the poor, poverty is concentrated among the aged—one out of every five poor families is headed by an aged person.

The Uneducated. Poverty rates vary inversely with the level of education. Low poverty rates are associated with high education levels and high poverty rates with low education levels. Only 2 percent of families headed by persons with four years of college are poor. In contrast, 23 percent of the families headed by persons with less than eight years of schooling are poor.

The Unemployed. Heads of families who are unemployed for any significant period of time are normally forced to draw on their savings to support their families. After their savings are depleted, a drastic cut in their living standard occurs. In 1971, there were 1,559,000 families headed by unemployed persons. More than one out of every five of these families lived in poverty.

The Working Poor. A job is no guarantee that a person or a family will not be poor. In 1971, there were 2,247,000 poor families that were headed by persons with jobs. These poor families headed by working persons represented 43 percent of all families that lived in poverty.

The Nonworking Poor. Many families lose hope, give up, live on welfare, and are not included in the labor force. There were approximately ten million families like this in 1971. About 27 percent of these families, or 2,650,000, lived in poverty in 1971. This group of families represents about one half of the families living in poverty.

Rural People. Poverty is widespread among families that live in rural areas. In some instances poverty in rural areas may not be as visible as it is in an urban environment. Poverty rates are almost two times higher among farm families than among nonfarm families. For example, the poverty rate was 17.4 percent among farm families as compared to 9.6 percent among nonfarm families in 1971. Job opportunities and family incomes are higher in urban areas than in rural ones.

POVERTY IN TERMS OF INCOME DISTRIBUTION

The second approach to poverty considers the distribution of income in the United States. We have said that the poverty problem in this country is mainly one of income distribution. This means that the level of income in our country is high enough so that a more equal distribution of income should mitigate the poverty problem and reduce its significance.

Income Equality

Economists usually explain income equality and income inequality by reference to a curve called a Lorenz curve, after M. O. Lorenz. Income equality among families means that any given percent of families receives an equal percent of family income; 10 percent of families receive 10 percent of income, 20 percent of families receive 20 percent of income, and 100 percent of families receive 100 percent of income. In Figure 7–2, equal percentages of families and incomes can be measured along the two axes. Income equality is shown by a 45-degree line starting at the origin. At any point on the 45-degree line, the percent of families shown receive an equal percent of total family income.

Income Inequality

Income inequality can be illustrated graphically by lines that deviate from the line of income equality. A Lorenz curve derived from actual data on income distribution will usually lie to the right of the line of income equality (the 45-degree line). The further to the right of the 45-degree line it lies, the greater the inequalities in income distribution. Lorenz curves are useful in making income distribution comparisons in a given year among different countries or in the same country over time.

Table 7–3 divides U.S. families into five numerically equal groups, or quintiles, and indicates the distribution of personal income among these groups. The table also shows the income share of the top 5 percent of families. It can be observed that income is very unequally distributed. The highest 20 percent of families re-

TABLE 7–3
Percent of Income Received by Each Fifth and Top 5 Percent of Families in Selected Years, 1950–70

Quintile of families	1950	1955	1960	1965	1970
Lowest fifth	4.5%	4.8%	4.9%	5.3%	5.5%
Second fifth	12.0	12.2	12.0	12.1	12.0
Third fifth	17.4	17.7	17.6	17.7	17.4
Fourth fifth	23.5	23.7	23.6	23.7	23.5
Highest fifth	42.6	41.6	42.0	41.3	41.6
	100.0%	100.0%	100.0%	100.0%	100.0%
Top 5 percent	17.0%	16.8%	16.8%	15.8%	14.4%

Source: U.S. Department of Commerce, Bureau of the Census, *Statistical Abstract of the United States,* 1972, p. 324.

ceived almost 42 percent of income in 1970, and the lowest 20 percent received 5.5 percent. The top 5 percent of families received 14.4 percent of income. These data on income inequality are shown by the Lorenz curve drawn in Figure 7–2.

Income inequality was reduced during the 1930s and the years of World War II. The share of income received by the top 5 percent and the highest 25 percent decreased between 1929 and 1944, while the share received by the lowest 25 percent of families increased. It is generally agreed that the two main reasons for this trend toward greater income equality were that property income fell drastically during the Great Depression of the 1930s, and the gap between low-paid and high-paid workers was reduced when full employment was reached during World War II.[3]

Since the 1950s, the trend toward greater income equality has not been so pronounced. The shares of income received by the top 5 percent and top 25 percent have decreased slightly, from 17 percent and 43 percent, respectively, in 1950 to 14.4 percent and 42 percent, respectively, in 1970. The share of income received by the lowest one fifth of families increased from 4.5 percent in 1955 to 5.5 percent in 1970. The shift in income since 1950 has been away from the upper income groups and toward the lower income ones. The striking feature concerning the distribution of income during the past two decades is the stability of the income distribution pattern, especially the share of income received by middle-income families.

---

[3] Joseph A. Pechman, "The Rich, the Poor and the Taxes They Pay," *The Public Interest,* No. 17 (Fall 1968).

FIGURE 7–2
Lorenz Curve Plotted with Data on U.S. Family Income, 1970

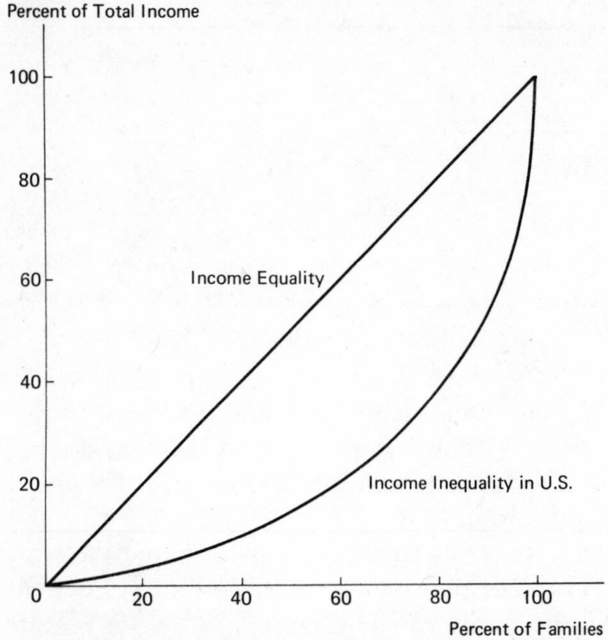

Percent of Total Income

Percent of Families

The Lorenz curve shows the existing degree of income inequality. The horizontal axis measures the percent of families,
starting with the poorest. Thus the 20 percent mark represents
the lowest earning fifth of the population. In 1970, the lowest
20 percent earned 5.5 percent of the total income, and the
lowest 40 percent earned 17.5 percent of total income. This
means that the fourth quintile (the families included between
the 20 percent and the 40 percent marks), earned 12.0 percent
of the total income (17.5—5.5). If perfect income equality
existed, the Lorenz curve would be the 45-degree line.

Source: Data from U.S. Department of Commerce, Bureau of the Census,
Statistical Abstract of the United States, 1972, p. 324.

THE ECONOMIC CAUSES OF POVERTY

Determinants of Resource Prices and Employment

Family incomes depend on the quantities of resources that families can place in employment and the prices received for those
resources. To understand poverty, then, it is important to understand what determines the prices paid for human and capital re-

sources and what determines the quantities that can be employed.

Wage Rate Determination.   Under competitive market conditions, the basic principle of wage rate determination is that units (man-hours) of any kind of labor tend to be paid a price equal to any one worker's (hourly) contribution to his employer's total receipts. In other words, a worker is paid about what he is worth to his employer. What a worker is worth to his employer is referred to by economists as the worker's marginal revenue productivity. Suppose the marginal revenue productivity of the worker is $4 per hour; that is, an hour of labor is contributing $4 to the receipts of the employer. Then the worker is worth $4 an hour to his employer and would be paid that amount under competitive conditions. If a worker were paid less than what he is worth to his employer, he would also be paid less than he would be worth to *other* employers. Consequently, other employers would bid for his services, driving the worker's wage rate (hourly wages) up to what he *is* worth. On the other hand, rather than pay him $5 an hour, an employer would lay him off.

This principle can be seen more clearly with reference to Figure 7–3. The demand curve for labor (*DD* in the figure) shows what employers are willing to pay at different quantities of labor (man-hours per month), or, alternatively, how much a unit of labor is worth at different possible employment levels. The supply curve for labor (*SS* in the figure) shows the quantity of labor that will be placed on the market at different wage rates. Labor is paid less than it is worth at the wage rate w_0. Only q_0 units of labor want to work at this wage rate. However, at this employment level, labor is worth w_2 to any employer. Thus, a shortage exists; that is, at the wage rate w_0, the quantity of labor demanded is greater than the quantity supplied, and wage rates will be driven up to w_1. Labor is paid about what it is worth to any employer at w_1. At a wage rate above w_1, however, the quantity of labor supplied is not worth that wage to employers. A surplus exists; that is, the quantity of labor supplied is greater than the amount demanded. Thus the wage rate will return again to w_1.

The Price of Capital.   In a competitive market the price of a unit of capital, say a machine, is determined in a way similar to the price of a unit of labor. The price of any kind of capital depends upon the demand for and supply of units of capital and, at market

FIGURE 7–3
Wage Rate Determination under Competition

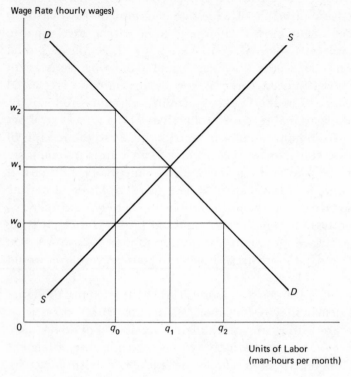

equilibrium, the price of capital equals what that capital is worth to its employer.

Determination of Individual or Family Income

The income of a person depends upon the *price* he or she receives for his or her resources, labor and capital, and the *quantities* of resources he or she can place in employment. For example, the monthly family income from labor equals the quantity of its labor employed, multiplied by the wage rate. From capital, its income equals the quantity of capital employed, multiplied by the price of each unit of capital. Total monthly family income, then, is a summation of the two monthly income flows.

Determinants of Income Distribution

The distribution of income among persons and families depends upon the distribution of resource ownership and the prices paid for resources of different kinds in different employments. The ownership pattern of resources is unequally distributed among persons and families. This unequal ownership pattern of resources gives rise to an unequal distribution of income in our society. People at the bottom of the income ladder own a small share of the nation's resources, and the market places a low value on the resources they do own. People at the top of the income ladder own a large share of the nation's resources on which the market places a high value.

Causes of Differences in Labor Resource Ownership

Brains and Brawn. The inheritance of mental and physical talents is not equally distributed among people. Some people have greater capabilities than others. Some families' labor resources have exceptional learning abilities; others' labor resources have special talents—acting, singing, playing baseball or football. Other families are not so fortunately endowed.

Skill Levels. Skill levels vary among individuals. Differences in skills among persons are primarily due to differences in inherited capabilities, training opportunities, and discrimination. Some persons inherit specific abilities to do certain tasks better than others. Most often people with high skill levels have acquired them from their training and education. In some instances, people have low skill levels because they have been discriminated against and have not had equal opportunities for training and education. Even with the same training, certain groups, say females, may not receive the same pay as others, although they perform the same tasks. In general, persons with highly developed skills are worth more and, therefore, are paid more in the market than are unskilled or semiskilled workers.

Causes of Differences in Capital Resource Ownership

Inheritance. Some persons and families inherit real property and claims on real property such as stocks and bonds. These people have a head start on those who do not begin with inherited capital resources.

Luck. Luck is not evenly distributed among the population. Some families may be at or near the bottom of the income pyramid because of bad luck. A business failure caused by a depression, a prolonged illness, a fatal accident, or a natural disaster may leave persons and families without income or the ability to earn an adequate income.

Propensities to Accumulate. People vary as to their propensities or tendencies to save and accumulate capital resources. Those who are strongly motivated are willing to forego consumption today in order to enjoy greater income in the future. Others are more concerned about their current consumption standards. They do not save and do not accumulate capital resources.

Summary of the Causes of Poverty

Several things are clear about the poor and about low-income families. They have small quantities and low qualities of resources. The market places a low value on the services they provide in the market. The low productivity and, therefore, the low pay of the poor are due to low levels of training and education, misfortune, relatively small inheritances, and discrimination. The poor are in a vicious circle which is difficult to escape. What they need in order to move out of poverty they do not have and cannot afford to acquire. So they remain poor.

GOVERNMENT ATTEMPTS TO ALLEVIATE POVERTY

Two approaches to poverty are suggested by the foregoing analysis. First, the productivity of the employable poor can be increased. This can be accomplished through subsidized education of the children of the poor, adult training and education programs, counseling and guidance, job placement programs, and the elimination of discrimination. Second, a minmum annual income can be guaranteed. This is essential if no one is to live in poverty. Some people, such as the very young, the very old, the disabled, and the ill, are poor because they cannot produce at all, and others are poor because they cannot produce enough. Income-support programs are required to aid persons who are unproductive and those who have low productivity.

Government Measures to Increase Productivity

The federal government has a variety of programs designed to increase the quality of human resources. These may be classified as manpower training programs and the provision of goods and services, such as education and health, which will enhance productivity. Many of these programs are not exclusively for the poor and, therefore, benefit the rich as well.

Manpower training programs were launched in a big way in the 1960s. They can be grouped into training programs, job creation programs, and information services.[4] Training programs include vocational education, adult education, vocational rehabilitation, and special training programs for technologically displaced and disadvantaged persons and those on welfare. To complement the training programs, other programs were designed to create jobs for the poor. The aim of the job creation programs is to pave the way for jobs in private industry and in government for the poor and disadvantaged. In addition, the productivity of the poor has been increased through the services of the U.S. Training Employment Service, which provides information to the poor concerning employment opportunities and training programs.

Government Income-Support Programs

Government programs to support the income of individuals and families are numerous and large in dollar amounts (approximately $100 billion in fiscal year 1973). They were developed in a piece-meal fashion over a number of years and vary as to purpose, benefits, eligibility requirements, and method of financing. Most government income-support programs are not restricted to families who live in poverty; they are designed to assist any family who happens to fall in a specific category, such as the disabled, the blind, the aged, and female heads of families with dependent children. In

---

4 Sar A. Levitan, *Programs in Aid of the Poor for the 1970s* (Baltimore: Johns Hopkins Press, 1969), pp. 50–61.

some income-support programs, benefit payments are related to previous contributions (social security) or past services (veterans' payments). In other income-support programs, such as public assistance, individual benefits are not related to individual costs or contributions.

Income-support programs may provide benefits in the form of cash or goods such as housing, food, medical care, and education. Benefits under income-support programs may not be uniform in all states; for some income-support programs, for example, benefit levels and eligibility requirements are determined by each state.

Retirement and Related Programs.   The amount of federal funds spent on retirement and related programs in 1973 was $72.6 billion, or about 70 percent of the total amount spent on all income-support programs (Figure 7–4). These programs are aimed pri-

FIGURE 7–4
Federal Expenditures for Income-Support Programs in 1960 and 1973 (est.)

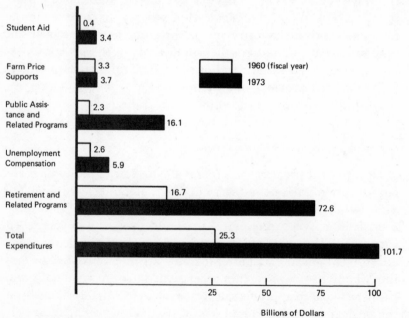

Total expenditures for income-support programs have increased by 300 percent between 1960 and 1973.

Source: Charles L. Schultze and others, *Setting National Priorities: The 1973 Budget* (Washington, D.C.: Brookings Institution, 1972), p. 176.

marily at providing retirement income and medical and disability benefits to persons over 65 years old who have employment records in civil service, the armed forces, and private industry. They are only indirectly related to poverty and are financed largely out of current tax revenues. The largest of these programs, the Old Age, Survivors, Disability and Health Insurance Program (OASDHI), is financed by social security taxes—half collected from the employer and half from the employee. The growth in expenditures on OASDHI from $10.8 billion in 1960 to $55.1 billion in 1973 reflects increases in the number of persons reaching the retirement age, the proportion of the population covered by social security, and the average benefit payment.[5]

Unemployment Compensation. Unemployment compensation payments were $5.9 billion in 1973. This program was established in 1935 under the Social Security Act. Its purpose is to provide income support to persons who have a temporary loss of income due to unemployment. The program is administered at the state level and financed by a tax on the employer. Eligible persons may receive unemployment benefits for a period of 26 weeks, and benefits may be extended for an additional 13 weeks if the unemployment rate among the eligible workers equals or exceeds 4.5 percent for three consecutive months. Like retirement programs, unemployment compensation is not directly aimed at aiding the poor.

Public Assistance. Public assistance is directly concerned with alleviating poverty. A person or family must meet a "needs" test to be eligible to receive it. The federal government spent an estimated $16.1 billion in 1973 on public assistance programs. These programs include cash benefits to the aged, disabled, and blind who are not covered by social security, cash benefits to families who have dependent children, and goods and services (medical services, food, housing subsidies, etc.) to persons and families who are poor.

The major crisis in public assistance involves the program called Aid to Families with Dependent Children (AFDC). The major criticisms of this program are: (1) it is unfair because eligibility standards and benefit levels vary from state to state, (2) it does not include many poor families, primarily families headed by a male earning a

---

[5] Charles L. Schultze and others, *Setting National Priorities: The 1973 Budget* (Washington, D.C.: Brookings Institution, 1973), p. 180.

low income, and (3) it discourages work, since earned income is taxed at a very high rate. Until 1967, a dollar of earned income was taxed at 100 percent; that is, dollar benefits were reduced by every dollar earned. The public assistance law now permits persons to keep $30 per month and one third of earned income. The tax rate on earned income remains high at 67 percent.

Farm Price Supports.   The major aim of the government's farm price support program is to maintain the incomes of farmers. Both poor and rich farmers benefit from the program, but the benefits flow largely to farmers who are relatively well off. A study revealed that in 1969 the top 19 percent of farmers, classified by their sales, received 63 percent of farm program benefits. At the other end of the scale, 50 percent of the farms classified by their sales as at the bottom of the scale received only 9 percent of the benefits.[6]

Aid to Students.   The first major attempt to support the incomes of students in higher education took place after World War II, when veterans were provided education benefits in the form of tuition and cash benefits. Education benefits have since been extended to veterans of the Korean and Vietnam wars. In addition to cash benefits to veterans to cover tuition and living expenses, an increasing amount of federal dollars in grants, low-interest loans, and fellowships have been made available to students who are not veterans. Most of these funds go to the financially needy.

Evaluation of Government Programs

Government measures to increase the productivity of labor resources, particularly those of the handicapped, disadvantaged, and other poor, are an essential part of any antipoverty program. Most people agree that close and continuous scrutiny of these programs is necessary to improve their efficiency, that it is especially important for these programs to concentrate on the young, and that the long-run solution to alleviating poverty among the employable poor is through manpower training programs of some sort.

Opinion is divided with respect to what constitutes equity and what constitutes efficiency in income maintenance programs. How-

---

6 Charles L. Schultze, *The Distribution of Farm Subsidies: Who Gets the Benefits?* (Washington, D.C.: Brookings Institution, 1971), p. 29.

ever, there is some common ground. For one thing, it is agreed that the public assistance program is badly in need of reform because of its unequal treatment of families in similar circumstances, its built-in incentives for persons not to work, and its inadequate coverage. In addition, there is growing acceptance that the income of the poor may be best supported through a negative income tax plan—a guaranteed annual income plan based on the idea that when you have taxable income you pay money to the government (positive taxes), and when you have negative taxable income the government pays you (negative taxes).

NEGATIVE INCOME TAX PROPOSALS

In this final section two alternative proposals for income support are presented. The negative income tax is the major feature in both.

The two proposals differ in the degree in which the negative income tax replaces existing income support programs. Before discussion of these proposals, including the pros and cons of each, we shall look into the essential features of a negative income tax.

The Negative Income Tax

There are three variables common to every negative income tax scheme, as noted in Table 7–4. These variables are the guaranteed level of income, the negative tax rate, and the break-even level of income. In the example in Table 7–4, the guaranteed level of

TABLE 7–4
Negative Income Tax Plan for a Family of Four

Minimum Guaranteed Income	Earned Income	Negative Tax or Subsidy ($4,000 − 50% of Earned Income)	Disposable Income (Earned Income plus Negative Tax)
$4,000	$ 0	$4,000	$4,000
4,000	1,000	3,500	4,500
4,000	2,000	3,000	5,000
4,000	3,000	2,500	5,500
4,000	4,000	2,000	6,000
4,000	5,000	1,500	6,500
4,000	6,000	1,000	7,000
4,000	7,000	500	7,500
4,000	8,000	0	8,000

income is $4,000, and the negative tax rate is 50 percent. The break-even level of income, that is, the level of earned income at which negative taxes or government subsidies are zero, is $8,000.

The relationship among these variables may be seen from the formulas $Y = rB, r = Y/B$, or $B = Y/r$, where

Y = guaranteed annual income
r = negative tax rate
B = break-even level of income

In the example of a negative income tax plan in Table 7–4, the guaranteed annual income and the negative tax rate are given. Thus, the break-even level of income may be calculated—$B = \$4,000/.5 = \$8,000$. Under the plan a family of four earning $2,000 would have a disposable income of $5,000. This family would receive negative taxes of $3,000 ($4,000 − 50 percent of earned income), plus $2,000 in earned income. (Before going further, examine Table 7–4 carefully in order to be certain that you understand this illustration of a negative income tax plan.)

The level of income that will be guaranteed to every family, along with negative tax rate, will be determined by whatever society believes to be acceptable. It should be pointed out, however, that the costs of negative income tax plans vary directly with the guaranteed level of income and inversely with the negative income tax rate. For example, an increase in the guaranteed level of income increases the cost of a scheme, given the negative tax rate; and an increase in the negative tax rate, given the guaranteed annual income, decreases the cost of a plan.

The negative income tax scheme is simple and easy to administer, and incentives to earn income are built into the program. Under a negative income tax plan, people are always better off if they earn income than they are if they do not earn it, and the more they earn, the better off they will be. Two alternative proposals concerning the negative income tax will be considered in the sections below.

Alternative 1

One alternative is to replace the public assistance program with a negative income tax plan, keeping the other income-support programs essentially as they are. Under this approach, income-support programs are viewed as having multiple objectives. For example, retirement programs are considered on their own merits as "rights to retirement income" that people have built up over their lifetimes. Similarly, benefit payments to veterans are thought of as payment for past services and past contributions to society.

The cost of replacing the public assistance program with a plan that would move every person and family above the threshold level of poverty is estimated to be in the neighborhood of $30 to $35 billion. Since the current cost of public assistance is about $16 billion, the added or marginal cost of alternative 1 is between $14 and $19 billion.

Alternative 2

A second alternative is to replace all income-support programs with a negative income tax plan, that is, a plan based on the single objective of eliminating poverty. The underlying idea of this alternative is that the only justification for income support is poverty. A person who is over 65 years old, who is disabled, or who is a veteran may or may not be poor. A person who is a farmer may or may not be poor, and so on. In this view, the sole purpose of government transfer payments is to increase the purchasing power of the recipients, at the expense of the purchasing power of those who pay taxes. The presumption is that the alleviation of poverty by transfers from those above the poverty line to those below it is the primary legitimate use of transfer payments.

It has been stated that the cost of moving all persons above the poverty line is between $30 billion to $35 billion. Thus, if a transfer payment program aimed only at eliminating poverty replaced the current income-support programs, there would be substantial savings to society of between $65 billion to $70 billion.

Advantages and Disadvantages

Several advantages are claimed for alternative 2. One, inequalities in present antipoverty measures would be eliminated by concentrating transfer payments on the poor. Two, the coverage of the poor would be universal, and payments to the poor would exceed

in many instances what they receive from present transfer programs. Three, special-interest groups such as veterans, farmers, and
the aged are not subsidized unless they are poor. Four, the cost of
this alternative is substantially less than the cost of current transfer
programs.

There are also disadvantages associated with alternative 2.[7] In
the first place, this alternative will encounter strong political opposition. The idea of a negative income tax is simple but novel, and
it represents a fundamental departure from providing transfer payments based on specific categories such as the aged to providing
transfer payments based strictly on financial need.

Second, it is argued that providing cash benefits on the basis of
need is not an adequate substitute for many social service programs.
The mere payment of money may not solve all the problems of the
poor. Many social service programs for the poor, such as child health
and maternity programs, services to crippled children, medical aid,
and vocational rehabilitation, may need to be improved and expanded.

Third, a negative income tax plan, as other subsidization programs, may discourage persons who are working and earning low
incomes. Suppose that in the absence of such a plan a person is
earning $4,000 a year and receives no public assistance benefits.
After personal deductions this individual is likely to pay a tax at a
rate of 14 percent on taxable income, which is the lowest present
personal income tax rate. Under a negative income tax plan, earned
income is likely to be taxed (his subsidy is likely to be reduced) at
a much higher rate, such as 50 percent. However, the disposable
income of a person or family will still be directly related to earned
income under a negative income tax plan; that is, the more you
earn, the better off you are in terms of disposable income.

The main advantage of alternative 1 over alternative 2 is that
the former is more likely to receive political support. The disadvantage of alternative 1 in comparison with alternative 2 is that
there would still be many income-support programs not directly
related to aiding the poor.

---

[7] Joseph J. Klos, "Public Assistance Family Allowances, or the Negative Income
Tax?" *Nebraska Journal of Economics and Business*, Spring 1969, pp. 26–28.

SUMMARY

Progress has been made in the United States toward the reduction of poverty. There are fewer persons and families living below the poverty line, and income inequality has been reduced. Still, more progress is needed. Too many persons and families remain poor, and the distribution of income remains very unequal.

The incidence of poverty is extremely high among blacks, the young, the aged, the uneducated, the unemployed, the working poor, the nonworking poor, and farm families. One out of four to one out of five families with any of these social characteristics is living in poverty.

A program to alleviate poverty should (1) increase the productivity of the poor and (2) guarantee a minimum annual income to families who cannot work and those who cannot earn that minimum when they do work. Government measures to increase the productivity of the poor have, in part, been successful.

A guaranteed annual income plan in the form of a negative income tax scheme would appear to be more efficient than our current public assistance program. Two important aspects of a negative income tax scheme are that (1) only the poor receive negative taxes (subsidies) from the government and (2) the recipients of government subsidies are encouraged to earn income.

SUPPLEMENTARY READINGS

Green, Christopher. *Negative Taxes and the Poverty Problem*. Washington, D.C.: Brookings Institution, 1967.

> The idea of the negative income tax is fully developed (Chapter 4), and the common features of negative income tax schemes are presented (Chapter 5).

Kershaw, Joseph A. *Government against Poverty*. Chicago: Markham Publishing Co., 1970.

> Discusses different types of income maintenance problems. The advantages and disadvantages of the negative income tax scheme are covered in Chapter 6, which could be used to supplement the section above on the negative income tax.

Levitan, Sar A. *The Great Society's Poor Law*. Baltimore: Johns Hopkins Press, 1969.

Chapter 3, "Programs for the Employable Poor," is suggested to contribute to the understanding of manpower programs designed to increase the productivity of the poor.

Sackrey, Charles. *The Political Economy of Urban Poverty*. New York: W. W. Norton & Co., 1973.

A critical analysis of the way poverty is usually studied. Chapter 3, "Economics and Black Poverty," attacks the methodology and theories of economists concerning poverty.

Scoville, James G. *Perspectives on Poverty and Income Distribution*. Lexington, Mass.: D. C. Heath & Co., 1971.

A selection of readings. Some of the readings in Part 3, which covers the incidence and causes of poverty, can be used effectively to supplement the sections above on the economic causes of poverty.

Thurow, Lester C. *Poverty and Discrimination*. Washington, D.C.: Brookings Institution, 1969.

Extent of poverty is covered in Chapter 2, and the income distribution patterns for whites and blacks are examined. Chapter 3 is good on the causes of poverty.

Chapter 8

DISCRIMINATION

CHECKLIST OF ECONOMIC CONCEPTS

Market Discrimination
Wage Discrimination
Employment Discrimination
Occupation Discrimination
Price Discrimination
Nonmarket Discrimination
Monopoly Power
Exploitation
Tastes for Discrimination
Economic Cost of Market Discrimination

8

DISCRIMINATION
The High Cost of Prejudice

Outfielder King is going to be taught a lesson. Outfielder King is not going to mess up the exact extent of children's rights as the Little League, in its own infinite adolescence, knows them to be. Outfielder King is going to be the reason all of Ypsilanti, Michigan, blows its Little League charter.

Parents can act like idiots in the grandstand and on the coaching lines, kids can have psyches bent, bruised and embarrassed. But no girl is going to set foot on a Little League diamond and that's that.

Carolyn King is 12 years old and, given her choice, she doesn't feel that nature has preordained her to a recreational life of jacks and jump ropes.

She went out for and earned a place on a Little League team in Ypsilanti, Michigan. Somebody pulled out the Little League charter and found a clause barring girls from competition. The 10 coaches voted and it came up 8–2 in outfielder King's favor.

Yesterday, Bob Taylor, the Ypsilanti Little League Vice-President, was advised by telephone that Ypsilanti could play gorillas, iguanas and even girls if it chose to do so from here on in because the deep thinkers at national headquarters wouldn't have to deal with Ypsilanti as it was then constituted any more. Ypsilanti was being kicked out of the league.

"People," Taylor reported, "are being sent out here from national headquarters to organize a new franchise."

"Listen kid, they tell me you're pretty quick with the bat. Have a fresh slice of bubble gum, kid. That's O.K., there's plenty where that

209

*came from. Now listen, we got the old, established Little League, kid. I
mean a guy makes it. Well, he wants to make it against the best."*[1]

Discrimination shows its ugly face through varied expressions.
At its worst, discrimination attacks heart and soul, takes away all
or large chunks of freedom and rights, robs people of human dignity
and, in the end, enslaves them. In its milder form, discrimination is
an unintentional by-product of decision making. For example, a
famous restaurant in the French Quarter in New Orleans will not
take a reservation unless there are at least four persons in the party.
Parties with three or less persons are denied access to a service because of the decision of the restaurant to exclude or discriminate.
However, the decision of the restaurant to restrict reservations to
parties based on size was undoubtedly motivated not by the desire
to discriminate but by desire to use its facilities efficiently. Also,
this form of discrimination leaves open access to the restaurant to
everyone in a party of four or more.

WHAT IS DISCRIMINATION?

The Public View

Most people relate discrimination to what they consider to be
unfair treatment of some sort. Discrimination is viewed as the opposite of social justice. A person who is discriminated against is one
who is treated unjustly.

There is nothing wrong in relating discrimination to unfair
treatment. The shortcoming of this view is that it does not go far
enough. It leaves unanswered the vital question: What is unfair
treatment?

The Dictionary Definition

Webster's dictionary defines discrimination as the act of discriminating—"to make a difference in treatment or favor on a
basis other than individual merit." Accordingly, discrimination
does not enter into human behavior unless a person is treated differ-

---

[1] Jerry Izenberg, "Little League Faces a Major Crisis in Ypsilanti," *The Daily
Oklahoman*, May 10, 1973, p. 64.

ently on grounds other than individual merit, such as the grounds of religion, race, sex, income, speech, appearance, social position, and so on. Differences in treatment should reflect only differences in individual merit. Differences based on anything else introduce discrimination into the equation of human conduct.

A Working Definition

Discrimination as we use it means that equals are treated unequally or that unequals are treated equally. More specifically, discrimination exists in a labor market when persons with equal productivity are paid different wages or persons with differences in productivity are paid equal wages. Discrimination exists in the product market when consumers pay different prices for the same product.

Market discrimination exists, then, when the terms on which market transactions are based are not the same for all persons. A seller who charges different prices to different consumers for essentially the same product or service is practicing price discrimination. A buyer who pays different wages for identical units of labor provides another illustration. Sellers who cannot sell in a certain market and buyers who cannot buy in a certain market for reasons other than price provide examples of complete market discrimination.

ECONOMIC ANALYSIS OF DISCRIMINATION

Sources of Market Discrimination

Market discrimination may be traced to two primary sources. These are the power to discriminate in the market and the desire to discriminate.

Monopoly Power. Monopoly power may exist on the selling and buying sides of markets. In Chapter 2 we defined a monopolistic market as one in which the seller is able to manipulate the product price to his own advantage and can keep potential competitors out of the market. A monopsonistic market was defined as a market in which the buyer is able to control resource prices. This *monopoly* control over price and impediments to entry in markets which are not competitive makes it possible for consumers and workers to be *exploited.* Consumers are exploited when the price of a product is above the cost per unit of producing it, and workers are exploited when the wage rates paid are below their marginal productivity— below their contributions to the receipts of their employer.

Exploitation may exist without discrimination. For example, both blacks and whites with the same productivity may be paid equal wages that are below their productivity. However, monopoly power is a source of discrimination. In the exercise of monopoly power, a seller may segregate the market and charge consumers different prices for the same product. A monopsonistic buyer may segregate the job market and practice discrimination by paying workers on bases other than merit or productivity.

Taste for Discrimination. Some people have a taste for discrimination and strive to satisfy this taste or desire. An employer has a taste for discrimination when he acts as if nonmoney costs were connected with hiring women, blacks, Chicanos, Indians, or Puerto Ricans.[2] The result is that resources are allocated on bases other than productivity, and the incomes of minority groups are reduced.

Kinds of Market Discrimination

There are different kinds of market discrimination. The major ones are wage, employment, occupation, and price discrimination.

Wage Discrimination. The U.S. Census Bureau reported that in 1971 the average household income of males ($11,832) was over twice that of females ($5,294).[3] Is this evidence of wage discrimination by sex? Differences in wages and incomes of males and females may arouse the suspicion that discrimination exists, but they are not by themselves evidence that discrimination does exist in fact. Wage and income differences among people may reflect differences in productivity. Wage differences between males and females would indicate discrimination, then, only if both sexes were contributing the same to the receipts of their employers.

---

[2] Douglass C. North and Roger Leroy Miller, *The Economics of Public Issues* (New York: Harper & Row, Publishers, 1971), p. 136.

[3] U.S. Bureau of the Census, *Consumer Income,* Current Population Reports, Series P–60, No. 83 (July 1972), p. 7.

The meaning of wage discrimination can be elucidated further by the slogan "equal pay for equal work." Suppose a male and female complete their Ph.D. degrees at the same time and place, have identical records and recommendations, are hired by the same university to teach speech, and differ in only one respect—the male is paid $14,000 a year and the female is paid $12,000 a year to teach. This is a case of discrimination. Two workers have the same productivity but are paid unequal wages.

It is often difficult to be sure that wage discrimination exists because the person who discriminates may deny it, and the relative productivities of labor may be difficult to measure. A discriminator may say that qualified blacks cannot be found or that females are paid less than males because their productivity is less. In some instances, the discriminator may be right; in others, he may only be trying to hide his discriminatory behavior.

The meaning of wage discrimination is clear enough—unequal pay for equal contributions. But the proving of discrimination depends upon being able to distinguish among individuals on the basis of individual efforts and productivity. Generally speaking, human resources, like any other resources, are paid approximately what they are worth in a competitive economy. Thus, wage differences where competition exists reflect differences in labor productivity. Wage discrimination that does exist in the economy means that the market is not working perfectly in allocating resources among alternative uses.

Employment Discrimination. Employment discrimination means that some persons are not hired because of noneconomic characteristics such as race or sex. Two persons with the same training, education, and experience apply for a job. One is black and one is white. If both do not have the same chance of getting the job, discrimination has entered into the decision-making process.

Employment discrimination, like wage discrimination, is difficult to identify positively. Differences in unemployment rates among whites and minority groups and between males and females may suggest discrimination but do not prove that it exists. However, when you consider all low-productivity families and discover that unemployment rates are much higher among blacks than whites, or when you look at families with identical education levels and find unemployment rates higher among black families than white fami-

ilies, the evidence of employment discrimination becomes more conclusive.

Occupation Discrimination. There is a growing belief that discriminatory differences in pay, especially sex differences in pay,
occur largely because of occupational segregation. In general, men
work in occupations that employ very few women, and women
work in occupations that employ very few men. Barbara Bergman
points out that the economic results of occupational segregation
for women are low wages.[4] She observes that women are relegated
to occupations where productivity and experience have little to do
with their status as they advance in age.[5] Another study confirms the
concentration of women in low-paying occupations and points out
further that women are found in occupations where opportunities
for overtime and premium pay are limited.[6]

Why do women fail to enter the high-paid occupations? Male
prejudice has been an important factor, but in some cases women
have imposed discrimination upon themselves along occupational
lines. Women are usually taught early in life to believe that their
economic role will be unimportant. "They are socialized to expect
that they will spend their lives as housewives and mothers—for
toys they are given the tools of their trade: dolls, tea sets, frilly
dresses, and so on."[7] Until women begin to think in terms of careers,
prepare themselves for them, and break completely away from self-
imposed economic exile, the male-female pay gap is likely to remain
sizable.

The women's liberation movement has probably had little impact thus far in changing the distribution of women among occupations. Clare Boothe Luce entitled her article in the *1973 Britannica
Book of the Year,* "Woman: A Technological Castaway." She states
that men make all important decisions and there are not 100 women
who occupy critical policy-making positions. "The only institution

4 Barbara R. Bergman, "The Economics of Women's Liberation," *Challenge,*
May–June 1973, p. 12.

5 Ibid.

6 Mary Hamblin and Michael Prell, "The Incomes of Men and Women: Why Do
They Differ?" *Monthly Review,* Federal Reserve Bank of Kansas City, April 1973,
p. 10.

7 Marilyn Power Goldberg, "The Exploitation of Women," in David Mermelstein
(ed.), *Economics: Mainstream Readings and Radical Critiques,* 2d ed. (New York:
Random House, 1973), p. 52.

in which women appear in equal numbers with men is our institution of monogamous marriage."[8]

Price Discrimination. A shopping study in New York City revealed that an Admiral 19-inch screen, portable television set varied in price from $179 to $200 on the lower east side and that an identical set was sold in a downtown discount house for $139. Three different prices were quoted for a set by one lower east side store—$125 for a white law student, $139 to a Puerto Rican housewife, and $200 to a black housewife.[9] Is this evidence that the lower east side consumers are discriminated against?

The price differential for the identical TV set between the lower east side store and the downtown discount store does not by itself indicate price discrimination. The price difference between the lower east side store and downtown discount store may reflect costs differences. The former may have higher costs in the form of higher insurance rates, higher bad-debt rates, higher theft rates. It may be an inefficient supplier of TV sets.

There is evidence of price discrimination on the part of the lower east side store because different prices were quoted to different customers for the same set. Even here more information is needed about the payment record of each customer. We have defined price discrimination as charging different prices to different consumers for the same product or service. We need to qualify this definition of price discrimination. We must add the assumption that costs in the form of risks of payment are constant or do not account for the differences in price.

Price discrimination may take the form of preventing a person, because of race, from having access to a given market. The housing market has been mentioned in this regard. Another illustration is the refusal to allow blacks equal access to the capital or credit markets. The purchase of real capital—equipment, machinery, buildings, etc.—is usually financed from borrowed money. The complete or partial barring of blacks from the credit market may result in low ratios of capital to labor for blacks and, consequently, low produc-

---

[8] Elsie Shoemaker, "Famous Woman Has Full View of Liberation Movement," *Stillwater (Oklahoma) News Press*, April 4, 1973, p. 28.

[9] Warren G. Magnuson and Jean Carper, *The Dark Side of the Market Place* (Englewood Cliffs, N.J.: Prentice-Hall, 1972), p. 37.

tivity. Their production efforts are thus limited to products and services where high ratios of labor to capital are required.

Economic Costs of Discrimination

The economic costs of discrimination are both individual and social in nature. The individual costs of discrimination are those imposed on individuals or groups who lose one way or another because of discrimination. The social cost of discrimination is in the form of a reduction in total output in the economy due to discimination.

Individual Losses and Gains. Individual losses and gains flow from discrimination. Individuals discriminated against, or the discriminatees, suffer losses in the form of reduced living standards. They tend to be paid less for what they sell, to pay higher prices for what they buy, to have fewer employment opportunities, and to be segregated in low-paying occupations. Individuals who discriminate, the discriminators, may gain and may lose. An employer-discriminator may gain if a female worker can be hired at a lower wage than a male worker, assuming both are equally productive. The wages of whites may be kept artificially above blacks if blacks are shut off from jobs and occupations because of race. Discriminators, however, may lose by having to forfeit income in order to satisfy their taste for discrimination. For example, an individual who refuses to sell a house to a black may end up selling the house at a lower price to a white. Or, an individual who refuses to hire a woman may end up paying a higher price for a male with the same productivity.

Output Reduction. We have said that the cost to society of discrimination is the reduction in the nation's output of goods and services resulting from discrimination. In the *Economic Report of the President,* the President's Council of Economic Advisors estimated in 1966 that if the unemployment rate and average productivity of blacks were equal to those of whites, total production in our economy would expand by $27 billion.[10] Lester Thurow argues that discrimination causes a large reduction in the potential level of output of the American economy and that losses

---

[10] *Economic Report of the President, 1966,* p. 10.

caused by discrimination against blacks amount to approximately
$19 billion per year.[11] Add to this discrimination against females,
Chicanos, Puerto Ricans, and Indians, and you have a huge annual
loss of goods and services to the American society.

Discrimination causes losses of goods and services to society because it results in unnecessarily low levels of economic efficiency.
Without discrimination, resources would tend to be allocated on
the basis of their productivities. Units of any given resource would
tend to be used where their productivity is the greatest.

The production possibilities curve shown in Figure 8–1 illus-

FIGURE 8–1
Production Possibilities with and without Discrimination

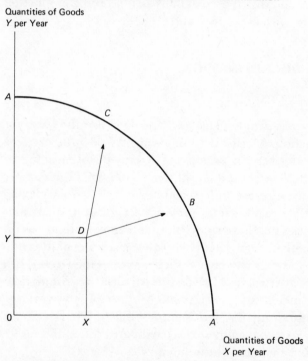

Point D = combination of X and Y with discrimination.
Points B and C = combination of X and Y without
   discrimination.
Line AA = production possibilities curve.

11 Lester C. Thurow, *Poverty and Discrimination* (Washington, D.C.: Brookings
Institution, 1969), p. 158.

trates the impact of discrimination on production of goods and services in the economy. Point D represents the combination of goods X and Y produced in the economy when discrimination exists, with its resultant inefficiency. Without discrimination, the quantities of goods X and Y may be expanded to points like B and C.

Discrimination prevents the efficient use of resources, causing the combination of goods and services that is produced to lie below the production possibilities curve. The elimination of discrimination makes possible the production of those combinations of goods and services that lie on the curve. The social cost of discrimination is equal to the difference between the gross national product represented at point D and that represented by points on the production possibilities curve, such as points B and C.

NONMARKET DISCRIMINATION

Social Discrimination

Social tastes and attitudes, customs, and laws are the bases for social discrimination. Social discrimination may take the extreme form of preventing certain persons or groups from engaging in social interaction. The direct quote at the beginning of this chapter concerning a Little League rule that prevents girls from playing baseball in Little League games provides an illustration. Fraternities and sororities that have rules limiting membership to certain races provide another. Segregated schools are examples of discrimination based on customs and laws. Societies such as the Deep South and South Africa are structured along lines of social discrimination. Under these arrangements, discrimination by race is a way of life, sanctioned by custom and frequently enforceable by law. Deviations from the legal segregated manner of behavior are crimes, and severe punishment may be handed out to offenders.

Social discrimination is difficult to root out, since it is based on deep-seated beliefs and customs often supported by law. In contrast to market discrimination, it is difficult to associate monetary costs with social discrimination. Persons who may with joy vote to keep certain persons from joining their country club often with the same joy sell products to them in the market. Although the source of much market discrimination is social discrimination, the self-interest motive in the market tends to overcome and reduce the effectiveness of discrimination in the marketplace.

Educational Discrimination

It is generally believed that if everyone had equal access and opportunity to training and education, many of the major issues in our society, such as poverty and extreme income inequality, would be significantly alleviated, perhaps even eliminated. Unfortunately, however, inequality and discrimination exist in our public school system.[12]

A great deal of the inequality in public education is due to the way it is financed. The public school system is a highly decentralized system composed of thousands of school districts charged with the responsibilities of providing education. School districts pay for education with revenues from the local property tax and grants-in-aid, primarily from the state. Variations in the market value of property give rise to variations in per pupil expenditures on education within a given state and among states. A poor district (one with low property values) within a state and a poor state will have low per pupil expenditures and may have high property tax rates. This regional and state inequality in the allocation of resources for the purpose of public education has led to court decisions opposing the way public education is financed. In the meantime, however, resources are unequally distributed and the rich receive better education than the poor.

Discrimination in the public school system is indicated by the allocation of experienced and highly paid teachers.[13] The worst teachers, the least experienced and the lowest paid, are concentrated in the ghettos. Also, there is a regional bias to discrimination. Effective discrimination in public schools is more evident in the South; in some cases it reaches complete segregation, "with all black stu-

---

[12] John D. Owen, "Inequality and Discrimination in the Public School System," in David Mermelstein and Robert Lekachman (eds.), *Economics: Mainstream Readings and Radical Critiques* (New York: Random House, 1970), pp. 137–44.

[13] Ibid., p. 141.

dents taught by black teachers and all white students taught by white teachers."[14]

WHAT CAN BE DONE ABOUT DISCRIMINATION

Markets and humans are not perfect. Perfection may be beyond reach. However, movements in the direction of perfection are possible. What courses of action can be taken to move in the right direction? What policy implications can be drawn from our analysis?

Reduce Tastes for Discrimination

If discrimination resulting from tastes is to be reduced, people must be persuaded that they should alter their views and behavior. Tastes for discrimination may be reduced by education, by legislation, and by the use of government subsidies to discourage discrimination.

Education. A task of education is to teach people to understand one another and to be unprejudiced. Unfortunately, this task of education is hampered by discrimination in education itself, especially in regard to the allocation of resources for primary and secondary education. Although not a panacea, a more equal distribution of resources for public education would reduce inequality in per pupil educational services, and it could contribute toward reducing tastes for discrimination.

Legislation. It is difficult to change the tastes of people by coercion, that is, by passing laws. Laws are usually effective only when they are supported by or coincide with people's beliefs. However, the framework for reducing tastes for discrimination can be established by laws. The Civil Rights acts of 1964 and 1965 make certain acts of discrimination illegal. They provide the legal basis for protecting the rights of people who may be treated harmfully— for example, denied employment or opportunities for advancement because of race, sex, or religion. These laws have reduced discrimination by imposing greater risks and higher costs on discriminators. A persons who satisfies a taste for discrimination by

---

14 Ibid., p. 144.

refusing to sell a house to a black breaks the law and risks prosecution.

Government Subsidies. If the sole goal is to eliminate discrimination, government subsidy payments may be used to encourage employers not to discriminate. Subsidy payments would be made to employers who do not practice discrimination in hiring, wages, and promotions. Employers who discriminate would be sacrificing subsidy payments. Thus an incentive is provided not to discriminate. The alternative cost of discrimination is equal to the subsidy payment. Government subsidy payments will reduce discrimination if the subsidy payments are equal to or greater than the nonmonetary gain the discriminator receives from discrimination.

Reduce Market Imperfections

Market defects such as scarce labor market information, imperfect competition, and immobility of labor constitute a major source of market discrimination. Some people receive low wages, that is, wages below what they could earn in alternative employments, because they are unaware of other job openings. Improved job information would make it less necessary for one to receive income below what he would be paid on a similar job.

The market for goods and the market for resources may not work well at all if there is little competition in these markets. In imperfect markets, discrimination may be prevalent. A seller or a buyer has control over the price of what he sells or buys in highly monopolized markets. Other potential sellers or buyers are shut out of the market. Price, wage, employment, and occupational discrimination may remain unchallenged in the absence of competitive forces and in the presence of monopolistic controls. Antitrust action to strengthen competition and reduce barriers to entry into markets would be an important way to eliminate or at least lessen discriminatory market behavior.

The government has an important role to play in the elimination of discrimination when it is due to the use of monopoly power. First, it is the responsibility of the government to reduce monopoly power and restore competition in markets where competition is lacking through the vigorous use of antimonopoly laws. Second, a great deal of monopoly power is derived from and granted by government.

Thurow notes that "The institutions of government are an important link in implementing discrimination. Either directly through
legal restrictions or indirectly through harassment and expenditure
decisions, the coercive power of the white community flows through
local, state, and federal government institutions."[15]

Reduce Discrimination in Development of Human Capital

Investment in human capital, that is, spending on education,
training, and health, provides a high rate of return in the form of
increased productivity and income. Blacks and other minority
groups generally do not and cannot invest enough in human capital,
and public investment in human capital is unequally distributed.
The elimination of human capital discrimination would tend to
make most forms of market discrimination, such as wage and employment discrimination, less effective. The reason for this is that
it is difficult to treat human resources unequally if they are productive and have access to other jobs. Thurow, who believes human
capital investment holds the key to nondiscrimination, states, "Attacking human capital discrimination will not raise Negro incomes
by itself, since wage, employment, and occupational discrimination
would also have to be eliminated, but eliminating human capital
discrimination would make the enforcement of these other types
difficult in the absence of government discrimination."[16]

Reduce Occupational Segregation

Women, blacks, and other minority groups have been pushed
into low-wage occupations. The effect of segregation by occupations
is twofold. First, the supply of labor is increased in those occupations restricted to minority groups, depressing wages in those
occupations. Second, the supply of labor is decreased in those occupations closed off to minority groups, thus increasing wages in those
occupations. The result of these effects is to create a wider gap between low and high wage occupations.[17]

---

15 Thurow, *Poverty and Discrimination,* p. 158.

16 Ibid., p. 138.

17 Daniel R. Fusfeld, *The Basic Economics of the Urban Racial Crisis* (New York:
Holt, Rinehart & Winston, 1973), pp. 64–68.

In addition, if a member of the minority group crosses over into segregated occupations usually closed to members of the group, he or she has typically not received equal pay for equal work. For example, a black male with a Ph.D. in chemistry who works as a research chemist for an oil company may be discriminated against in wages and opportunities for advancement because he has a position typically reserved for whites. In recent years this situation has been reversed in many cases by the Equal Opportunities Act. Employers are virtually required to bid for minority group personnel. The small supplies available of these workers who are qualified assure they will receive salaries *above* those of white employees.

However, segregation by occupations would be difficult to maintain if minority groups were relatively well educated and well trained. Education and training open up job opportunities. Those who have job opportunities cannot easily be forced into designated occupations; they are mobile and can cut across occupations. Providing improved job opportunities for minority groups is one way to break up segregation by occupations.

SUMMARY

Market discrimination means that people with the same economic characteristics are not treated equally. For example, workers who have the same productivity receive different wages, and consumers are charged different prices for the same product.

Discrimination comes from two sources—market and human imperfections. Market imperfections are due to imperfect knowledge, immobility of resources, and imperfect competition. Human imperfections are revealed in the tastes and preferences that some people have for discrimination. Market discrimination exists in the form of wage, employment, occupation, and price discrimination.

Discrimination is costly both to individuals and to society. There are individual welfare gains and losses from discrimination. It is difficult to say who gains and who loses. Sometimes the discriminator can lose. It is certain that there is a loss to society from discrimination, in the form of a reduction in output.

The economic analysis of market discrimination stresses two related points: (1) the observed differences in wages and prices may reflect differences in productivity and (2) market discrimination exists only to the extent that wage and price differences cannot be explained on the basis of productivity. Competitive markets tend to minimize the extent and degree of discrimination. Occupational segregation explains to a large extent differences in wages and income, and social discrimination, especially in the field of public education, is the source of much inequality.

Several policy conclusions may be drawn from our analysis. One, tastes for discrimination have to be reduced. This can be done by changing the tastes of people concerning discrimination through education, preventing by law the fulfillment of tastes for discrimination, and encouraging people not to discriminate by the payment of subsidies to employers who refrain from discriminating. Two, the source of exploitation and much discrimination—the exercise of monopoly power—has to be reduced. The way to reduce the use of monopoly power is to reduce that power itself through vigorous antimonopoly laws. A great deal of market discrimination is primarily due to human capital discrimination. If there were no discrimination in regard to investment in human capital (education, training, and health), segregation by occupations would be dealt a serious blow. It is difficult to discriminate in the market against people who are productive and have job choices.

SUPPLEMENTARY READINGS

Fusfeld, Daniel R. *The Basic Economics of the Urban Racial Crisis.* New York: Holt, Rinehart & Winston, 1973.

Presents an economic theory of discrimination that is different from the two theories presented in this chapter: the crowding theory. This theory holds that minority groups are forced into menial occupations, which causes an increase in the supply of labor and a decrease in wage rates for these occupations. Chapter 5 is the relevant one.

Magnuson, Warren G., and Carper, Jean. *The Dark Side of the Market Place.* Englewood Cliffs, N.J.: Prentice-Hall, 1968.

Easy reading and personalized in style. Many illustrations of market imperfections are presented. There is a bibliography at the end of the book, but footnoting is not used.

Mermelstein, David (ed.). *Economics: Mainstream Readings and Radical Critiques.* 2d ed. New York: Random House, 1973.

Includes several good essays on discrimination, particularly "The Structure of Racial Discrimination," by Raymond Franklin and Solomon Resnick, and "The Economic Exploitation of Women," by Marilyn Power Goldberg.

Schiller, Bradley R. *The Economics of Poverty and Discrimination.* Englewood Cliffs, N.J.: Prentice-Hall, 1973.

Primarily treats the poverty problem, but Chapter 9 would be a good supplement to the section above on discrimination in education.

Thurow, Lester C. *Poverty and Discrimination.* Washington, D.C.: Brookings Institution, 1969.

Covers the economic theories of discrimination. In Chapter 7, various kinds of market discrimination are presented and analyzed.

Part III

STABILIZATION

Chapter 9

UNEMPLOYMENT ISSUES

CHECKLIST OF ECONOMIC CONCEPTS

Potential GNP
GNP Gap
Involuntary Unemployment
Frictional Unemployment
Structural Unemployment
Cyclical Unemployment
Circular Flow of Production and Income
Leakages
Injections
Aggregate Demand
Aggregate Supply
Monetary Policy
Fiscal Policy

9

UNEMPLOYMENT ISSUES

Why Do We Waste Our Labor Resources?

I'd get up at five in the morning and head for the waterfront. Outside the Spreckles Sugar Refinery, outside the gates, there would be a thousand men. You know dang well there's only three or four jobs. The guy would come out with two little Pinkerton cops: "I need two guys for the bull gang. Two guys to go into the hole." A thousand men would fight like a pack of Alaskan dogs to get through there. Only four of us would get through. I was too young a punk.

So you'd drift up to Skid Row. There'd be thousands of men there. Guys on baskets, making weird speeches, phony theories on economics. About eleven-thirty, the real leaders would take over. They'd say: O.K., we're going to City Hall. The Mayor was Angelo Rossi, a dapper little guy. He wore expensive boots and a tight vest. We'd shout around the steps. Finally, he'd come out and tell us nothing.

I remember the demands: We demand work, we demand shelter for our families, we demand groceries, this kind of thing. . . .

I remember as a kid how courageous this seemed to me, the demands, because you knew that society wasn't going to give it to you. They'd demand that they open up unrented houses and give decent shelters for their families. But you just knew society wasn't yielding. There was nothing coming.[1]

---

[1] Studs Terkel, *Hard Times* (New York: Random House, Pantheon Books, 1970), p. 30.

SOME EFFECTS OF UNEMPLOYMENT

Both economic and social effects are associated with unemployment. The economic effects are related to the impact of unemployment on the nation's production of goods and services, that is, the GNP. The social effects of unemployment are more difficult to pin down and measure, but they are just as real as the economic effects.

Effects on GNP

Idle human resources represent a waste, a loss of goods and services, and, therefore, a loss of real income. Unemployed resources could have contributed to society's well-being; the economic value of this lost contribution of goods and services is the economic cost of unemployment. The difference, then, between what may be produced at full employment and what is produced at less than full employment measures the total cost of unemployment. In 1971 and 1972, the total or aggregate cost of unemployment, or, as shown in Figure 9–1, the gap between actual and potential GNP, was in excess of $50 billion.

Unemployment may affect not only current production of goods and services but also future production. During periods of unemployment, machines as well as men are idle. Capital goods, plant and equipment, become obsolete and are not replaced. The productivity of labor and the overall ability of the economy to produce in the future are reduced during periods of unemployment.

Effects on Social Relations

Unemployment threatens the stability of the family as an economic and social unit. Without income or with a loss of income, the head of the family cannot play the role in which he or she was cast. Family wants and needs are not fulfilled, and family relationships suffer as a consequence. Economic and social dependency and important family ties may be in jeopardy and may eventually be severed by prolonged unemployment.

Human relationships outside the family are also seriously affected by unemployment. An unemployed person loses his self-respect and

FIGURE 9-1
Actual GNP and Potential GNP

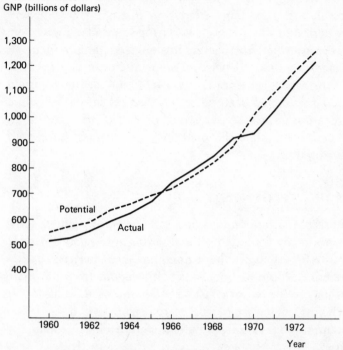

GNP (billions of dollars)

The potential GNP is what it would be if the economy were operating at full employment. The difference between potential GNP and actual GNP is called the GNP gap. The GNP gap can be estimated using the formula:

$$\text{GNP gap} = 3(U - .04)(\text{GNP}),$$

where U equals the actual unemployment rate, a *4 percent* unemployment rate is assumed to represent full employment, and GNP equals the actual GNP. Also, a change in the unemployment rate above or below 4 percent is assumed to be associated with a 3 percent change in the real GNP. After the GNP gap is calculated, potential GNP is equal to the actual GNP plus the GNP gap.

his influence among the employed. He may be rejected by his working companions and lose his pride and confidence. In the end, the unemployed may become spiritually disabled persons.

Although there may be a few families who are economically and socially prepared for unemployment, it tends to strike families who are least capable of withstanding either its economic or its so-

cial effects. Also, the incidence of unemployment, like family instability and crime, is high among low-income groups.

The social and economic effects of unemployment extend
beyond the period in which it occurs. During a period of high unemployment, consumption and savings are reduced, debt is incurred,
and, for many unemployed persons, home and auto loans may be
defaulted. Afterwards, when work is available and income is earned,
debts must be paid and savings replenished. It may take a long
period before the living standards that prevailed prior to the unemployed period can be reattained and even longer before self-
esteem is restored.

WHAT IS UNEMPLOYMENT?

It would seem that unemployment could be easily defined. However, there are many complexities and ramifications concerning its
meaning. The first thought about unemployment may be that the
unemployed are people without jobs. This may be true, but many
people without jobs are not considered unemployed. What about
a person who prefers leisure to work? Are persons over 65 to be considered unemployed? Is a college student included in the unemployment count?

Our approach to unemployment in this section is, first, to give a
general definition of unemployment, and, second, to elucidate the
meaning of *involuntary* unemployment—the unemployment that is
of major economic concern. The subsequent section probes deeper
into the meaning of unemployment.

General Definition

In general, unemployment may be defined as a situation in which
persons who are qualified for a job, willing to work, and willing to
accept the going wage rate cannot find jobs without considerable
delay. There are three important aspects to this definition.

First, a person has to be qualified for a job. A person is not in-
voluntarily unemployed if he seeks jobs which he is precluded from
obtaining because of a lack of training, experience, and education.
For example, he cannot be considered an unemployed truck driver
if he cannot drive a truck.

Second, a person is not considered unemployed if he is not seeking a job and willing to work at the market wage rate. Some may decide to withdraw their labor services because they prefer leisure to work at the market rate. These persons represent a type of unemployment, but not the kind that usually presents a problem.

Third, it may take time to find a job that a person is qualified for and is willing to accept at the going wage rate. However, the delay in finding a job should be of a short duration. The time delay should probably not extend beyond a 30- or 60-day period for most occupations. Some may believe that this time period is too long for people to be without jobs.

Involuntary Unemployment

The economic aspect of unemployment originates from a situation in which the quantity of labor demanded is less than the quantity supplied at the market wage rate. This results in involuntary unemployment. Involuntary unemployment occurs when wage rates are too high, that is, above competitive levels. The solution to involuntary unemployment is to expand demand or, if competitive forces are operating, to rely upon automatic market forces to drive wage rates down to the level at which the amount of labor demanded equals the amount supplied.

Figure 9–2 is shown to clarify the meaning of involuntary unemployment in a competitive economy. DD and SS are the demand and supply curves for labor. The wage rate is w_1. The amount of labor demanded at this wage rate is e_0, and the amount of labor supplied is e_1. The difference between e_0 and e_1 is equal to the distance AB, which is the excess of the amount of labor supplied over the amount of labor demanded. In a purely competitive situation, wage rates would be forced downward to w, and involuntary unemployment would disappear.

ANALYSIS OF THE UNEMPLOYMENT PROBLEM

Types of Unemployment

The meaning of unemployment may be elucidated further by distinguishing among different types of unemployment. Three major types are frictional, structural, and cylical unemployment.

FIGURE 9–2
Involuntary Unemployment in a Competitive Market

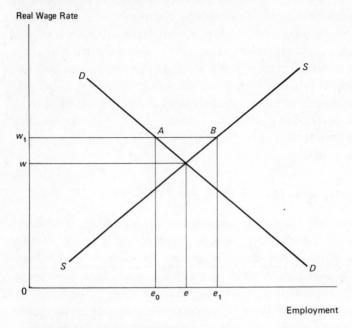

DD = Demand curve for labor.
SS = Supply curve for labor.
e_0 = Amount of labor demanded at w_1.
e_1 = Amount of labor supplied at w_1.
e_1 $- e_0$ = Involuntary unemployment.

Frictional Unemployment. Frictional unemployment is transitional or short run in nature. It usually originates on the labor supply side; that is, labor services are voluntarily not employed. A good illustration is the unemployment that occurs when people are changing jobs or searching for new jobs. The matching of job openings and job seekers does not always take place smoothly in the economy and, as a consequence, people are without work.

The important thing about frictional unemployment is that it does not last. Frictional unemployment may exist at all times in the economy, but for any one person or family it is transitional. Therefore, frictional unemployment is not considered a significant economic problem. It can be reduced by improvements in the flow of information concerning job openings.

Structural Unemployment. Structural unemployment is usually long run in nature and usually originates on the demand side of labor. Structural unemployment results from economic changes that cause the demand for specific kinds of labor to be low relative to its supply in particular markets and regions of the economy.

A relatively low demand for labor in a given market may be due to several factors. Technological change, although expected to reduce costs and expand the productive capacity of the overall economy, may have devastating effects in a particular market. Changes in consumer preferences for products expand production and employment in some areas but reduce them in others. Immobility of labor prolongs the period of unemployment which may have originated due to technological change and changes in consumers' tastes. A reduction in job opportunities should induce the unemployed to move, but immobility may prevent this from taking place.

Cyclical Unemployment. Unemployment caused by economic fluctuations is called cyclical unemployment. Cyclical unemployment is due to reductions in aggregate or total demand for goods and services in the overall economy. A decline in aggregate demand in the economy reduces total production and causes general unemployment throughout the economic system. Cyclical unemployment is usually the culprit when the unemployment rate goes above 4 percent.

Further Dimensions of the Unemployment Problem

The Unemployment Rate. The unemployment rate (UR) equals U/L, where U equals the number of persons included in the labor force who are unemployed and L equals the number of persons in the labor force. The unemployment rate underestimates the number of persons without work. Only those who are in the labor force are considered to be unemployed when they are without jobs. Those who have withdrawn from the labor force, that is, persons who are not actively seeking employment, are not included in the labor force.

Full employment is often defined for economic policy purposes in terms of a maximum acceptable unemployment rate. An unemployment rate of 4 percent has been arbitrarily used in recent years as the dividing rate to determine whether the economy is at full or less than full employment. Using this definition of full employment, the economy was operating at less than full employment in six of the ten years during the 1960s and in the first two years of the present decade. With a labor force of over 80 million people, a 4 percent unemployment rate means that between three and one-half million people are unemployed when the economy is said to be at full employment.

Who Are the Unemployed? Unemployment rates vary by age, sex, and color. The highest unemployment rates are among the young between the ages of 16 and 19 (Table 9–1). These rates of

TABLE 9–1
Unemployment Rates By Sex, Age and Color, 1960–72 (percent)

Year	All Workers	Both Sexes, 16–19 Years	Men 20 Years and Over	Women 20 Years and Over	White	Negro and Other Races
1960	5.5	14.7	4.7	5.1	4.9	10.2
1961	6.7	16.8	5.7	6.3	6.0	12.4
1962	5.5	14.7	4.6	5.4	4.9	10.9
1963	5.7	17.2	4.5	5.4	5.0	10.8
1964	5.2	16.2	3.9	5.2	4.6	9.6
1965	4.5	14.8	3.2	4.5	4.1	8.1
1966	3.8	12.8	2.5	3.8	3.4	7.3
1967	3.8	12.8	2.3	4.2	3.4	7.4
1968	3.6	12.7	2.2	3.8	3.2	6.7
1969	3.5	12.2	2.1	3.7	3.1	6.4
1970	4.9	15.2	3.5	4.8	4.5	8.2
1971	5.9	16.9	4.4	5.7	5.4	9.9
1972	5.6	16.2	4.0	5.4	5.0	10.0

Source: *Economic Report of the President, 1973,* p. 223.

unemployment are usually three times higher than the rates among all workers. For example, in 1970 the overall unemployment rate was 4.9 percent, as compared to 15.2 percent among young people. Men 20 years and older have an unemployment rate lower than women in the same age bracket. Also, the unemployment rate among whites is usually half the unemployment rate among blacks.

The overall unemployment rate does not reflect, of course, this wide variation in unemployment rates among people of different age and socioeconomic backgrounds. The unemployment rate was 3.5 percent in 1969. Yet, in the same year 12.2 percent of the young people in the labor force and 6.4 percent of nonwhites were unemployed. A full-employment economy, as defined by a 4 percent unemployment rate, fails to provide ample job opportunities to all groups.

WHAT CAUSES PEOPLE TO LOSE THEIR JOBS?

People lose their jobs in a recession when production in the economy is falling. But what causes the recession? What causes a decline in production? Economists have searched for a single answer and have found many—not enough spending, too much saving, wages too high, and so forth. Thus the answer is neither simple nor single. There are many contributing causes; we shall try to explain those that seem to be the most important.

Circular Flow of Economic Activity

To understand why people lose their jobs it is necessary to understand how jobs are created. This is not difficult in terms of the forces of supply and demand pertaining to products in individual markets. We have established an understanding of equilibrium prices and quantities for individual commodities like wheat, automobiles, dresses, television, ice cream, necklaces, and all other commodities produced in our economy—and demanded. We will move now from demand and supply curves for individual products to a demand and supply curve representing all commodities. This will be done by presenting an overview of the operation of the economy which economists call the *circular flow of economic activity*.

The circular flow is illustrated in Figure 9–3. The relationships it shows are important in understanding the operation of the economy. (Look at this figure and study it carefully.)

Income and jobs are created in a society when goods and services are produced. Owners of resources—labor, capital, and natural resources—sell their productive services to producers who, in turn, pay them money in the form of wages, interest, rent, and profits. The flow of productive services to producers represents the supply of resources, and the flow of money payments from producers represents the demand for resources. Producers transform productive services or resources into goods and services through the production

FIGURE 9–3
Flow of Production and Income in a Stationary Economy

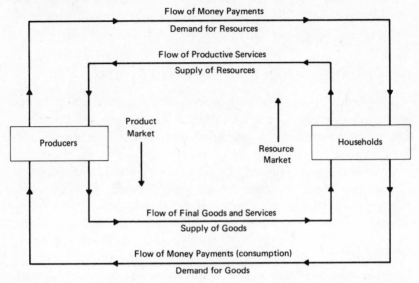

process and sell the goods and services to households. They receive
a flow of money payments from households in exchange. The flow
from producers to households represents the aggregate supply of
goods and services, and the flow of money payments from households to producers represents the aggregate demand for them.

There are several points to remember about the circular flow.
First, there are two markets—a resource market and a goods market.
The prices of resources and employment are determined in the
resource market, and the prices of goods and production are determined in the goods market. Second, the resource and goods
markets are interrelated. The demand for goods creates a demand
for the resources that are used to produce goods. The costs of producing goods depend upon the prices paid and the quantities of
resources used in production. Third, there are two circular flows
involved in the economy—a real flow of productive services (labor,
capital, and natural resources) and goods (autos, dresses, medical
services, etc.), and a flow of money payments to owners of resources
for productive services and to producers for goods and services.
Fourth, real income is determined by the physical goods and ser-

vices produced, and money income is the money value of the physical goods and services produced.

The circular flow of economic activity shows in a simple way how the overall economy operates. It emphasizes the interdependency of economic variables—the dependency of income on production, production on spending, spending on income, demand for resources on the demand for products, and so on. Now we shall turn to the products market in order to find possible reasons why people lose their jobs.

Aggregate Demand

Aggregate demand is a schedule showing output demanded in the economy at different prices. Since we are concerned with the prices of all goods and services, we must view prices as an average, or as a price level. Since we are also concerned with the quantities of all goods and services, we must view the quantities demanded as composite units of goods and services—each unit composed of shirts, tables, food, fuel, and the other items that comprise the real output of the economy.

Aggregate demand is illustrated in Figure 9–4. At the price level p_1, 200 units of goods and services are demanded; at the price level p, output demanded is 400 units, and so on. The output demanded of goods at any price level is the summation of the outputs of goods and services purchased by *consumers,* such as shoes and steaks, the outputs purchased by *investors,* such as new plant and equipment, and the outputs purchased by *government,* such as highways and recreational services. A change in the output demanded at a given price level by these groups—consumers, investors, and government —will change aggregate demand. For example, if consumers begin to buy greater quantities of consumer goods at all prices than they did previously, aggregate demand will increase—shift to the right, indicating that greater outputs are demanded at all prices.

The distinction between a change in demand and movement along a given demand curve is as important to remember in reference to aggregate demand as it is in the case of an individual demand curve. In a movement along the aggregate-demand curve, output demanded is inversely related to the price level—at a low price level output demanded is greater than it is at a high price level. This is

FIGURE 9–4
Aggregate Demand

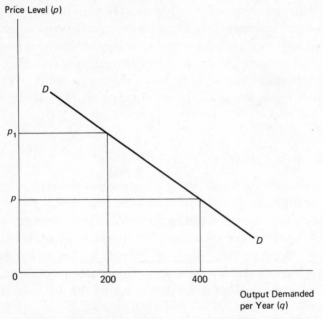

Price Level (p)

p_1

p

0   200   400

Output Demanded
per Year (q)

DD is an aggregate-demand schedule which shows the output
demanded at different price levels. For example, at price level p_1,
200 units of goods and services are demanded.

the principle of demand. A change in aggregate demand refers to a
shift in the entire aggregate-demand curve.

This discussion of aggregate demand leads to the question of why
people lose their jobs. Suppose aggregate demand becomes deficient;
that is, total spending in the economy has become too low to buy all
the goods and services that have been produced at the current price
level. The effect of this on jobs can be seen most easily in an individual market. Toward the end of 1973 automobile manufacturers
were having trouble selling all the cars they were producing—
especially the big ones. As the energy crisis hit, demand for automobiles with poor gasoline mileage decreased. Consumers no
longer desired the gas eaters that Detroit produced. Simultane-
ously, surpluses occurred in the recreation vehicle industry, the steel
industry, and many other industries throughout the economy.
People lost their jobs because of those surpluses—at the current

price level, quantity demanded was less than quantity supplied, so production levels were decreased.

Once a surplus appears in a market—watch out! It does not always spread to other markets, but it can. Every job loss is a loss in someone's income and results in a cut in spending for many products. General surpluses in the economy lead to losses of many jobs, reducing national income.

Aggregate Supply

Aggregate supply is a schedule showing the output supplied at different prices. In discussing the role of aggregate supply in the unemployment picture, we shall consider prices as a price level and quantities in terms of composite units of goods and services.

Unemployment is closely linked to aggregate supply. New jobs are created when the level of goods and services produced expands, and existing jobs are destroyed when it contracts. Producers hire more people to produce goods and services when profits increase. When profits decrease and losses are incurred, production is cut and jobs are lost.

To illustrate what causes changes in profits and losses, we shall use the resource of labor to see how a change in labor costs affects profits and hence aggregate supply. In general, labor is paid what it is worth to the employer. Now, if the contribution of a unit of labor to the receipts of employers does not change, higher wages will lead to a decrease in profits and a decrease in aggregate supply. By the same reasoning, if wages stay the same and workers begin to contribute more to the receipts of employers, profits increase and aggregate supply increases.

The relationship between wages, profits, and prices is complex. It may be helpful to remember that producers are trying to make money, and therefore they will tend to produce more at higher prices and less at lower prices. They will also produce more if costs are lower and less if costs are higher.

Aggregate Demand and Supply

Employment and job opportunities depend upon both aggregate demand and aggregate supply. Figure 9–5 shows aggregate supply,

FIGURE 9–5
Unemployment Equilibrium and Full Employment Output

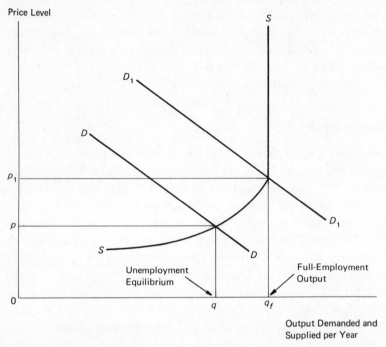

Unemployment equilibrium is an output level (q) where output demanded and output supplied are equal at less than the full-employment output (q_f). Full-employment output is the output level where production in the economy is at its maximum and cyclical unemployment is zero.

SS, and two aggregate demands, *DD* and D_1D_1. Given *DD* and *SS,* output demanded and output supplied are equal at an output of *q* and at a price level of *p.* The price level, *p,* and the output, *q,* are the equilibrium levels of price and output. Can aggregate demand be deficient at an equilibrium price and output?

Full-employment output is represented by q_f in Figure 9–5. This is the output where production is at its maximum and cyclical unemployment is zero. You can see that aggregate demand, *DD,* is deficient. A deficient aggregate demand in this instance means that at the equilibrium price level, output demanded falls short of the full-employment output.

Now look what happens when aggregate demand increases to

D_1D_1. The price level increases to p_1, and the output demanded and output supplied are equal at the full-employment output. People who were thrown out of work when aggregate demand was deficient now have jobs at D_1. At the higher price level p_1 it is profitable to produce more goods and services, and output supplied increases to the full-employment output, q_f.

What would happen if aggregate demand increased to D_1D_1 but the price level were not permitted to rise because of government controls? There would be no incentive for producers to increase output supplied. Output supplied would stay at q_1 and shortages would appear. People would remain out of work because at the controlled price level it would not be profitable to employ more labor.

Reasons for Deficient Aggregate Demand

We have said that producers may not produce an output that represents full employment because it may not be profitable to do so. But aggregate demand may fail to provide full employment, for a number of reasons.

Saving and Investment. The circular flow of economic activity shows that income is created in the process of production, and income created in production may return to producers in the form of spending for the products produced. However, there may be breaks in the circular flow. These breaks are called *leakages* and *injections*. Figure 9–6 shows the leakages and injections in the circular flow of economic activity.

Leakages, or withdrawals from the flow of economic activity, may be offset by *injections,* or additions to the flow of economic activity. An example of a leakage is *saving,* and an example of an injection is *investment*. Saving means that people are not spending part of the income created in production on the purchase of consumer goods such as radios, apples, cigarettes, ties, or refrigerators. This may turn out all right. Saving is required for the economy to invest in new plant and equipment and to grow. If the rate of saving at full employment returns to the circular flow of economic activity through investment (that is, the purchase of investment goods such as plant and equipment), aggregate demand will be sufficient to buy all of goods and services produced. If full-employment saving is

FIGURE 9–6
Breaks in the Circular Flow of Economic Activity: Leakages and Injections

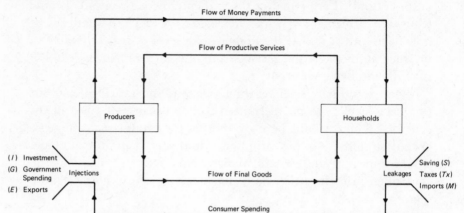

greater than full- employment investment, then aggregate demand will be deficient unless other injections into the circular flow happen to be greater than other leakages by the amount of difference between saving and investment. When aggregate demand is deficient, part of the income created by production does not return to producers in the form of spending. This results in surpluses at current market prices and employment levels. Producers respond to a surplus market situation by reducing production (and, therefore, income), which causes people to lose their jobs.

Taxes and Government Purchases. Another example of a leakage is government *taxes,* and the corresponding example of an injection is *government purchases.* Taxes are similar to saving in the sense that they represent a withdrawal from the circular flow of economic activity. Taxes reduce private spending and, therefore, reduce aggregate demand. Government purchases of goods and services increase aggregate demand. Aggregate demand may be deficient because taxes are too high in relation to government purchases.

Imports and Exports. Do you know why we have been so concerned about the *deficit* in the U.S. international balance of payments? A deficit in international trade means we are buying more products and services from other countries than they are buying from us. An *import* is a leakage from the circular flow of economic activity, and an *export* is an injection. A deficit, an excess of imports and exports, tends to decrease aggregate demand and contributes to the difficulty of reaching the level of aggregate demand required for full employment.

Summary. Aggregate demand may be deficient for a number of reasons. The cause may be that saving is greater than investment, taxes are greater than government purchases, and so on. There are more questions we could ask, such as: Why do people save? What determines investment? But the temptation will be resisted because we might begin to lose sight of the major issue—the wastes of unemployment.

COMBATING UNEMPLOYMENT

The type of unemployment must be identified before policies can be designed to cope with it. Among the three types of unemployment—frictional, cyclical, and structural—the first does not present a serious problem because of its transitional nature. Cyclical and structural unemployment do present problems, and policies must be designed to deal with them.

Cyclical Unemploymnt

Government Fiscal Policy. Cyclical unemployment, which is unemployment caused by a deficiency in aggregate demand for goods and services, may be controlled by the appropriate use of government fiscal policy in its tax-expenditure policy. An increase in government spending relative to tax collections will increase total spending in the economy. The relative increase in government spending may be in the form of an increase in the level of government spending, holding tax rates constant, or in the form of a decrease in tax rates, holding government spending constant. In the former case, aggregate demand increases primarily due to an increase in government demand, and in the latter the increase in aggregate demand is due primarily to the increase in private demand made possible by tax cuts. In both cases, a relative rise in government spending and a relative decline in tax collections, aggregate demand is stimulated and cyclical unemployment is reduced.

Federal Reserve Monetary Policy. Aggregate demand for goods and services is influenced by changes in the growth of the money supply. An increase in the money supply tends to increase aggregate demand, and a decrease in supply tends to decrease demand. The money supply is controlled largely by Federal Reserve monetary policy. The Federal Reserve System and the tools used to control the money supply are covered in the following chapter. However, it is important to indicate here that Federal Reserve monetary policy may play an independent or positive role in stimulating aggregate demand. It must play at least an accommodating role if government fiscal policy, such as an increase in government spending, is to have its maximum effect in stimulating aggregate demand and reducing cyclical unemployment.

Structural Unemployment

Additional measures are needed to cope with structural unemployment. Expansionary monetary and fiscal actions, assuming structural unemployment, will tend to increase resource and product prices without significantly reducing unemployment. Structural unemployment may be reduced by government policies designed to (1) relocate human resources from surplus labor areas to those where jobs are available, (2) foster wage and price flexibility, and (3) improve job opportunities of people who have a high incidence of unemployment.

It is difficult to design government policies which will successfully foster the voluntary movement of labor from depressed economic areas. There are social as well as economic costs involved in a human resource relocation program. Monetary incentives may be provided in the form of "free" transportation, low-cost housing, and job assurances. However, the social cost of moving and the government programs designed for different purposes, such as a guaranteed income program, may discourage the mobility of resources.

Government policies designed to foster competition and manpower training programs are more likely to reduce structural unemployment and to encourage resource mobility. In competitive labor and product markets, wage-price adjustments take place which tend to eliminate unemployment. Unemployment is much lower among the skilled and the highly trained and educated because of their relative scarcity and adaptability to technological changes and demand changes. Government policies designed to remove price fixing, whether by labor, business or government, and manpower training programs may contribute significantly toward alleviating the problem of structural unemployment.

SUMMARY

There are economic and social effects of unemployment. The economic effect involves the waste and loss of goods and services when resources are unemployed. The social effect involves the breaking up of human relationships within the family and outside it.

Involuntary unemployment, in a competitive framework, means that some people want to work but cannot find jobs because the amount of labor supplied is greater than the amount demanded at existing wage rates. The general solution to involuntary unemployment is a reduction in real wage rates until the amount of labor demanded equals the amount supplied. In a competitive market, the reduction in real wage rates would take place automatically.

There are three types of unemployment—frictional, cyclical, and structural. Frictional unemployment is not a serious economic issue, but cyclical and structural unemployment are. Cyclical unemployment may be kept under control by the appropriate use of monetary and fiscal policy. Structural unemployment may be reduced by policies designed to foster competition and to improve the long-run job prospects of persons who are not adaptable to a changing economy.

The economic forces operating in the economy which determine the levels of production and employment were analyzed with the help of concepts such as the circular flow of production and income and demand and supply curves. Employment rises and unemployment falls when injections into the circular flow are in excess of the leakages or, alternatively, when aggregate output demanded is greater than output supplied at current levels of prices and production. Employment falls and unemployment rises when injections into the circular flow of production and income are less than leakages or, alternatively, when aggregate output demanded is less than output supplied at current price and production levels.

SUPPLEMENTARY READINGS

Economics '73–'74. Guilford, Conn.: Dushkin Publishing Group, 1973.

An especially well-written book. Unit 20 would be an excellent supplement to the chapter above.

Hutchinson, Harry D. *Economics and Social Goals.* Chicago: Science Research Associates, 1973.

Analytical tools are developed in a lucid manner in this one-semester principles text. Chapters 7 and 8 are suggested as supplementary reading.

Miller, Roger L. *Economics Today.* San Francisco: Canfield Press, 1973.

Readings and issues are integrated with text materials in this well-organized two-term principles text. Chapter 7 and Issue VII are suggested readings.

Phillips, James, and Pearl, Carl. *Elements of Economics.* New York: Macmillan, 1973.

A one-term principles text written primarily for nonmajors in economics. Chapter 11, "What Are Inflation and Depression?" and Chapter 12, "What Is Fiscal Policy?" are suggested readings.

Rogers III, Augustus J. *Choice.* Englewood Cliffs, N.J.: Prentice-Hall, 1971.

Aggregate economic analysis is developed with the use of aggregate demand and aggregate supply curves in Chapter 6, which examines the determinants of national income using the same approach taken in the chapter above.

Chapter 10

INFLATION

CHECKLIST OF ECONOMIC CONCEPTS

Inflation
Price Index Numbers
Equity
Efficiency
Demand-Pull Inflation
Cost-Push Inflation
Money Supply
Equation of Exchange
Quantity Theory of Money
Legal Reserve Requirement
Open Market Operations
Discount Rate
Inflation-Unemployment Dilemma

10

INFLATION
How to Gain and Lose at the Same Time

We had sold out almost our entire inventory and, to our amazement, had nothing to show for it except a worthless bank account and a few suitcases full of currency not even good enough to paper our walls with. We tried at first to sell and then buy again as quickly as possible—but the inflation easily overtook us. The lag before we got paid was too long; while we waited, the value of money fell so fast that even our most profitable sale turned into a loss. Only after we began to pay with promissory notes could we maintain our position. Even so, we are making no real profit now, but at least we can live. Since every enterprise in Germany is financed in this fashion, the Reischsbank naturally has to keep on printing unsecured currency and so the mark falls faster and faster. The government apparently doesn't care; all it loses in this way is the national debt. Those who are ruined are the people who cannot pay with notes, the people who have property they are forced to sell, small shopkeepers, day laborers, people with small incomes who see their private savings and their bank accounts melting away, and government officials and employees who have to survive on salaries that no longer allow them to buy so much as a new pair of shoes. The ones who profit are the exchange kings, the profiteers, the foreigners who buy what they like with a few dollars, kronen, or zlotys, and the big entrepreneurs, the manufacturers, and the speculators on the exchange whose property and stocks increase without limit. For them practically everything is free. It is the great sellout of thrift, honest effort, and respectability. The vultures

253

flock from all sides, and the only ones who come out on top are those who accumulate debts. The debts disappear of themselves.[1]

Inflation is considered by most people as equal to or second only to unemployment among the nation's major aggregate economic problems. In almost every presidential campaign, candidates call inflation a bad thing and vow to control it once elected. The rising cost of groceries, auto repairs, medical services, clothes, travel, and everything else is a main topic of conversation among consumers. Business firms realize that higher prices for materials, labor, equipment, and other things they buy will reduce business profits unless they are successful in passing these higher costs on to the consumer in the form of higher consumer prices. Inflation is a prime bargaining consideration in labor union negotiations. A stated national goal of government economic policy is to stabilize the price level. All groups comprising the population—consumers, unions, business firms, and government—are concerned about inflation.

MEANING AND MEASUREMENT OF INFLATION

Most people have a good idea of what is meant by inflation. They know that it causes a sack full of groceries to cost more money. They know that buying Christmas presents costs more. They know that it is more expensive to eat out, to go to a movie, to take a vacation, or to buy a car. They know they will be generally worse off in the future unless their pay can keep up with inflation.

Inflation Defined

Inflation means that the general level of prices is rising. That is, enough commodity prices are rising so that, on the average, prices in general are rising. During inflation some commodities may be falling in price and some may be rising, but the commodities rising in price are dominant, and they exert an upward force on the general price level.

---

[1] Erich Maria Remarque, *The Black Obelisk* (Greenwich, Conn.: Fawcett Publications, 1957), pp. 43–44.

Further Aspects of Inflation

Dynamic Aspects.　An aspect of inflation that needs to be stressed is its dynamic and self-sustaining properties. Increases in the price level induce economic groups to react to rising prices, causing further increases in prices. For example, consumers expecting increases in prices may increase current consumer spending, causing current market prices to rise. During periods of rising prices, producers are not inclined to resist increases in wages and other costs, since higher production costs may be shifted forward to consumers in the form of higher prices. These increases in prices, however, become the basis for further increases in production costs and still higher prices.

Inflation without Rising Prices.　Inflation is not always observable in the form of rising prices. It may be suppressed; market prices may not reflect the inflationary forces operating in the economy. *Suppressed inflation* is usually associated with an attempt on the part of the government to control prices. For example, the government decreed a 90-day price freeze period beginning August 15, 1971. During the freeze period prices remained about the same. Inflationary forces, however, continued to exist. The reason is that the government did not do anything to alter the relationship of demand and supply. Inflation existed in the economy because aggregate output demanded exceeded aggregate output supplied at existing market prices.

Measurement of Inflation

Inflation is measured by price index numbers. Price index numbers indicate the general level of prices in reference to a base year. For example, the consumer price index in 1970 was 116.3, using 1967 as the base year. This means that prices on the average were 16.3 percent above prices in 1967. The consumer price index increased further, to 121.3, in 1971. What was the rate of inflation between 1970 and 1971? The answer is 4.3 percent. This was derived as follows:

$$\text{Rate of inflation} = \frac{121.3 - 116.3}{116.3} = 4.3\%$$

Consumer and Wholesale Price Indices. Table 10–1 shows the behavior of consumer and wholesale prices between 1929 and 1973. The U.S. Bureau of Labor Statistics computes both of these series of price indices. The consumer price index, sometimes referred to as the cost-of-living index, includes commodities which city wage earners and clerical workers buy, such as food, housing, utilities, transportation, clothing, health, and recreation. The wholesale price index includes hundreds of commodities such as farm products and processed foods, as well as industrial commodities, such as textiles, fuels, chemicals, rubber, lumber, paper, metals, machinery, furniture, nonmetallic minerals, and transportation equipment.

TABLE 10–1
Consumer Price Index and Wholesale Price Index in Selected Years, 1929–73 (1967 = 100)

Year	Consumer Price Index	Wholesale Price Index
1929	51.3	49.1
1940	42.0	40.5
1950	72.1	81.8
1960	88.7	94.9
1962	90.6	94.8
1964	92.9	94.7
1966	97.2	99.8
1968	104.2	102.5
1970	116.3	110.4
1971	121.3	113.9
1972	125.3	119.1
1973	132.4	137.7

Source: *Federal Reserve Bulletin,* August 1973.

Construction of a Price Index. Since inflation is measured by price index numbers, it is important to understand how price index numbers are derived. A simple illustration can point out the essential principles underlying their construction. Suppose a family spends $10,000, $10,500, and $11,000 in 1970, 1971, and 1972, respectively, for identical baskets of goods. If 1970 is used as the base year, the index number for the goods for that year is 100. It is 105 for 1971, calculated by dividing the cost of the basket in the base year ($10,000) into the cost in 1971 ($10,500) and multiplying by 100 in order to remove the decimal. Using the same procedure, the index number in 1972 is 110, or

$$\frac{\text{Cost of market basket (1972)}}{\text{Cost of market basket (1970)}} \times 100 = \frac{\$11,000}{\$10,000} \times 100 = 110.$$

The basket of goods used to compute price index numbers is a representative sample. The quantities of each good in the basket—the number of dresses, shirts, loaves of bread, gallons of gasoline, movie tickets, TV sets, autos, and so forth—bought during the year are specified. The summation of the price times the quantity of each good in the basket gives the value of the basket. After the value of the basket is calculated, the final step in the construction of a price index is to select the base year and compute the index numbers as illustrated.

A set of price index numbers is not a perfect measure of inflation. Only a sample of commodities is included in the index. What constitutes a representative sample is difficult to determine, and it changes over time in response to changes in tastes and preferences of people. It is also difficult to account for changes in the quality of goods that occur over time; for some goods and services, higher index numbers reflect higher costs for a better commodity rather than higher cost for the same commodity. Despite these imperfections, price index numbers still provide useful indicators of trends in the level of prices.

ECONOMIC EFFECTS OF INFLATION

Inflation affects the distribution of income, the allocation of resources, and the national output. The effects of inflation on the distribution of income are referred to as the *equity* effects, and its effects on resource allocation and national output are called the *efficiency* and *output* effects of inflation, respectively.

Equity Effects

The impact of inflation is uneven. Some people benefit, and some are worse off due to inflation. Because inflation alters the distribution of income, a major concern is the degree of equity or fairness in the distribution of income.

Anyone who is on a fixed income is hurt by inflation, since it reduces real income. For example, a person who earns $10,000 a year during an inflationary period in which there is a 25 percent increase in the price level suffers a cut in real income equivalent to the rate of inflation—$2,500 in this illustration. Examples of those whose incomes often do not rise as fast as the price level are retired persons on pensions, white-collar workers, civil servants, persons on public assistance, and workers in declining industries.

People who hold assets in the form of money and who have fixed claims on money may be worse off by inflation. Suppose a person deposits $1,000 in a savings account and receives a 5 percent interest rate, or $50 during the year. If the rate of inflation is in excess of 5 percent, the real value of the original savings of $1,000 plus the $50 earned on the savings for a year is reduced to less than the original $1,000. Creditors and owners of mortgages and life insurance policies are hurt by inflation, since the real value of their fixed money claims is reduced. People who bought government savings bonds for $18.75 and were paid $25.00 at maturity ten years later have sometimes discovered that the $25.00 would not buy the same quantity of goods and services as the $18.75 would have bought ten years earlier.

Inflation benefits people who have income that rises faster than prices and those who hold assets whose values rise faster than the price level. Wages and salaries of workers in rapidly growing industries are likely to rise faster than the price level. Teachers' salaries grew faster than the price level during the 1960s; therefore, teachers enjoyed absolute and relative real income gains during the period, due to the relative expansion in the demand for education. Strong unions are sometimes successful in bargaining for wage increases that are greater than the increases in the price level. People who depend upon income in the form of profits—owners of stocks and business enterprises—may have increases in real income, depending upon the rate of increase in profits in comparison to prices. The value of land and improvements on land may rise during inflation; if they rise in value faster than the rate of inflation, owners of property will benefit.

In summary, inflation alters the distribution of income and wealth.[2] Inflation is like a tax to some people and like a subsidy to others. Persons whose real incomes are reduced by inflation are those who have fixed incomes and hold assets in the form of money.

---

[2] It is assumed that inflation is unanticipated. A fully anticipated inflation may not alter the distribution of income and wealth.

Persons whose real incomes are increased by inflation are those who have money income that increases faster than prices and hold real assets that appreciate in value faster than inflation. The arbitrary manner in which inflation may change the pattern of income distribution gives support to the claim that inflation is inequitable.

Efficiency Effects

Inflation tends to change the pattern of resource allocation. In a competitive market the prices of different goods and services reflect differences in consumer valuations of the quantities made available. Inflation causes demands for different goods and services to increase, but demands for some increase more rapidly than those for others. Increases in demands evoke supply responses, the extent of which varies from product to product. Thus inflation changes relative demands, relative supplies, and relative prices of different goods and services. The pattern of resource allocation, then, is not the same pattern that would exist in the absence of inflation. It is not certain that the pattern of resource allocation with inflation is less efficient (that is, results in lower economic welfare) than the pattern without inflation.[3] However, many economists argue that inflation distorts the pattern of resource allocation, implying a less efficient pattern when inflation occurs.

Inflation encourages economic groups to spend time and resources in an attempt to adjust to inflation. For an example, since inflation reduces the purchasing power of money, it encourages everyone to economize or minimize their money balances, that is, assets which are held in the form of money. The time spent and the resources used in adjusting to inflation could have been used to produce goods and services. Thus, inflation, by encouraging everyone to make adjustments and divert time and resources away from production, reduces economic efficiency.

Output Effects

The preceding discussion of the equity and efficiency effects of inflation was presented on the assumption of levels of real output

---

[3] Frank G. Steindl, "Money Illusion, Price Determinacy and Price Stability," *Nebraska Journal of Economics and Business* 10 (Winter 1971): 26–27.

and production that lie on the economy's production possibilities curve. This was done in order to focus attention on how inflation may alter the distribution of real income among people (equity effects) and the allocation of resources (efficiency effects). To state this simply, a certain size pie was assumed in the previous discussion, and the concern was how inflation altered the slices of pie and how inflation affected the use of resources in making the pie. Now we shall consider what the effects of inflation are on the size of the pie. What are the effects of inflation on the level of output of goods and services?

Inflation may have a stimulating effect on production and employment in the economy. The argument in support of this proposition can be presented as follows: During inflation money wages lag behind price increases. Thus, real profit income is increased. Under the stimulus of higher profits, producers expand production and employ more people.

The argument that inflation may stimulate production and employment should be qualified. Runaway or hyperinflation may depreciate the value of money so drastically that it loses its acceptability as a medium of exchange. Under these circumstances a barter economy develops, accompanied by lower production levels and higher unemployment. If the economy is operating at full capacity and full employment, then, of course, inflation cannot stimulate them further. Inflation at full employment is referred to usually as *pure* inflation.

The impact of inflation differs depending upon whether or not inflation is associated with increases in production and employment. As long as production is rising, there is a check on inflation since, although lagging behind demand, supply is increasing, thus tending to mitigate inflationary forces. Also, the equity effects of inflation are minimized if production and employment are rising. However, as the economy approaches full employment, the seriousness of inflation increases. The possibility of an accelerated rate of inflation is nearer, and the possible beneficial effects of inflation on production and employment are remote.

ROLE OF MONEY IN THE INFLATIONARY PROCESS

It is important to understand the role of money in the inflationary process. After a discussion of the meaning and functions of money, we shall discuss the significance of money as an economic variable. This discussion centers around a development of the so-called "equation of exchange" and the quantity theory of money.

Meaning and Functions of Money

Money serves three basic functions: a medium of exchange, a measure of value, and a store of value. We use it first as the *medium of exchange;* goods and services are paid for in money, and debts are incurred and paid off in money. Without money, economic transactions would have to take place on a barter basis. Thus money facilitates the exchange process. Second, the values of economic goods and services are measured in money. Money as a *measure of value* makes possible value comparisons of goods and services and the summations of quantities of goods and services on a value basis. Concerning this last point, it is not possible to add apples and oranges, but it is possible to add the *values* of apples and oranges. Third, wealth may be held in the form of money. Money balances held by people in demand deposits at banks or at home in a sock are noninterest-bearing assets. Money serves as a *store of value.*

TABLE 10–2
Movements in the Money Supply in Selected Years 1960–72 (billions of dollars, seasonally adjusted)

Year (Dec.)	Total Money Supply	Currency	Demand Deposits
1960	141.7	28.9	112.8
1962	148.1	30.6	117.6
1964	160.5	34.2	126.3
1966	171.7	38.3	133.4
1968	197.4	43.4	154.0
1970	214.8	49.0	165.8
1971	228.2	52.5	175.7
1972	246.9	56.9	190.0

Source: *Economic Report of the President,* Jan. 1973.

Economists use the words *money supply* to mean the quantity or stock of money in the economy. The nation's money supply is composed of demand deposits (checking accounts) and currency in circulation (paper currency and coins). Table 10–2 shows the breakdown of the money supply between demand deposits and currency and the growth in the money supply since 1960.

The Equation of Exchange

A simple way of establishing the relationship between the money supply and the price level is provided in the following equation: $MV = PT$, in which M is the money supply, V is the velocity of circulation or the number of times the average dollar is spent per year, P is the price level or price index, and T is the physical volume of goods and services traded per year. The equation states that the supply of money times the velocity of money equals the price times the quantity of goods traded. Another way of looking at the equation is that the amount of money spent (left-hand side of the equation) equals the value of the goods sold (right-hand side of the equation). Surely no one doubts that the monetary value of purchases must equal the monetary value of sales. Then what is the importance of the equation of exchange?

Quantity Theory of Money

The equation of exchange is the starting point for the understanding and development of the *quantity theory of money*. This theory places prime importance on changes in the money supply. It states that the price level and output tend to move in the same direction as the money supply. Now return to the equation. If the money supply increases and the velocity of money stays the same, prices and output must rise. In these circumstances, if the economy were at full employment, an increase in the money supply would bring a proportionate rise in prices. This is the same conclusion arrived at in the preceding chapter in the discussion of aggregate-demand analysis. An increase in aggregate demand, assuming full employment, will increase prices only. The quantity theory of money is an alternative way of explaining and understanding the economic forces determining prices, output, and employment in the economy.

The quantity theory of money stresses a couple of points that may have been overlooked in the previous analysis. Inflation due to a demand pull is possible only if the money supply expands or the velocity of circulation increases, or both. It is usually correct to say that behind every great inflation there is a relatively great expansion in the money supply. In the section to follow on the causes of inflation, it is assumed that the money supply increases with increases in demand for money.

CAUSES OF INFLATION

Before policies can be designed to deal with inflation, the causes of inflation must be understood. We know from the quantity theory of money that a *basic* cause of inflation is *excess* aggregate demand generated by expansions in the money supply. Are there other causes?

Demand-Pull Inflation

Economists agree that most inflations are demand-pull inflations. This type of inflation is initiated by an increase in aggregate demand and is self-enforcing by further increases in aggregate demand. A demand-pull inflation is associated with increases in production and employment until the economy reaches full employment. Once full employment is reached, further increases in demand increase prices only.

Figure 10–1 depicts a demand-pull inflation. Beginning at the price level p and production q, an increase in aggregate demand to D_1 means that all of demand cannot be satisfied at p. Thus, the price level rises to p_1, and production rises to q_1. Then demand increases to D_2, causing the price level and production to rise further to p_2 and q_2, respectively. This inflationary process continues as long as aggregate demand increases, since all of demand can be satisfied only at higher prices.

Cost-Push Inflation

It is difficult to explain some of the inflationary periods in the 1950s and 1960s only on the basis of a demand-pull inflation. The economy experienced both inflation and recession together at certain times. How can this be? A demand-pull inflation is characterized by *rising* prices and *rising* production until full employment is reached. Inflation and recession at the same time mean *rising* prices and *falling* production.

The only way the economy can experience simultaneous infla-

FIGURE 10–1
Demand-Pull Inflation

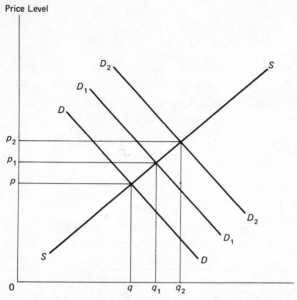

Inflation is due to the increases in aggregate demand from DD to D_1D_1 to D_2D_2.

tion and recession is for inflation to be initiated by a decrease in aggregate supply. This type of inflation is called a *cost-push infla-tion*. Increases in costs cause aggregate supply to decrease, which reduces the quantity of goods produced and increases prices.

Figure 10–2 illustrates a cost-push inflation. Beginning at price level p and production q, aggregate supply decreases to S_1. Now all of demand cannot be satisfied at p, that is, aggregate output de-manded is greater than aggregate output supplied. As a conse-quence, the price level rises to p_1. Aggregate supply decreases fur-ther, to S_2. Again, all of demand cannot be satisfied, and prices rise to p_2. This inflationary process continues until there are no further decreases in aggregate supply. It can be observed in Figure 10–2 that a cost-push inflation is characterized by rising prices and falling production.

A demand-pull inflation is explained in terms of theory—aggre-gate-demand theory and the quantity theory of money. A cost-push

FIGURE 10–2
Cost-Push Inflation

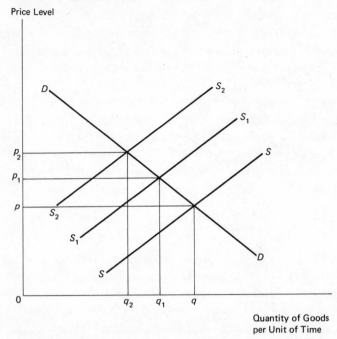

Inflation is due to a decrease in aggregate supply from SS to S_1S_1 to S_2S_2.

inflation is explained in terms of the market power possessed by unions and producers in certain industries. In highly monopolized industries, unions and management may use their market power to determine wages and prices independently of market forces. One explanation is that unions increase wages in excess of productivity increases. The effect of this is to increase labor cost per unit of output. With control over price and production, producers respond by decreasing supply and shifting higher unit labor costs to consumers in the form of higher prices.

Demand-Pull and Then Cost-Push Inflation

It may be misleading to look upon demand-pull and cost-push as two separate inflationary processes. They may be part of the same one, in that a single inflationary period may consist of both demand-pull and cost-push pressures.[4] Increases in aggregate demand start the inflationary process. Prices, production, and employment rise in response to the pull of demand. Money wages rise, but with a lag behind prices. Unions realize eventually that wages have lagged behind prices and begin to try to catch up by demanding wage increases in excess of productivity increases. Once this happens, cost-push pressures begin to reenforce demand pressures.

The end of an inflationary process may not coincide with the moment that demand-pull pressures no longer exist. Prices may continue to rise for a period because of cost-push pressures. These pressures operating alone sustain the inflation temporarily, even though production and employment are falling. However, without demand-pull pressures, inflation eventually stops.

CONTROL OF INFLATION

With reference to the equation of exchange—$MV = PT$—inflation results when MV is rising faster than T. Consequently, it should be controllable if one or more of these variables can be controlled. During an inflationary period M almost invariably is expanding, causing an increase in MV, or aggregate demand. The velocity of circulation, V, is also likely to be expanding, reflecting a decrease in people's desires to hold onto their money when it is going down in value. The volume of trade, T, reflecting primarily the total output of the economy, tends to increase if there are unemployed resources in the economy. However, its rate of increase will be impeded if the factors underlying cost-push inflation are present. In this section we shall consider how these variables can be controlled by means of monetary policy, fiscal policy, and the antimonopoly policy of the federal government.

Monetary Policy

Monetary policy refers to the control exercised over the money supply, M, by the federal government. Demand deposits are far and away the largest component of the money supply—in 1972 the

---

[4] Samuel A. Morley, *The Economics of Inflation* (Hinsdale, Ill.: Dryden Press, 1971), pp. 4–6.

average amount of demand deposits in existence was $190 billion, while the average quantity of the currency was $57 billion. Therefore they represent the immediate target of control measures. How is control of the amount of demand deposits available for use accomplished? To answer this question, we must sketch out the structure and operation of the U.S. banking system.

Creation of Demand Deposits. The hundreds of commercial banks in which we have our checking accounts and do our borrowing generate the demand deposit component of the money supply. Demand deposits come into existence in two ways. First, when we deposit currency in our banks the demand deposits of the banking system are increased by the amount deposited. Second, when we borrow from our banks, they give us the loans in the form of additions to our checking accounts, thus generating new demand deposits.

Deposits arising when we take currency to the banks do not increase the total money supply, M. The currency turned over to the bank is no longer in circulation, so M is decreased by that amount. The deposits generated are equal in amount to the currency turned over to the bank. The whole process is a straightforward exchange of currency for demand deposits, with no net change in M.

Deposits arising from borrowing are a different story. When we borrow we give our banks promissory notes—which are not money. In exchange, the banks increase our demand deposits—our checking accounts—by the amount borrowed. These additions to demand deposits are money, so the lending activities of banks serve on balance to increase M.

The deposit component of the money supply is decreased by the inverse of the processes discussed above. When we need currency we write checks to "cash." Our banks give us the currency and reduce our bank accounts by the same amount. Note that this does not change M, however. When we repay bank loans, we write checks to our banks—thus reducing our demand deposits. They give us nothing in return but our cancelled promissory notes! So this process operates to reduce M.

Three fundamental principles characterizing the effects of commercial bank operations on M emerge from the foregoing discussion. First, when commercial banks are making new loans in greater amounts than old loans are being paid off, demand deposits and, consequently, M will be expanding. Second, when the amounts of new loans being made are less than the amounts of old loans being paid off, M will be contracting. Third, when the amounts of new loans being made are just equal to the amounts of old loans being paid off, M is neither expanding nor contracting.

Unfortunately, when banks are left to follow their own individual interests, their actions augment inflationary forces. It is precisely when economic expansion and inflation are occurring that it is most profitable for banks to expand their loans. Business firms want to borrow, and their demands for loans raise the interest rates that banks can charge (note the 10 percent interest rate that existed in mid 1973). The dangers of defaults by borrowers are minimal. The resulting increases in M add fuel to inflationary fires.

Federal Reserve Control of Demand Deposits. The federal government has sought to limit this economically perverse tendency of commercial banks by means of the Federal Reserve System established by the Federal Reserve Act of 1913. Under the act 12 Federal Reserve banks were established—one in each of the Federal Reserve Destricts into which the United States is divided. These act in a coordinated way as the central bank of the United States, with their activities controlled by a seven-man Board of Governors. A central bank acts as a banker's bank. Commercial banks themselves hold deposits at Federal Reserve banks and may also borrow from them. A second function of a central bank is to control the demand deposits that exist in the economy.

The bulk of the total demand deposits of individuals and businesses at commercial banks is held in banks that are members of the Federal Reserve System. Many commercial banks are national banks, receiving their charters from the federal government. All of these are required by law to be members of the system. The rest are state banks, chartered by individual states. Membership in the Federal Reserve System is optional for them, but it offers sufficient advantages so that many elect to join.

The feature of commercial banks that enables the Federal Reserve Board of Governors to exercise control over their total demand deposits is the reserves that they hold against their deposits. Reserves are in the form of commercial bank deposits at Federal Reserve banks, but they may also be held in the form of currency. The historical purposes of reserves are twofold. They serve to take care of both current routine needs of customers for currency and any extraordinary demands for currency that customers may have. The larger the ratio of a bank's reserves to the total demand deposits of its customers, the safer the bank is thought to be. Before the Federal Reserve Act was passed, experience indicated that prudent banking called for ratios of reserves to deposits—called *the reserve ratio*—of somewhere between 5 and 20 percent.

The Board of Governors can influence the quantities of reserves available to commercial banks and can set the minimum reserve ratio below which member banks of the Federal Reserve System cannot go. Both of these are indirect controls over the total volume of demand deposits in the economy.

To combat inflation, the Board of Governors can bring about reductions in the reserves of commercial banks through *open market operations* in government securities. Both commercial banks and Federal Reserve banks own large quantities of government bonds and treasury bills. By offering to sell at extraordinarily low prices, the Federal Reserve authorities can induce commercial banks to buy quantities of the securities from the Federal Reserve banks. Commercial banks use their reserves (deposits held at a Federal Reserve Bank) to buy them. As their reserves are reduced, so are their capacities to make new loans and to expand M.

A second means available to Federal Reserve authorities for reducing member bank reserves is elevation of the *discount rate*—the rate of interest charged commercial banks when they borrow from Federal Reserve Banks. At any given time some part of total commercial bank reserves consists of such borrowing. When a member bank borrows from a Federal Reserve Bank it receives the loan in the form of a deposit at the Federal Reserve Bank; such deposits serve as reserves for member banks. Consequently, when Federal Reserve authorities raise the discount rate, making it more expensive for member banks to borrow, the total amount of member bank borrowing shrinks, making the total reserves of member banks smaller. This in turn reduces the capacities of member banks to make new loans and expands M.

A third method of reducing the tendency of commercial banks to expand demand deposits during periods of inflation is Federal Reserve control of the *minimum required reserve ratio* that member banks may hold. Suppose, for example, that the minimum required reserve ratio of member banks is 10 percent, total reserves are $50 billion, and total demand deposits are $250 billion. The actual reserve ratio of all banks together is 20 percent—$50 billion/$250 billion. If inflation is occurring, member banks could expand their total deposits to $500 billion, thus contributing to further inflation. However, if the Federal Reserve authorities increase the minimum required reserve ratio to 20 percent, the $50 billion in reserves will permit no expansion at all in new loans and demand deposits.

We should note that all of the three means available to Federal Reserve authorities for controlling demand deposit expansion during inflation can operate in reverse to encourage expansion of demand deposits during recession. Open market purchases of government securities by Federal Reserve banks will increase member bank reserves. So will decreases in the discount rate. Further, decreases in the minimum required reserve ratio will permit demand deposit expansion.

Fiscal Policy

Fiscal policy refers to federal government decision making with respect to its tax receipts and its expenditures. The relative magnitudes of these factors have important effects on aggregate demand and, therefore, on the price level and the level of employment in the economy. Given the level of government expenditures, increases in tax collections will reduce aggregate demand, whereas decreases in tax collections will increase it. On the other hand, given the level of tax collections, increases in government expenditures will increase aggregate demand, while decreases in government expenditures will reduce it. Thus changes in either or both tax collections and expenditures should provide means of attacking either inflation or unemployment.

When the economy is experiencing a period of inflation, the government can combat it by raising taxes, reducing expenditures, or both. To the extent that rising aggregate demand is causing demand-pull inflation, such measures will serve to slow or stop it. If, however, cost push is the primary cause of inflation, fiscal policies of this sort acting on aggregate demand will serve to increase unemployment at the same time that they slow down the rate of inflation.

Output Expansion Policies

Since inflation occurs whenever MV is increasing faster than T, it follows that anything that increases T or the output of the economy will be helpful in mitigating it. Obviously T can rise most easily when there is slack or unemployment in the economy, as there was in 1960. From 1960 through 1965 aggregate demand was increasing, but inflation was mild because T was increasing rapidly also. Once the economy approaches full employment of its resources, output expansions are difficult to achieve.

One possible way to encourage output expansion is through anti-monopoly policies. Business monopolies tend to restrict production and hold prices higher than they would be in a more competitive economy. This can, of course, lead to unemployment of resources or an inefficient allocation of resources among different uses. Similarly, union labor monopolies tend to press wage rates higher, causing the employment level to be lower than it would be in their absence. Both business and labor monopolies tend to keep prices artificially high—higher than they would be under more competitive conditions.

A second way to encourage an expansion of the goods and services available to be purchased is through decreasing the restriction of imports from abroad. With reductions in tariffs and allowable quotas of foreign goods, more foreign goods will be imported and sold. These larger quantities amount to increases in T which help to hold the price level down.

THE INFLATION-UNEMPLOYMENT DILEMMA

A major problem in controlling inflation once it has gotten underway is that effective control measures almost inevitably cause unemployment. This happened as monetary and fiscal policies were tightened to control inflation from 1969 through the summer of 1971. By August 1971 what had been a 6 percent inflation rate was down to approximately 3.5 percent. But over the same period unemployment increased from less than 4 percent of the labor force to over 6 percent. This type of thing has led many people to raise the question: Can aggregate demand be controlled by monetary and fiscal policy so that the economy can operate at a stable price level and full employment?

The Tradeoff Problem

Some economists advance the argument that full employment and a stable price level are incompatible policy goals. They argue that an increase in aggregate demand, at less than full employment, will expand production and employment but will be associated with a cost-push inflation before full employment is reached. Also, they argue that an attempt to reduce inflation by reducing aggregate demand will prevent the economy from reaching full employment or move it away from full employment if it is already there.

Therefore, it is concluded that economic policies designed to control aggregate demand, such as monetary and fiscal policy, cannot achieve both full employment and a stable price level. Instead, there is a policy choice between full employment and some rate of inflation or between a stable price level and some rate of unemployment. This policy dilemma may be referred to as the tradeoff problem. How much unemployment should be traded for stable prices, or how much inflation should be traded for full employment?

Possible Inflation-Unemployment Combinations

Paul Samuelson and Robert Solow studied the relationship between changes in the price level and changes in the unemployment rate in this country over a 25-year period and derived a tradeoff curve similar to the TT curve depicted in Figure 10–3.[5] The tradeoff curve shows the various combinations of inflation and unemployment that are possible, given the competitive behavior of buyers and sellers and the market structure of the economy. Look at points A, B, and C on the tradeoff curve (TT). Point A shows a combination of a 3 percent unemployment rate and 5 percent inflation. Point B shows a combination of a 4 percent unemployment rate and a 3 percent inflation, and point C a stable price level associated with a 5.5 percent unemployment rate. Points between A and B and C show other possible combinations of unemployment and inflation.

The tradeoff curve indicates the policy choices. Can anything

---

[5] Paul A. Samuelson and Robert M. Solow, "Our Menu of Policy Choices," in Arthur M. Okum (ed.), *The Battle against Unemployment* (New York: W. W. Norton & Co., 1965), pp. 71–76.

FIGURE 10–3
Possible Combinations of Inflation and Unemployment

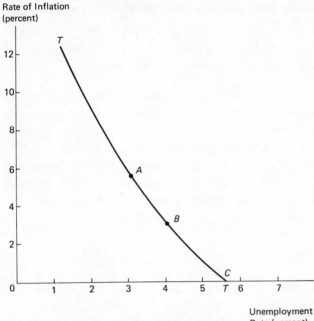

Any point on the tradeoff curve, *TT,* shows a combination of inflation and unemployment which is possible, given the degree of competition in the economy. For example, point *B* represents a combination of 3 percent inflation and 4 percent unemployment.

be done to improve these choices, that is, to make stable prices and full employment more compatible? In terms of the tradeoff curve, this means a shift of the curve to the left, indicating a reduction in tradeoff costs—a lower rate of inflation associated with any given rate of unemployment.

The tradeoff curve could be shifted to the left and even made to disappear if noninflationary monetary and fiscal policies were pursued and if the economy were perfectly competitive. Some inflation may be necessary to bring us out of a recession in which there is substantial unemployment. But over time, given monetary and fiscal policies that are not inflationary, people will come to expect and depend on stable prices. This in turn will induce them to price their goods and resources so that surpluses and unemployment do not occur. The more competitive the market structures of the economy, the more likely it is that stable prices and full employment will be compatible.

EXPERIENCES WITH WAGE-PRICE CONTROLS

The Nixon administration became convinced that monetary and fiscal policy could not cope with the economic situation existing in the economy in the summer of 1971. The economy was suffering from a high rate of inflation and unemployment. Although the rate of inflation was slowing down, it was argued that a new course of action was required to deal with both inflation and unemployment. The new course of action turned out to be a policy of wage and price controls.

The Four Phases

Phase One. A policy of wage and price controls was initiated by the Nixon administration on August 15, 1971, with the announcement of a 90-day freeze period. The freeze period, Phase One, has been followed by Phases Two, Three, and Four. During Phase One, plans were developed for the operation of a wage and price control scheme. Wages and prices did not rise much during the freeze period, since by government decree they were not suppose to increase. However, economic forces operating behind demand and supply are not affected by government decrees, and inflationary forces were continuing to build during the freeze period. In an attempt to explain why the freeze was a mistake, Milton Friedman stated, "Freezing individual prices and wages in order to halt inflation is like freezing the rudder of a boat and making it impossible to steer, in order to correct a tendency for the boat to drift one degree off course."[6]

Phase Two. Phase Two covered a 14-month period from November 14, 1971, to January 11, 1973. The wage and price control scheme was a mandatory scheme, that is, wage and price increases in

---

[6] Milton Friedman, "Why The Freeze Is a Mistake," *Newsweek*, August 30, 1971, p. 22.

industries under the controls had to be justified and approved by government. The wage and price guidelines were a 5.5 percent wage increase and a 2.5 to 3 percent price increase. The record during Phase Two was good if judged against these guidelines. During Phase Two food prices rose 6.5 percent, the cost of living increased 3.6 percent, and wages increased 5.9 percent.

Phase Three. Phase Three covered five months from January 11, 1973, to June 13, 1973. Under Phase Three the wage and price control scheme was voluntary. Wage and price guidelines were to be adhered to voluntarily, with the threat of government action in the event that they were not followed. Phase Three proved to be disastrous; wage and price controls completely broke down. This was partly because it was a voluntary scheme but primarily because of the adverse effects of price controls on supply and an increase in demand. The money supply rapidly increased during the period, making it possible for goods and services to be purchased at higher price levels.

Phase Four. A full cycle—from freeze to freeze—was completed on June 14, 1973, with the announcement of a 60-day freeze period. This was a half freeze, since some goods and services were not frozen (food and health) and some were frozen (meat, nonfood products, gasoline, etc.). After the 60-day freeze, on August 15, 1973, a system of mandatory wage and price controls was established. This marked the beginning of Phase Four; it is uncertain as to the phases to follow. One thing is certain—wage and price controls have been far from successful.

What Have We Learned from Wage-Price Controls?

Our recent experiences with wage and price controls reflect some important lessons of economics. Lesson No. 1 is that a wage and price freeze does not prevent wage and price increases—it only postpones them. Lesson No. 2 is that a price control scheme that keeps market prices below market equilibrium prices creates shortages. Lesson No. 3 is that mandatory wage and price control schemes appear more effective than voluntary schemes, but both types of schemes treat the symptoms, not the cause, of inflation. Lesson No. 4, a concluding lesson, is that wage and price controls cannot resolve the inflation-unemployment dilemma.

Where Do We Go from Here?

Monetary and fiscal policy cannot cope with the inflation-unemployment dilemma. Wage and price controls have also proved unsuccessful. What choices remain? One possibility is to pursue policies that would tend to remove the cause of the problem, namely, policies designed to restore competition where it does not exist and foster more competition where it is restricted. The inflation-unemployment dilemma would not exist in a highly competitive economy. If the consequences of this choice are too extreme, a second course of action would be to select a set of inflation and employment goals that would be consistent with our present institutional framework. A stable price level and full employment have proved to be incompatible goals. Other goals may not be incompatible; for example, a steady rate of inflation, such as 6 percent a year, and a 5 percent unemployment rate may both be feasible. A third choice which may be considered is a mixture of choices 1 and 2. We could design and pursue economic policies which would foster competition, perhaps, beginning in markets where the greatest monopoly power is exercised. At the same time we could pursue a monetary and fiscal policy that would direct the economy toward a realistic set of inflation and unemployment objectives.

SUMMARY

Inflation means that the general level of prices is rising. It means that it takes more money to buy the same quantity of goods and services. Inflation may be suppressed. This occurs when quantity demanded is greater than quantity supplied at the current price level, but the price level does not rise because of government price controls.

The three effects of inflation are the equity, efficiency, and output effects. The equity effects involve the impact of inflation on income distribution. The people who lose during inflation are those receiving fixed incomes, holding assets in the form of money, and having fixed money claims. The people who gain during inflation are those whose money incomes rise faster than prices and who hold assets which rise in value more than the increases in the prices of goods and services.

The efficiency effects of inflation involve the impact of inflation on the allocation of resources. Inflation changes the allocating of resources, since inflation alters relative commodity prices. It is not certain that this change in resource allocation is a less efficient allocation. However, some economists argue that the allocation of resources is distorted by inflation and results in a less efficient allocation of resources.

The impact of inflation on national production of goods and services (output effects) may be to encourage production. Before the economy reaches full employment, rising prices tend to go hand in hand with rising production. The same forces that cause prices to rise cause production to rise. However, the continuation of inflationary forces at full employment leads to pure inflation, that is, rising prices not associated with rising production.

It is very important not to allow inflation to get out of hand. Whereas a steady rate of inflation of 5 percent per year may not be the ideal situation, it does not represent the kind of problem that an accelerated inflation does. The key to controlling inflation is to control the growth in the money supply. The growth in the money supply may be controlled by Federal Reserve monetary policies.

The economic situation in the summer of 1971, rising prices and high unemployment rates, brought on an era of wage and price controls which are not proving to be successful. Wage and price controls do not treat the cause of inflation and will be eventually laid aside. Where will we go from here? One choice is to get at the cause of the inflation-unemployment dilemma by pursuing policies that enhance competition. A second choice is to decide upon a set of inflation and employment objectives so that monetary and fiscal policy may have a good chance of reaching them. A third choice is to pursue a "mix" of choices 1 and 2.

SUPPLEMENTARY READINGS

Economics '73-'74. Guilford, Conn.: Dushkin Publishing Group, 1973.
See especially Unit 21, "The Problem of Inflation," and Unit 29, "The Current Dilemma: Unemployment and Inflation Together."

Hutchinson, Harry D. *Economics and Social Goals,* chaps. 8 and 9. Chicago: Science Research Associates, 1973.

Levy, Fred D., and Sufrin, Sidney C. *Basic Economics,* chap. 5. New York: Harper & Row, 1973.

Morley, Samuel A. *The Economics of Inflation.* Hinsdale: Dryden Press, 1971.

   An intermediate-level treatment of inflation. Chapters 1 and 2 are suggested.

Part IV

EPILOGUE

Chapter 11

THE ENERGY CRISIS

CHECKLIST OF ECONOMIC CONCEPTS

Supply
Demand
Equilibrium Prices
Inflation
Ceiling Prices
Shortages
Rationing
Allocation Priorities
Coupon Rationing
Black Markets
Efficiency
Per Unit Taxes
Subsidies

11

THE ENERGY CRISIS
Must Simple Things Be Made Complex?

ELI HIGGENBOTTEM pulled his sweater a little more tightly around his shoulders as he walked into the hallway to check the thermostat. It confirmed his suspicions; it read 60° instead of the 68° that he scrupulously maintained, indicating that the oil tank was empty. The next delivery was supposed to arrive about 8:30 the next morning, so it looked like a cold night was in the cards. Eli would be late for work because he would have to wait around and relight the furnace after the oil arrived. He would miss his carpool, of course, and would be forced to drive his own car, using up some of the family's precious gasoline supply.

The gasoline supply was another sore point around the Higgenbottem household. Eli and his wife, Ellen, had decided to make that long-postponed trip from Pennsylvania to California next summer. Ellen and the kids had never been west of the Mississippi River. They had looked forward to a leisurely four weeks' drive through the Midwest, Oklahoma, the Painted Desert, the Grand Canyon, and then on to Disneyland. Now the trip would have to be postponed indefinitely, since pleasure driving was frowned upon and no end to the energy crisis was in view.

Another dream of Eli's bit the dust when gasoline priorities were announced. For years his favorite Sunday afternoon activity had been to drive to the airport to watch the airplanes—the Cessna 150's and the Piper Cherokees loaded with students and their instructors taxiing and shooting touch and go landings. At last Eli had reached an income level—and was fearful of passing the age—at which learning to fly was in the realm of possibility. He and Ellen had agreed that he would start in the spring. But now because of the reduction in gasoline made available for general aviation, he had been informed by the Flight Training Center that they would be unable to take on new students.

THE PROBLEM

As if Watergate and inflation were not enough, the U.S. public in late 1973 came face to face with an energy problem. It became apparent as the year progressed that an energy-hungry economy would become increasingly hard pressed to satisfy its appetite. Then in October the Arab nations of the Middle East and North Africa shut off their crude oil exports to the United States and curtailed them to most of Europe and Japan, in retaliation against support of Israel in the Israeli-Egyptian conflict. Congress and the Nixon administration were spurred by the embargo to take actions to meet the "crisis."

The crisis in the United States has centered primarily on petroleum, since this energy source provides some 50 percent of the total energy requirements of the economy. Natural gas fills another 30 percent of the requirements and will surely receive increasing attention as the crisis intensifies. About 15 percent of the requirements are met by coal, while the remaining 5 percent is taken care of by nuclear and hydroelectric energy sources.[1]

In a televised address on November 26, 1973, President Nixon estimated that energy shortages could run *as high* as 17 percent in 1974. Presumably this means that estimated quantities of energy supplied will cover all but 17 percent of the estimated quantities of energy demanded. Almost everyone—the President, the Congress, and the general public—views this shortfall as a crisis. We constantly read in the news media and hear on television pessimistic forecasts of things to come.

What are the expected results of the crisis if we fail to shape up

---

[1] *Newsweek,* November 19, 1973, p. 112.

and cut back on nonessential uses of petroleum? The most critical expectation is a decrease in gross national product and an increase in unemployment. Magnitudes discussed are a 1 to 2 percent decrease in GNP and an increase in unemployment to somewhere around 10 percent of the labor force. These are the predicted consequences if industry is unable to get the fuel oil and electric power it needs to keep its wheels turning. In order to get the required quantities of fuel and power to industry, there is talk of shutting down schools, extensive power brownouts, homes colder than usual, and severe curtailment of transportation via autos, buses, trucks, and airplanes.

THE ECONOMIC BACKGROUND OF THE CRISIS

The crux of the energy crisis in the United States is that the demand for energy is increasing faster than the supply. Further, since 1971 the U.S. government has pursued a set of policies that has insured the development of shortages.

Demand

For energy sources in general a little less than one half of the total direct demand originates with *industrial* users. *Transportation* users create an additional one fourth, while residential and commercial users generate a little over one fourth of the total demand. For the petroleum component of energy, transportation users demand the largest amounts. Next in line are residential and commercial users, followed by industrial users. Electricity-generating plants, classified here as industrial users, provide a secondary source for energy users of all types. They obtain about half of their primary energy from coal, with the rest coming from natural gas, petroleum. hydropower, and nuclear power, in that order.

In the transportation area, automobiles, trucks, buses, and airplanes are the important petroleum energy users. The number of automobiles, trucks and buses on the road has almost tripled since World War II, and, in contrast to Europeans, our tastes have been strong for large, powerful cars that consume prodigious amounts of fuel. Our concern with environmental quality in recent years has led to mandatory antipollution devices on our motorized vehicles that have in turn reduced the miles per gallon obtained and increased their total fuel consumption. In commercial aviation, piston engine airplanes have been replaced by the fuel-hungry blowtorches that we call jets. Even the number of piston engine general aviation airplanes has been increasing rapidly, although quantitatively these are not yet a large factor in the total demand for petroleum products.

Increasing residential and commercial demand for petroleum products reflects general economic expansion and rising affluence. The population is growing; greater numbers of houses are being built; and houses are larger in size. Central heating and air conditioning induce us to heat more rooms in our homes than we did with the space heaters and floor furnaces of a few years ago. Numbers of commercial establishments and the average size of the areas enclosed by them . . . have been increasing commensurately.

Industrial demand for petroleum products rises continually for two reasons. The first and most obvious reason is the expanding industrial activity associated with economic growth. The second is the continuing shift away from coal and toward petroleum as an energy source. To be sure, the industrial demand for coal continues to increase, but industrial demand for petroleum products—fuel oil—increases faster. The important factors causing the relative shift are: (1) environmental considerations—coal is the dirtier fuel —and (2) what has been the relatively low cost of petroleum energy.

It should come as no surprise that the demand for petroleum by electricity-generating plants is growing rapidly. Again, economic growth and rising affluence creates rising needs for electricity for lighting, heating, and cooling and for running the ever-growing masses of appliances that come on the market. Power-generating plants have relied heavily on coal as a fuel, but the same factors that tend to shift other industrial plants toward petroleum affect power plants, too.

Supply

Energy supplies in the United States have been increasing over time but have not kept pace with the increasing demands for them. The production of bituminous coal has been increasing steadily over the past ten years, but the output of the cleaner-burning Pennsylvania anthracite has been decreasing. Natural gas production has been increasing slowly, largely because relatively low price ceilings have been set by the Federal Power Commission, making it unprofitable to increase production significantly. Nuclear power has not yet been tapped in any sizable quantities, but its use is growing rapidly as the costs of alternative energy sources rise. Thus, petroleum, which accounts for over half of our energy supplies, has been the crucial element in the supply picture over the past decade and will continue to be for several years to come.

The production of crude oil in the United States rose steadily until 1970. Most people believed that the annual increases in output

FIGURE 11–1
U.S. Production of Crude Oil, 1965–73

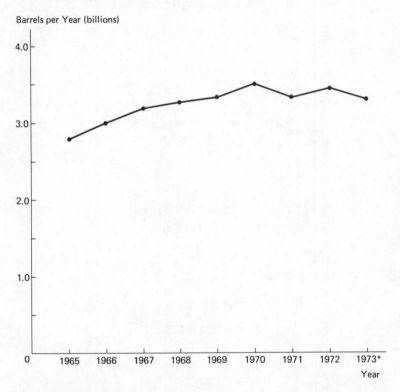

Barrels per Year (billions)

ᵒ Estimated.
Sources: U.S. Department of the Interior, Bureau of Mines, Mineral Industry Surveys, *Crude Petroleum, Petroleum Products, and Natural Gas Liquids*, 1965–73 issues; *Oil & Gas Journal*, July 30, 1973, p. 99.

2 *Oil and Gas Journal,* July 30, 1973, p. 99.

TABLE 11–1
Total Supplies of Crude Oil in the United States, 1960 and 1965–73 (1,000 barrels)

Year	Domestic Production	Imports — Arab Countries*	Imports — Percent of Total U.S. Supply	Imports — Total	Imports — Percent of Total U.S. Supply	Total U.S. Supply
1960	2,574,933	114,342	3.9%	371,575	12.6%	2,946,508
1965	2,848,514	137,941	4.2	452,040	13.7	3,300,554
1966	3,027,763	133,608	3.8	447,120	12.9	3,474,883
1967	3,215,742	84,588	2.3	411,649	11.4	3,627,391
1968	3,329,042	124,716	3.3	472,323	12.4	3,801,365
1969	3,371,751	125,256	3.2	514,114	13.2	3,885,865
1970	3,517,450	86,674	2.2	483,293	12.1	4,000,743
1971	3,453,914	150,505	3.7	613,417	15.1	4,067,331
1972	3,459,052	197,879	4.6	811,135	19.0	4,270,187
1973†	3,364,935			1,171,650	25.8	4,536,585
1st half 1973	1,673,077	143,052	6.4	550,873	24.8	2,223,950

* Egypt, Iran, Iraq, Libya, Saudi Arabia, United Arab Emirates.
† Estimated.

Sources: U.S. Department of the Interior, Bureau of Mines, Mineral Industry Surveys, *Crude Petroleum, Petroleum Products, and Natural Gas Liquids*, 1960, 1965–1973 issues; *Oil and Gas Journal*, July 10, 1973, p. 99.

could go on forever. However, U.S. production of crude oil peaked in 1970 and declined somewhat in 1971. A slight increase over 1971 was registered in 1972, and a slight decrease from 1972 was projected for 1973.[2] These trends through 1973 are shown in Table 11–1 and Figure 11–1.

Imports of crude oil largely complete the supply picture. Over the years the percentage of crude oil supplies imported to total crude oil supplies available (including imports) rose from 12.6 percent in 1960 to 19.0 percent in 1972. In 1973 we depended even more heavily on imports. For the first half of the year 24.8 percent of total supplies were imported. Estimates for the entire year are about the same.[3] The trends are shown in Table 11–1 and Figure 11–2. Total supply trends for the same period are shown in Figure 11–3.

FIGURE 11–2
U.S. Imports of Crude Oil, 1965–73

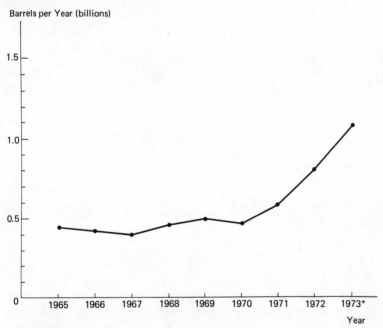

Barrels per Year (billions)

* Estimated.
Sources: U.S. Department of the Interior, Bureau of Mines, Mineral Industry Surveys, *Crude Petroleum, Petroleum Products, and Natural Gas Liquids,* 1965–73 issues; *Oil & Gas Journal,* July 30, 1973, p. 99.

3 Ibid.

FIGURE 11-3
Total Supply of Crude Oil in the United States, 1965-73

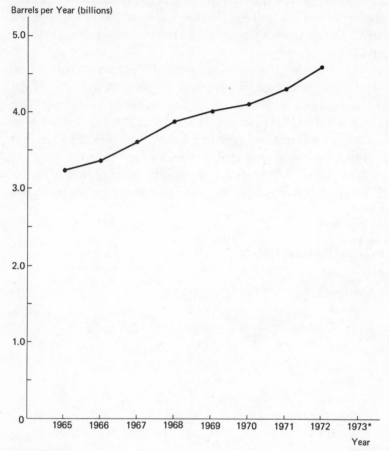

Barrels per Year (billions)

° Estimated.
Sources: U.S. Department of the Interior, Bureau of Mines, Mineral Industry Surveys, *Crude Petroleum, Petroleum Products, and Natural Gas Liquids,* 1965–1973 issues; *Oil & Gas Journal,* July 30, 1973, p. 99.

Contrary to popular opinion, most of the U.S. imports of crude oil do not come from the Middle East. Canada supplies large amounts, as do Nigeria, Venezuela, and Indonesia. Not shown in our tables and diagrams are the large amounts imported of finished petroleum products—mostly residual fuel oil, but also motor gasoline, jet fuel, and distillate fuel oil. In 1972 total imports of these items were 846,988,000 barrels, as compared with crude oil imports of 811,135,000 barrels. These finished products come mostly from Central America, the Caribbean, and South America.[4]

Nevertheless, it was the embargo that the Arab countries placed on shipments of crude oil to the United States that triggered the energy crisis of 1973. As Table 11–1 shows, from 1965 through 1970, United States imports from the Arab countries fluctuated up and down, with a predominantly downward trend. In 1971, 1972, and the first half of 1973 they increased sharply as U.S. production dropped off. As Table 11–1 shows, in 1971 Arab oil comprised 3.7 percent of the total crude available to the United States. In 1972 it made up 4.6 percent of the total, and for the first half of 1973, it was 6.4 percent. For the month of June 1973, it was 7.3 percent of the total.

While the Arab cutoff of crude oil shipments to the United States triggered the crisis, it does not appear that it was in itself sufficiently important to *cause* the crisis. At the most, it should reduce supplies by not more than 10 percent below what they would otherwise be. It is worth noting, also, that *even without Arab oil the total amount available to the United States for 1974 should be approximately as much as was available in 1972, including imports from the Arab countries.* It seems that supplies equal to 1972 levels should be sufficient to prevent the kind of frantic talk and the governmental warnings of dark, cold days ahead that were so prevalent in late 1973. Isn't there a missing link somewhere in the chain of events leading to the "energy crisis"?

Governmental Policies

There is indeed such a missing link, and it is called policies of the federal government. The problem is not that the government has failed to do enough to avert a crisis, as many seem to believe. Rather, it appears that the government has done too much; its actions have brought on the crisis.

Through 1970 there was no real hint of an energy crisis. We heard, of course, from geologists, oil companies, and others con-

---

4 U.S. Department of the Interior, Bureau of Mines, Mineral Industry Surveys, *Crude Petroleum, Petroleum Products, and Natural Gas Liquids, January, 1973* (April 18, 1973), p. 31.

TABLE 11–2
Total Supplies of Crude Oil in the United States, 1972 and January–June 1973 (1,000 barrels)

Year	Month	Domestic Production	Imports Arab Countries*	Percent of Total Supply	Total	Percent of Total Supply	Total U.S. Supply
1972	....	3,459,052	197,879	4.6	811,135	19.0	4,270,187
1973	January	284,551	19,108	5.2	84,693	22.9	369,244
	February	262,452	18,904	5.5	80,433	23.5	342,885
	March	284,421	28,661	7.5	98,021	25.6	382,442
	April	276,987	20,978	5.7	81,459	24.8	368,446
	May	288,405	28,112	7.2	99,654	25.7	388,059
	June	276,261	27,289	7.3	96,613	25.9	372,874
Total 1973	January–June	1,673,077	143,052	6.4	550,873	24.8	2,223,950

* Egypt, Iran, Iraq, Kuwait, Libya, Saudi Arabia, United Arab Emirates.
Sources: U.S. Department of the Interior, Bureau of Mines, Mineral Industry Surveys, *Crude Petroleum, Petroleum Products, and Natural Gas Liquids,* January–June, 1973; *Oil and Gas Journal,* July 10, 1973, p. 99.

cerned with energy supplies that on down the road there would be a day of reckoning when energy supplies would fail to meet rapidly expanding energy demands. But vocalizations of these sorts are commonly heard from producers' special-interest groups seeking governmental subsidization. There were no economic indications that we would be unable to buy as much gasoline and fuel oil as we desired. To put it in familiar economic terms, equilibrium prices prevailed in these markets until late 1971. Markets for crude oil and its products were in equilibrium. Using gasoline as an example, Figure 11–4 shows an equilibrium price of p_1 prevailing; buyers want quantity q_1 at that price, and suppliers are willing to place quantity q_1 on the market.

Now take inflation into account. As we noted in the preceding chapter, inflation occurs whenever aggregate demand is increasing

FIGURE 11–4
Equilibrium Price and Quantity of Gasoline

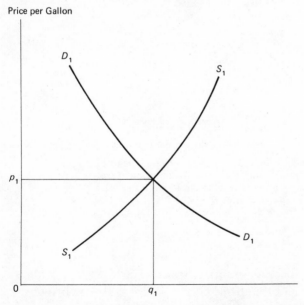

Gasoline (gallons per month)

Given the demand D_1D_1 and the supply S_1S_1 of gasoline, the equilibrium price will be p_1 and the equilibrium quantity will be q_1. At the equilibrium price there is neither a surplus nor a shortage.

faster than aggregate supply. The demands for petroleum products and other energy sources in an expanding inflationary economy tend to increase even more rapidly than the aggregate demand of which they are component parts. The results are illustrated for gasoline in Figure 11–5. An increase in demand from D_1D_1 to D_2D_2,

FIGURE 11–5
Effects of Changes in the Demand for and Supply of Gasoline with and without Price Controls

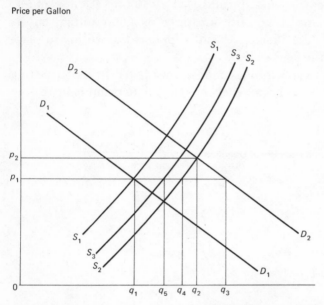

Price per Gallon

Gasoline (gallons per month)

An increase in demand from D_1D_1 to D_2D_2, accompanied by an increase in supply from S_1S_1 to S_2S_2, causes the price of gasoline to rise from p_1 to p_2, and there is no shortage. If the price is controlled at p_1, a shortage of q_4q_3 will occur. If supply then decreases to S_3S_3 and the price is held at p_1, the shortage will increase to q_5q_3.

which outstrips an increase in supply from S_1S_1 to S_2S_2, brings about a price increase in gasoline from p_1 to p_2. This is the nature of the inflationary process. As such, it is a part of the inflation problem, but it generates no energy crisis.

The energy shortages began to make themselves felt following the wage-price freeze of August 17, 1971. They became more and more intense through the various phases of price controls in 1972 and 1973. Then with the cutoff in Arab oil in October 1973, they suddenly began to appear catastrophic.

As we noted in the discussion of the meat crisis in Chapter 2, wherever price controls are effective in holding prices *below* their equilibrium levels, shortages occur. This is precisely what is happening in the petroleum case. Petroleum product prices are being held below equilibrium levels by the government, creating shortages of gasoline, jet fuel, and fuel oils. Consider Figure 11–5 again. When demand increases to D_2D_2 and supply increases to S_2S_2, suppose that price controls hold the price of gasoline at p_1. At that price level consumers now want q_3 gallons, but suppliers are willing to place only q_4 on the market, leaving a shortage of q_4q_3 gallons. Now, on top of this, the imposition of the Arab cutoff of crude oil shifts the supply curve for gasoline to the left, to S_3S_3. If a price ceiling of p_1 is maintained, the shortage increases to q_5q_3. We can expect shortages to continue as long as petroleum product prices are held by the government below their equilibrium levels.

PROPOSED SOLUTIONS TO THE CRISIS

Everyone feels the impact of shortages of petroleum products, although different persons may feel it in different ways. Some find themselves short on the gasoline they need to drive to work; others are short on fuel oil for heating. Some are unable to take the vacations on which they have been planning. Are there ways to cope with the shortage problem? Three major lines of attack that have been suggested are: (1) rationing and allocations of available supplies, (2) taxing purchases of the products in short supply, and (3) allowing prices of the products in short supply to rise to equilibrium levels.

Rationing and Allocations

If the prices of petroleum products are held below their equilibrium levels, the gap between the quantities that buyers want to buy and sellers want to sell at the controlled prices makes some kind of rationing scheme necessary. Several possibilities exist. First, the government may stay completely out of the rationing process and let individual sellers dispose of their limited supplies in any way they like—subject to the ceiling prices. Second, the government may intervene by establishing priorities for sellers to observe in allocating the short supplies to their customers. Third, the government may establish a coupon rationing system.

Rationing by Individual Sellers—No Priorities. When individual sellers are left to dispose of their supplies however they see fit, the simplest kind of rationing system exists. Sellers may use a first-come, first-served method of selling as long as they have stocks available. Or they may take care of friends, acquaintances, or old customers first and, if this does not exhaust their supplies, resort to first-come, first-served for the remainder.

Rationing by individual sellers has a number of faults and very few virtues. The prime virtue is its simplicity. An obvious fault is that prospective buyers must waste time waiting in line to be served. If time has value—and the alternative-cost principle indicates that it does—the true cost of the item to a customer who must stand in line for it exceeds the ceiling price he pays for it. Another fault is that there will always be persons toward the end of the line who are left out completely.

A third fault is that rationing of this type is inefficient in the sense that it does not place the short supplies in those uses where they are most valuable to buyers. Consider Figure 11–6, in which a price ceiling of p_0 is placed on gasoline. Sellers have only quantity q_0 to place on the market at the ceiling price. *For that quantity there are prospective buyers who can find uses for gasoline in which each gallon is worth p_2 or more.* This must be so, since for quantity q_0 there are enough buyers who would be willing to pay a price of p_2 per gallon to take the entire quantity. No buyer for whom the expected value of the use of a gallon of gasoline is *less* than p_2 would be willing to pay that price for it.

However, if buyers are prevented from paying more than p_0 per gallon, anyone who can put gasoline to uses in which its value to him is p_0 or more per gallon will want it. Some prospective buyers for whom it is worth less than p_2 but at least as much as p_0 per gallon will succeed in purchasing some of it. The result will be that many of the q_0 gallons available will be put to uses less valuable than p_2—some will be put to uses valued as low as p_0 per gallon, whereas the entire quantity could have been put to uses with values equal to or greater than p_2.

FIGURE 11–6
Comparative Effects of Rationing, Taxation, and Free-Market Pricing

Price per Gallon

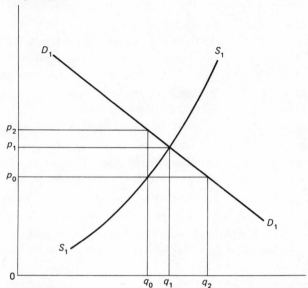

Gasoline (gallons per month)

If the price is controlled at p_o, suppliers will place quantity q_o on the market, but buyers want quantity q_2. Because of the shortage, the available supply must be rationed. If a per unit tax of p_op_2 is placed on buyers, they will reduce their purchases to q_o. If the price is allowed to find its equilibrium level, it will rise only to p_1; the quantity supplied will increase to q_1 and consumers will voluntarily limit themselves to the available supply.

Rationing by Individual Sellers—Priorities. The government may leave the actual rationing of short supplies to sellers while providing them with a pecking order of the buyer groups that are to be preferred. This was the initial approach taken by the government to meet the petroleum shortage.

Users of fuel oil were favored over users of motor fuels as refineries were asked to increase the fuel oil–motor fuels ratio of their outputs. Most industrial users of fuel oil were cut back to 90 percent of their calendar year 1972 base period deliveries. Deliveries of oil for heating purposes to both residential and commercial users were supposed to be cut enough to induce residential users to lower their thermostats by six degrees and commercial users to lower their thermostats by ten degrees.

Motor fuels of various kinds—gasoline, diesel fuels, and jet fuels —were to be sold on a first-priority basis to fuel producers and public passenger surface transportation lines. Jet fuel allocations for airlines were cut some 15 percent, while gasoline for general aviation was reduced by about 35 percent. Pleasure driving of automobiles was given an official frown by the closing of service stations from 9:00 P.M. on Saturday to midnight on Sunday.

Government priorities imposed on sellers have the same faults as sellers' rationing with no priorities, but presumably the faults exist in a lesser degree. Waiting in line or queuing may be reduced, except for those at the bottom of the priorities scale. Again, some people may be excluded altogether. Further, a priorities system does not provide safeguards against inefficient uses of the short supplies. A ceiling price set below the equilibrium price level will always induce some users to put the supplies they get to uses that are less valuable than some of the uses to which other users could put them.

Coupon Rationing. Under coupon rationing the government takes full responsibility for determining who gets how much of the available short supplies. Many people argue that the petroleum shortage will last long enough to force the government eventually into rationing gasoline in this way. The rationing system itself is not very complex—the government simply issues and distributes coupons good for the monthly (or other appropriate time period) quantities available. These can be distributed among potential users however the government desires.

Coupon rationing is thought somehow to allow for fair treatment of everyone. For example, what could be more fair than ten gallons of gasoline across the board for every automobile owned? Or should it be for every family? Or perhaps for every working member of each family? Or should it be for every driver? Some people live only short distances from work and from the store, while others live long distances away. Some have public transportation and carpools available and others do not. Some have big cars and others have small ones. A thousand and one other differences among the circumstances of different persons arise which in the name of equity would call for something other than equal amounts for everyone—if we could define who everyone is. Determining what constitutes equity is a difficult, if not impossible, task.

Coupon rationing eliminates the problem of lines of waiting customers and will usually insure that no one is left out completely; however, it suffers from the same kinds of inefficiencies in the use of the good in short supply as do the other rationing schemes. To elminate those inefficiencies some economists have recommended that once ration coupons have been distributed their holders should be free to buy and sell them for whatever prices they will bring.[5] In the case of gasoline, those to whom gasoline is most valuable will bid for coupons, while those who value the uses to which it can be put at less than the sum of the gasoline price plus the coupon price will sell their coupons.

In essence, a free-market equilibrium price of gasoline would be established—the free-market price being the ceiling price plus the price of a one-gallon coupon. Gasoline would be channeled toward its most efficient uses (those most valuable to users). In Figure 11–6 above, the one-gallon coupon price would become p_0p_2, with p_2 being the free-market price of quantity q_0 of gasoline and p_0 being the controlled ceiling price.

The primary problem with this so-called "white market" in ration coupons is that it provides no incentive to suppliers to increase gasoline output beyond q_0. The "profits" of the system, rather than going to suppliers and providing incentive for larger outputs, go to those who are issued ration coupons and who then sell them to the ultimate users. A second question that arises is, Why bother with the coupons at all? What useful function do they perform if they can be freely bought and sold that a free-market price cannot perform? The coupons are nothing but government subsidies equal to the value of the coupons issued to each person or family.

Some Comments on Rationing. All of the rationing schemes discussed contain built-in inducements for violation of the price control and/or rationing rules. Those responsible for dispensing units of the rationed product—whether they be private sellers or persons in governmental positions, face great temptations to play favorites. In some instances those favored will be family members and close friends. In other instances they will be persons with polit-

---

5 See Paul A. Samuelson, "Energy Economics," *Newsweek,* November 26, 1973, p. 96.

ical pull. Money talks, and so do promises of reciprocal favors. As economist Paul McCracken puts it,

Economies that are managed by license and edict and coupon books are also economies with pervasive corruption and graft. This is no accident. Those possessing the authority to grant favorable decisions possess something of great value and there will be growing numbers who are willing to pay the price. All they will need to do is look around them to conclude that almost "everybody does it."[6]

Wherever price ceilings are imposed, black markets tend to arise. A *black market* is essentially an illegal free market for the product that is subjected to controls. This illegality is not taken lightly in countries where price controls are widely used; the death penalty for black marketeers is not uncommon. Still, the black market tends to increase the efficiency with which items traded in it are used. Units of such items are withheld from lower value uses by those who provide supplies to the black market (those who have bought quantities of the good at ceiling prices) and are put to higher value uses by those who buy them from the black market. The economic shortcoming of the black market is that producers faced with ceiling prices have no inducements to expand their outputs. The gains from the higher black-market prices are captured by those who operate it.

Taxation

A proposed solution to the petroleum products shortage—particularly the gasoline shortage—bandied about considerably in late 1973 was a per unit tax on the product sufficient to induce buyers to cut back their purchases to the quantity available. In Figure 11–6 above, for example, a tax of $p_0 p_2$ per gallon of gasoline would induce buyers to voluntarily reduce their purchases to quantity q_0—they would not want more because total amount per gallon they would have to pay would be p_2, composed of the ceiling price p_0 plus the tax $p_0 p_2$.

The increased cost to consumers over and above the ceiling price for each gallon of gasoline would cause every consumer to examine

---

[6] Paul W. McCracken, "Coupon Book Economics," *Wall Street Journal*, November 26, 1973.

his uses of it. Those considering trading cars would be induced to consider carefully the virtues of an economy car as compared with those of a gas hog. Spur-of-the-moment trips to the store would be cut down. Public transportation would look more attractive. Vacations involving long-distance driving would become less attractive. Above all, each consumer, instead of being *coerced* into such things as reducing speed and eliminating Sunday driving, would *voluntarily* seek out and eliminate those uses of gasoline least important to him or her. People differ in their valuations of the various uses to which they put gasoline (or any other product, for that matter). The tax could be set at a high enough level to secure the same reduction in consumption as that obtained by the coercive rationing and allocation plans. But it would result in more efficient gasoline usage because consumers would be induced to put gasoline to its most valuable uses.

What are the magnitudes of taxes involved and what would be their impact on the level of economic activity? Guesses as to the tax per gallon that would be required to cut consumption to the level of quantities available at the ceiling price run in the neighborhood of 25 to 30 cents per gallon. It is also thought that each one cent per gallon tax would yield about one billion dollars per year in tax revenues to the government. An increase in annual tax collections of this size would have a depressing effect on economic activity unless government spending were increased or unless tax revenues from other sources were decreased by a like amount.

Suggestions have been made that the government could use the tax revenues so collected to stimulate increases in energy supplies. For example, the United States has vast reserves of oil-bearing shale deposits, but the technology for massive efforts at mining the shale, squeezing the oil out of it, and disposing of the resulting oilless shale have not been perfected. This kind of effort could be encouraged by government research grants to and/or subsidization of oil companies or others that undertake development of the appropriate technologies. It is thought, too, that governmental support of nuclear research and nuclear power facilities could expand substantially our total energy supplies. In addition, many argue that subsidization of exploratory and drilling activities is likely to result in the recovery of sizable additional amounts of domestic crude oil.

The Free Market

Basic economic principles—demand and supply analysis—suggest a simple solution to the petroleum shortage. It is that the government withdraw from rather than enter more extensively into the energy field—particularly the marketing area. The ceilings on prices of petroleum products would be abandoned, and prices would be permitted to rise to their equilibrium levels. This would cause the shortages to disappear, and governmental rationing and allocation decisions would be unnecessary.

The higher prices would affect the uses of petroleum products in the same way as would the suggested per unit taxes discussed in the preceding section. They would induce each user to eliminate the less important uses and concentrate available quantities on more important uses. But free market prices would do it more effectively than per unit taxes. Tax rates that would just induce users to buy the available quantities cannot be determined accurately in advance, but can only be approached by a trial and error process. This would be a slow, painful business. Free-market prices would move rapidly to whatever levels are necessary to alleviate shortages and just clear the markets.

The higher prices would also serve to increase to some extent the quantities of petroleum products made available on the market in the short run. Higher prices for gasoline and fuel oil would induce refiners to attempt to operate at maximum refinery capacities, and this would in turn bid up the prices of crude oil. Higher crude oil prices would result in some increases in U.S. production—bringing some oil out of stripper wells and other wells that cannot now be pumped economically at controlled prices. Higher prices would also make U.S. refiners more competitive in the world market for crude oil. Oil from Arab countries may even find its way to the United States via non-Arab countries.

In the long run, free-market equilibrium prices would be expected to increase energy supplies further. They would encourage exploratory and drilling activity, thus expanding both our reserves and our recovery rates. They would encourage the development of shale-oil recovery techniques and the actual recovery of oil from this source. Research in the conversion of coal to clean-burning forms and in the capture of solar energy would be encouraged by the higher payoff possibilities. Expansion of nuclear energy facilities would be stimulated.

The maximum impact of higher prices on crude oil supplies can be realized only if an additional government millstone around the necks of crude oil producers is removed. This millstone, hung by the states of Texas, Louisiana, New Mexico, Kansas, and Oklahoma, which collectively account for about two thirds of the crude oil production in the United States, is called *market-demand prorationing.*[7] Prorationing is accomplished by commissions in the individual states (in Texas by the Texas Railroad Commission and in Oklahoma by the Oklahoma Corporation Commission) for two stated purposes: (1) to conserve crude oil reserves and (2) to divide the market equally among producers.

In practice, prorationing serves as a government-supported monopolizing device that enables producers to act jointly to reduce supplies of crude oil placed on the market and to receive higher prices for their product than would be the case in competitive markets. The commission in a given state determines how much crude oil is to be produced and allocates quotas to the producers of the state. Ordinarily low-volume, high-cost wells are permitted to produce as much as they are capable of, while production from high-volume, low-cost wells is restricted. The results are restricted production and higher costs of recovery from wells that are operating currently, as well as reduced incentives for exploration and development of new oil fields. In the interests of expanding domestic production of crude oil, prorationing, as well as other monopolizing or restrictive devices, must be eliminated.

Free-market equilibrium prices would tend to be lower than the ceiling prices plus per unit taxes that would be necessary to induce consumers to reduce their total consumption level to the quantities available. This is illustrated in Figure 11–6 above. Given a ceiling price of p_0 suppliers would place q_0 gallons of gasoline on the market. A per unit tax of p_0p_2 would be necessary to induce consumers to reduce consumption to that level. However, if the tax *and* the price ceiling were withdrawn, the market price would rise only to p_1 because the rising price level would induce producers to increase

---

7 James C. Burrows and Thomas A. Domencich, *An Analysis of the United States Oil Import Quota* (Lexington, Mass.: D. C. Heath & Co., 1970), pp. 62–68.

their outputs. At price p_1, suppliers would be willing to place q_1 gallons on the market, and consumers would be just willing to take that amount off the market.

The free-market equilibrium price solution of the energy shortage problem has much to commend it. The primary argument in its favor is simply the argument for a private enterprise economic system *vis-à-vis* a socialistic economic system. The price system induces consumers to voluntarily limit their consumption of each good or service to the available supply. It also induces producers of each good and service to increase the quantity available, up to the point at which consumers value a unit of it at approximately what it costs to place it on the market. The price system also induces buyers of goods and services and resources to put available supplies to their most efficient uses. Relative prices, relative costs, and relative profits continually induce transfers of goods from less valuable to more valuable uses. All of this is done automatically and impersonally. No coercion is necessary. We avoid putting our economic fate in the hands of government bureaucrats who may or may not be knowledgeable of the consequences of their actions, regardless of how good their intentions may be. And Watergate has led many of us to have some doubts about the intentions of politicians and bureaucrats!

There are three primary arguments against the free-market price solution. First, people argue that it would enable oil companies to make large windfall profits. Second, they maintain that it would discriminate against the poor. Third, they fear that it would contribute to inflation. All of these are probably correct conclusions, but are they valid arguments against the free-market solution?

Consider the profit issue. Given our present corporate income tax structure, some 50 percent of any windfall profits made by oil companies would be paid in taxes to the government. The remainder would be left with the profit-making companies to encourage supply expansion. *All* of the solutions to the shortage problem recognize that supply expansion is desirable. Only the taxation and free-market solutions contain incentives to encourage it. But the rationing solution in and of itself ignores supply expansion. The taxation solution contains suggestions that tax receipts be used to subsidize oil companies to expand their outputs. How does this differ from windfall profits? Why not let the free market provide the incentives for output expansion directly and automatically without the government acting as an intermediary in the collection and disbursement of "profits"?

An increase in the prices of petroleum products from ceiling levels to equilibrium levels may or may not affect the poor in greater proportion than the more well-to-do. Only to the extent that the poor spend larger proportions of their total incomes on petroleum products than wealthier people do will an increase in the prices of those products reduce their real incomes in greater proportion. In any case, to the extent that we have poverty problems, those problems can be attacked most efficiently by direct means, as we noted in Chapter 7. Poverty problems result from low incomes, not from relatively high prices of specific products. Have rationing schemes as we have known them in the past ordinarily operated in ways that favor the poor?

The withdrawal of ceiling prices from petroleum products will surely result in price increases for those products. But consider the ceiling prices themselves—they, together with the shortages they induce, are evidence of *suppressed inflation*. Is a situation in which inflation is suppressed by price controls superior to one in which prices are permitted to seek equilibrium levels, even though general price levels rise? There are no unequivocal answers to this question. We argued in Chapter 10 that monetary policy, fiscal policy, and antimonopoly policy, rather than price controls, are the appropriate tools to use in combating inflation. These are consistent with the use of free-market prices to solve the energy problem.

SUMMARY

The U.S. public is confronted with an energy shortage that has caused pessimistic predictions for the level of GNP and employment for the next few years. The problem centers primarily on petroleum, which provides about half of our energy requirements.

Demand for petroleum products has been increasing faster than has supply. Price controls since 1971, together with the 1973 Arab embargo on crude oil shipments to the United States, have turned these supply-demand relationships into acute shortages.

Rising affluence and a growing GNP over time have caused rapid increases in demand for energy by transportation users, industrial users, and residential and commercial users. Domestic production of crude oil also increased through 1971 and then decreased slightly. Crude oil imports rose sharply from 1971 through 1973, thereby bringing about increases in total supplies available, until the Arab embargo hit in October 1973. With the embargo in effect, crude oil supplies available for 1974 should be in the neighborhood of those available in 1971 and 1972. Acute shortages have developed because of the government's price control policies which have held petroleum product prices below their equilibrium levels.

Three possible lines of attack on the problem have been suggested. First, most people seem to believe that rationing is in order. Possible rationing systems are rationing by individual sellers with no priorities assigned by the government, by individual sellers with certain groups of buyers given priorities, and by the government through a coupon system. Second, heavy per unit taxes on petroleum products could be levied to induce buyers to cut their purchases back to the quantities made available at the controlled prices. Third, price controls could be removed from petroleum products, allowing prices to rise. This would cause buyers to reduce their purchases to the amounts available and should at the same time call forth additional quantities of the products.

All of these plans have both advantages and disadvantages. Rationing schemes ensure that some of the available supplies will be used inefficiently, because product prices are controlled at below equilibrium levels. Also, rationing schemes as such do nothing to expand supply. Per unit taxes, if set at the correct levels, would induce purchasers to put the available supplies to their most efficient uses, but they do not serve to expand supplies unless the government uses the tax receipts to subsidize those who can bring about expanding supplies. Free-market prices would induce purchasers to put what they purchase to its most efficient uses and would also provide inducements to suppliers to expand their outputs. Free-market prices appear to be better geared to solving the energy problem than do the other schemes.

SUPPLEMENTARY READINGS

Friedman, Milton. "The Inequity of Gas Rationing." *Newsweek,* December 10, 1973, p. 113.

In assessing the equity of a rationing system, Friedman compares it with a subsidy system.

Friedman, Milton. "Why Some Prices Should Rise." *Newsweek,* November 19, 1973, p. 130.

Presents a case for using the price system rather than governmental allocations and rationing to meet the energy crisis.

Gramm, W. Philip. "The Energy Crisis in Perspective." *Wall Street Journal,* November 30, 1973.

Points out that the energy problem is nothing new and that if the price system were allowed to operate, forces would be set in motion that would solve the problem.

McCracken, Paul W. "Coupon Book Economics." *Wall Street Journal,* November 26, 1973.

Alternative means of rationing and consequent problems of each are examined in this article.

Samuelson, Paul A. "Energy Economics," *Newsweek,* November 26, 1973, p. 96.

Argues for governmental rationing and a white market for ration coupons.

"What U.S. Can Do to Tap Energy Sources Closer Home." *U.S. News and World Report,* December 3, 1973, pp. 25–26.

Catalogs the energy sources available to the United States in the face of the cutoff of oil shipments from Arab countries. These include crude oil reserves, shale oil reserves, natural gas, and nuclear energy in the United States, Canada, and Latin America.

INDEX

INDEX

311

Shortages, 46, 270, 284–85
Siddayao, Corazon M., 166 n, 174 n, 179
Social spillover benefits
of education, 82–83, 96, 100
of health services, 160
of semicollectively consumed goods, 114
Social spillover costs
of education, 82
of semicollectively consumed goods, 114
Solow, Robert M., 272
Somers, Herman M., 170, 170 n
Steindl, Frank G., 259 n
Stewart, Charles T., 166 n, 174 n, 179
Storage and loan programs
costs of, 57
economic effects of, 55–57
nature of, 55
and surpluses, 55–57
Student aid, 200
Subsidies
for energy development, 301
farm
economic effects of, 58–59
nature of, 58–59
Sufrin, Sidney C., 278
Sulfur oxide, 133
Supply
changes in, 43
definition of, 41
of health services, 166–70
of meat, 67
of petroleum, 286–91
restrictions in agriculture, 53–54
Surpluses
causes of, 46, 55–57
of farm products, 55–57

T

Taxes
and collectively consumed goods, 115–16
and fiscal policy, 247, 270
and higher education, 79–80, 90–91, 95–97
as leakages from the circular flow, 246

Taxes—*Cont.*
negative income, 201–4
and pollution control, 147–50
and population control, 25
as a rationing device, 300–301
Technology, 10
Thurow, Lester C., 206, 217 n, 222, 224

U

Underdeveloped countries, 16, 18
Unemployment
cyclical, 237
definition of, 234–35
effects of
on GNP, 232
on social relations, 232–34
frictional, 236
incidence of, 238–39
involuntary, 235
rates of, 237–39
structural, 237, 248–49
Unemployment compensation, 199
Universities; *see* Colleges and universities

W–Z

Wage controls
employment effects of, 243–45, 274–75
output effects of, 243–45, 274–75
Wage-price freeze, 274–75, 294–95
Wage rates
determination of, 193–94
flexibility of, 248–49
and unemployment, 235–36
Wants, 8
Waste disposal, 131–32
Wastes
biodegradable, 132
from economic activity, 131–32
recycling of, 131–32
Watergate, 111, 284
Weisbrod, Burton A., 104
Windham, Douglas M., 104
Worthington, Nancy L., 158 n
Zero population growth, 16, 23–24

This book has been set in 11 and 10 point Baskerville, leaded 2 points. Part numbers and chapter titles are 24 point (small) Univers Medium Extended. Part titles are 24 point (small) Univers Medium Extended. Chapter numbers are in 30 point Univers Bold Extended. The size of the type page is 26 × 43⅔ picas.